TEXT AND TRAUMA

An East-West Primer

Other books by Ian Richard Netton

Al-Farabi and His School

Allah Transcendent: Studies in the Structure and Semiotics of Islamic Philosophy, Theology and Cosmology

Arabia and the Gulf: From Traditional Society to Modern States (editor)

Golden Roads: Migration, Pilgrimage and Travel in Mediaeval and Modern Islam (editor)

Middle East Materials in United Kingdom and Irish Libraries: A Directory

Muslim Neoplatonists: An Introduction to the Thought of the Brethren of Purity (Ikhwan al-Safa')

A Popular Dictionary of Islam

Seek Knowledge: Thought and Travel in the House of Islam

TEXT AND TRAUMA

An East-West Primer

Ian Richard Netton

CURZON
PRESS

First Published in 1996
by Curzon Press
St John's Studios, Church Road, Richmond
Surrey, TW9 2QA

Typeset in Times by LaserScript Ltd, Mitcham
Printed and bound in Great Britain by
Biddles Limited, Guildford and King's Lynn

British Library Cataloguing in Publication Data
A catalogue record of this book is available from the British Library

Library of Congress Cataloguing in Publication Data
A catalog record for this book has been requested

ISBN 0–7007–0325–X (hbk)
ISBN 0–7007–0326–8 (pbk)

For my Family with much love

CONTENTS

PREFACE AND ACKNOWLEDGEMENTS

As Islam and the West approach the beginning of the twenty first century, it is clear from such events as the Rushdie affair, the arena of education, the Iran – Iraq War of 1980–1988, and the Iraqi invasion of Kuwait in August 1990, as well as many others, that the East and the West (if they may thus be monolithically characterised) speak different languages in more senses than one. This monograph attempts, *inter alia*, to highlight and explore aspects of that 'difference'. It does so in a very specific way, using *the text* as a primary vehicle, making particular reference to the concept of blasphemy and surveying how that concept has been understood. It presents a religious, cultural, historical and literary *archaeology* of three selected novels by Najīb Maḥfūẓ (Naguib Mahfouz), Salman Rushdie and Nikos Kazantzakis. These are: Maḥfūẓ's *Children of Gebelawi*, representing a novel which has been labelled as blasphemous by the Islamic East; Rushdie's *Satanic Verses*, execrated by Muslims in both the East and the West, and representing a link between those two spheres, for its author was born in the one, lives in the other and writes about both; and Kazantzakis' *Last Temptation* which is an example of a novel condemned as blasphemous in the Christian West. Reference is also made to Martin Scorsese's film of the last novel. An attempt is made to unpack the cultural and other baggage of the word *blasphemy* although it should be stressed here, right at the beginning, that no final definition is attempted. So this monograph tries to uncover the *past* embedded at several levels in the *contemporary* text which may have far-reaching repercussions in the present.

A variety of methodologies for the present project were considered. They ranged from the famous 'method' espoused by Bernard Lonergan[1] to the approach of Ninian Smart in *The Phenomenon of Religion*.[2] Finally, however, I decided to adapt the methodology of Fernand Braudel (1902–1985)[3] and combine it with the intertextual insights of

Julia Kristeva and others. Braudel adopted a method 'in which history is viewed and studied on three levels of (i) enduring geographic and economic structures, (ii) social structures and 'conjunctures', and (iii) events.'[4] I have devised for this monograph a literary method or sieve whereby the three main texts may be studied on the five levels of *Pre-Text*, *Text*, *Context*, *Intertext* and *Antitext*. It is hoped that, at the end of this work, the reader will at least be clear as to (a) why a text was considered offensive in the first place, (b) the political pattern of the alleged offence, and (c) the scope of that offence.

This book deals with other people's perceptions of blasphemy. Chapter Two, entitled *Text*, is a lengthy one since critics of the three main texts under discussion have often resorted to condemnation without a preliminary reading. The extensive summaries contained in this Chapter will enable the reader to perceive at a glance those areas of the texts which have given rise to controversy. They are not, however, to be regarded in any way as a substitute for reading the original texts.

I have many debts of gratitude to record. In the first place I must thank my wife and family for their indulgence and patience while I was writing yet another book. I am enormously grateful to the University of Exeter for the Study Leave on full pay which it awarded me during the Lent and Trinity Terms of 1992; this enabled me to do the basic research for the present monograph. I also thank my former colleagues in the Department of Arabic and Islamic Studies for their many kindnesses during my absence. As always, I appreciated the unrivalled help and efficiency of Miss Heather Eva, Director of Exeter University's Inter-Library Loans Department, and Mr. Paul Auchterlonie, Exeter University's unmatched Arabic Specialist Librarian. Professor David Catchpole, St. Luke's Foundation Professor of Theological Studies in that University, kindly supplied the names of relevant theological works when asked, with promptness and interest; while another dear friend and colleague, Dr. Rasheed El-Enany of the Department of Arabic and Islamic Studies at Exeter University, kept me supplied with an amazing stream of photocopies, book titles, stimulating ideas and enjoyable conversation. To these and to all who have followed the progress of this monograph with interest and concern, I express my warmest thanks.

March 1994

Ian Richard Netton
Professor of Arabic Studies
University of Leeds

NOTES

1 B.J.F. Lonergan, *Method in Theology*, (New York: Herder & Herder, 1971/2nd edn.: London: Darton, Longman & Todd, 1973); see also Hugo Meynell, 'Bernard Lonergan' in David F. Ford (ed.), *The Modern Theologians: An Introduction to Christian Theology in the Twentieth Century*, (Oxford: Basil Blackwell, 1989), vol. 1, pp. 205–216.

2 Ninian Smart, *The Phenomenon of Religion*, Philosophy of Religion Series, (London: Macmillan, 1973).

3 See his *Civilization Matérielle, Économie et Capitalisme (XV*ᵉ-XVIIIᵉ Siècle), (Paris: Librairie Armand Colin, 1979), 3 vols.; idem., *La Méditerranée et le Monde Méditerranéen à l'Époque de Philippe II*, (Paris: Librairie Armand Colin, 1949, 2nd rev. edn., 1966); see also Ian Richard Netton, 'Arabia and the Pilgrim Paradigm of Ibn Baṭṭūṭa: A Braudelian Approach' in Ian Richard Netton (ed.), *Arabia and the Gulf: From Traditional Society to Modern States*, (London & Sydney: Croom Helm, 1986), pp. 29–42.

4 Netton, 'Arabia and the Pilgrim Paradigm of Ibn Baṭṭūṭa', p. 31.

ABBREVIATIONS

AH	*Awlād Ḥāratinā*
BSOAS	Bulletin of the School of Oriental and African Studies
CG	*Children of Gebelawi*
CRE	Commission for Racial Equality
CSIC	Centre for the Study of Islam and Christian-Muslim Relations
edn.	edition
EI[2]	Second Edition of *The Encyclopaedia of Islam*
EIS	*Shorter Encyclopaedia of Islam*
ff	following
IFN	The Inter Faith Network for the United Kingdom
LT	*The Last Temptation*
Q.	*The Qur'ān*
reg.	(*regnabat*) he/she ruled
SV	*The Satanic Verses*
s.v.	(*sub verbo*) under the word
v.	verse
WCC	World Council of Churches

1

PRE-TEXT

> Most archaeologists are not working with the expectation of finding a king's tomb or similar riches. They are aiming at throwing light on some portion of man's past by the careful piecing together of evidence, much of it apparently insignificant in itself.
>
> Kenyon, *Beginning in Archaeology*, p. 9.

'Then the high priest tore his clothes and said, "He has blasphemed. What need of witnesses have we now? There! You have just heard the blasphemy. What is your opinion?" They answered, '"He deserves to die.'[1] The High Priest's words in the New Testament echo down the ages, and the response that death was the fitting penalty completes an archetypal paradigm in which blasphemy and consequent death are ineluctably linked. Yet while this paradigm still has the power to provoke, at the very least, a nod of recognition in the world of Islam, it has been emasculated and frequently overturned in the secular West.

The concept of blasphemy has been defined, *inter alia*, as 'profane speaking of God or sacred things; impious irreverence.'[2] Early examples of the word in English, which incorporate a definition, appear in such statements as 'Some haue fallen in to blasphemie whiche ben they that speken unhonestly of god' (Caxton, 1488), 'Blasphemy or evil speaking against God maliciously' (Milton, 1659), and 'Blasphemy against the Almighty, by denying his being or providence' (Blackstone, 1768).[3] In all these primary examples it is God Himself who is the object of man's evil speech.

In Arabic the word 'blasphemy' has been rendered by such terms as *tajdīf* and *sabb*. The former is the more religiously specific of the two words, implying an irreverent way of speaking about religious things; the word *tajdīf* does not, however, appear in the Qur'ān. Furthermore, it does not *necessarily* imply either 'heresy' (*ilḥād*), or 'unbelief' (*kufr*) or a 'charge of unbelief' (*takfīr*) though it is unsurprising that connotations of some or all of these frequently attach to the Arabic usage of *tajdīf*.[4] *Sabb*, by contrast, is a much more general noun deriving from a verb meaning 'to revile', 'to curse', 'to insult'. It need not have religious connotations at all although, interestingly, it *is* to be found in the Qur'ān in one form: 'Do not revile (*lā tasubbū*) those other than God to whom they direct their prayers in case they [in turn] revile (*yasubbū*) God in revenge and pure ignorance.'[5] Here the abuse is clearly associated both with pagan gods and idols as well as the God of the Qur'ān. With regard to the rendition of *tajdīf* as 'blasphemy', it is of considerable linguistic and theological interest that this Arabic word carries a primary linguistic baggage of denial or denigration of God's gifts and favours.[6]

If we turn now from the language dictionaries to the primal sacred texts of Christianity and Islam, the Bible and the Qur'ān, we find that the Bible is ostensibly stronger in its condemnation of blasphemy *qua* blasphemy than the latter text. *The Book of Leviticus*, for example, specified the fate of the blasphemer in no uncertain terms. Chapter Twenty Four describes the case of a man with an Israelite mother and Egyptian father who is brought before Moses charged with blasphemy. Yahweh orders Moses to have the blasphemer removed from the camp. Those who have heard the blasphemy are to place their hands on his head and the offender is then to be stoned to death.[7] Moses is to tell the Israelites:

> Anyone who curses his God will bear the consequences of his sin, and anyone who blasphemes the name of Yahweh will be put to death; the whole community will stone him; be he alien or native-born, if he blasphemes the Name, he will be put to death.[8]

The sentence pronounced by Yahweh is accordingly carried out.[9] We are reminded by the commentator that this ritual death for blasphemy in the Old Testament has a cleansing effect: 'The community, defiled by the curse, will be cleansed by the stoning of the guilty man; hands are imposed on him as on the sacrificial animal which is the community's substitute.'[10] As we have already seen in the stark quotation which began this chapter, the New Testament world of the Jewish High Priest still adhered to this paradigm: the penalty for blasphemy was, quite simply, death. We see this again vividly in the case of Stephen in *The Acts of the Apostles* where false witnesses are procured to testify 'We heard him using blasphemous language against Moses and against God.'[11] After a valiant and lengthy speech, Stephen is executed by stoning,[12] more the victim here of an enraged lynch mob than 'a judicial process.'[13]

The Old and New Testaments, then, condemn blasphemy in the strongest possible terms. The Qur'ān, by contrast, while never in any way condoning blasphemy, chooses primarily to focus upon *other* aspects of what might be termed 'religious sin'; we have already noted that the word *tajdīf* (blasphemy) does not appear in the Qur'ān. However, to state that fact is not to suggest that the Qur'ān refrains from all condemnations of blasphemy.

Yusuf Ali translates v.180 of the Qur'ānic *Sūra* 7 as follows:

> The most beautiful names
> Belong to God:
> So call on him by them;
> But shun such men as
> Use profanity [*yulḥidūna*] in His names:
> For what they do, they will
> Soon be requited.[14]

Arthur J. Arberry is even more specific in his rendition of the key Arabic verb here, *yulḥidūna*:

> To God belong the Names Most Beautiful;
> so call Him by them,
> and leave *those who blaspheme* [*yulḥidūna*] His Names –
> they shall assuredly be recompensed
> for the things they did.[15]

The Arabic verb *alḥada* has a range of meanings which include 'to deviate from the right course, digress from the straight path; to abandon one's faith, apostatize, become a heretic.'[16] But in the above Qur'ānic quotation, as the two translators have recognized, it is quite clear that it is *blasphemy* which is intended by this verb. It is equally clear from the text that punishment will follow upon such blasphemy, although the nature of this punishment remains unspecified here.

There is indirect or implicit condemnation of blasphemy in the Qur'ān as well. Much of what might normally be characterised as blasphemy, if we take the *Oxford English Dictionary* definition[17] as a criterion, is condemned *under another name*. It is ultimately a question of linguistic emphasis. But a brief glance at the following examples makes it clear that, while *kufr* (unbelief) and its closely related partner *shirk* (polytheism) are the prime surface targets of condemnation, there is a large unstated theological baggage also attaching to each verse of which blasphemy in its most basic sense is a major component. Furthermore, Izutsu reminds us that 'words or concepts are not simply there in the Koran, each standing in isolation from others, but they are closely interdependent and derive their concrete meanings precisely from the entire system of relations . . . In analyzing the individual key concepts that are found in the Koran we should never lose sight of the multiple relations which each of them bears to others in the whole system.'[18] There is what Izutsu calls 'a conceptual network or total Gestalt underlying the world-view of the Koran.'[19] A particularly striking example which this author provides is the Arabic word *taqwā*. Its 'cultural baggage' ranged from 'the basic semantic core' in Jāhilī times of the 'self-defensive attitude of a living being, animal or man, against some destructive force coming from outside' to the Islamic 'pious fear of Divine chastisement on the Day of Judgment' and, finally, 'personal "piety".'[20]

The Arabic word *kufr* moves, in the following verse, from having a primary cultural baggage of 'ingratitude'[21] to something much more akin to blasphemy: here the perpetrator of *kufr*, the *kāfir*, will have Hell as his reward:

> Such is their recompense: Gehenna, because they acted [in the world] as Kāfirs, making a mockery of My signs and My Apostles.[22]

Because *kufr* is 'man's denial of the Creator', it is hardly surprising that it 'manifests itself most characteristically in various acts of *insolence, haughtiness*, and *presumptuousness*.'[23]

Connotations of blasphemy lurk behind the term *shirk* in specific contexts as well. Semantically, such nouns as *shirk* and *kufr* and the Arabic verse *istahza'a* (which means 'to deride, to mock,'[24] 'to scoff') have much in common:[25]

> Therefore expound openly
> What thou art commanded,
> And turn away from those
> Who join false gods with God [*al-mushrikīn*].
> For sufficient are We
> Unto thee against those
> Who scoff, –
> Those who adopt with God,
> Another god: but soon
> Will they come to know.[26]

From these few examples, then, and the Qur'ānic usage of the Arabic verb *yulḥidūna* noted earlier, we may judge that such nouns as *kufr* (unbelief), *shirk* (polytheism), and *ilḥād* (heresy) share a common semantic field, to follow here the kind of analysis employed by Izutsu, of which the sense of 'blasphemy' is a common substratum.

Such examples also demonstrate how necessary it is to unpack the semantic, linguistic and cultural baggage of some of the earlier usages of Arabic words, as exemplified in the Qur'ān, and avoid the danger, inherent in every translation, of extrapolating from a *single* surface 'meaning'. In all this the Italian adage *traduttóre traditóre* (a translator is a traitor) can be only too true. Izutsu draws necessary attention to Morris Cohen's remarks, for example, on 'the danger of relying on the too easy equivalence of the Greek word *areté* with 'virtue' in discussing Aristotle's view of the 'virtuous' man. He remarks that the English word 'virtue', which is used almost exclusively as the equivalent of *areté*, is very misleading'; *areté* would be more accurately rendered as 'excellence', the object of admiration.'[27]

If, then, the very words which we are going to handle, translate and deploy – words like 'blasphemy' and 'apostasy' – are 'slippery' both in their Arabic originals and their translations, and are always culturally and temporally conditioned, how much more slippery must be their deployment in the modern age! How much more evanescent and 'exploitable' by different mutually opposed factions will such terms be, given the passage of times and cultures. And since, as we have seen, such terms are not concretised within one single meaning, within the primary sacred texts, it is fruitless to expect such texts to deliver a *single* authoritative usage. There may be several authoritative usages within the same text, competing for our attention and sometimes only capable of rationalisation by a literary or semantic version of the doctrine of abrogation.

Textual antecedents can be useful spotlights – and in this monograph we may ourselves choose to freeze one or other definitions as our primary parameter for the sake of the discussion – but it is recognised throughout that language, and the concepts it conveys, are ever changing in space, time and culture. All this may seem obvious enough but it needs, I believe, to be acknowledged once more before we proceed to sieve our three chosen texts through the four other selected layers, or levels, of Text, Context, Intertext and Antitext.

NOTES

1 Matthew 26:65–66, trans. in Henry Wansbrough (ed.), *The New Jerusalem Bible* (Standard Edition), (London: Darton, Longman & Todd, 1985).

2 J.A. Simpson & E.S.C. Weiner, *The Oxford English Dictionary*, 2nd edn., (Oxford: Clarendon Press, 1989), vol. 2 (B.B.C. – Chalypsography), p. 264 s.v. 'blasphemy'.
3 Ibid.
4 See Hans Wehr, *A Dictionary of Modern Written Arabic*, ed. J. Milton Cowan, 2nd Printing, (Wiesbaden: Otto Harrassowitz/London: Allen & Unwin, 1966), for basic definitions: p. 115 s.v. *tajdīf*, p. 392 s.v. *sabb*.
5 Qur'ān [hereafter referred to as Q.] 6:108 (my trans. and italics). (The noun *sabb*, as such, does not appear in the Qur'ān).
6 Edward William Lane, *An Arabic-English Lexicon*, Part 2 *Jīm-Khā'*, (Beirut: Librairie du Liban, 1968), p. 391 s.v. *jaddafa*.
7 *Leviticus* 24:10–15.
8 Ibid. 24:16, trans. in *The New Jerusalem Bible*.
9 Ibid. 24:23. See F.L. Cross (ed.), *The Oxford Dictionary of the Christian Church*, (London: Oxford University Press, 1957), p. 177 s.v. 'Blasphemy'; and *The Interpreter's Dictionary of the Bible: An Illustrated Encyclopedia*, vol. 1 A-D, (New York & Nashville: Abingdon Press, 1962), p. 445 s.v. 'Blasphemy'.
10 *The New Jerusalem Bible*, p. 167 n.24c.
11 *Acts* 6:11, trans. in *The New Jerusalem Bible*; see *The Interpreter's Dictionary of the Bible*, vol. 1, p. 445 s.v. 'Blasphemy'.
12 *Acts* 7.
13 *The New Jerusalem Bible*, p. 1811 n.7s.
14 Q.7:180, trans. by Abdullah Yusuf Ali, *The Holy Qur'an: Text, Translation and Commentary*, (Kuwait: Dhāt al-Salāsil, 1984), [Hereafter referred to as Yusuf Ali, *Qur'an*], p. 396.
15 Q.7:180, trans. by Arthur J. Arberry, *The Koran Interpreted*, (2 vols., London: Allen & Unwin/New York: Macmillan, 1971), [Hereafter referred to as Arberry, *Koran Interpreted*], vol. 1, p. 193 (my italics).
16 Wehr, *Dictionary of Modern Written Arabic*, p. 859 s.v. *laḥada*.
17 See above n.2.
18 Toshihiko Izutsu, *God and Man in the Koran: Semantics of the Koranic Weltanschauung*, Studies in the Humanities and Social Relations, vol. 5, (Tokyo: Keio Institute of Cultural and Linguistic Studies, 1964), p. 12.
19 Ibid.
20 Ibid., p. 18.
21 Ibid., p. 21. As Izutsu notes, the verb *kafara* (in the sense of 'to be ungrateful') is the direct opposite of *shakara* ('to be thankful'). I am grateful to my colleague Dr. Rasheed El-Enany for also drawing my attention to the 2nd form of the verb, *kaffara*, which had the older meaning of 'to prostrate oneself', 'to pay honour to a prince in bowing down'. (See J.G. Hava, *Al-Farā'id Arabic-English Dictionary*, (Beirut: Dār al-Mashriq, 1970), p. 660 s.v. *kaffara*). The noun *kafr* ('homage of Persians to their king') is phonetically close to *kufr* (unbelief). Thus, in Islam it is not an exaggeration to say that *kufr* carried a hidden cultural baggage, by virtue of its root, of prostrating oneself before false gods.
22 Q.18:106, trans. by Toshihiko Izutsu, *Ethico-Religious Concepts in the Qur'ān*, McGill Islamic Studies 1, (Montreal: McGill University Press, 1966), p. 153. See Hava, *Al-Farā'id*, p. 660 s.v. *kufr*.

23 Izutsu, *Ethico-Religious Concepts*, p. 120 (my italics).
24 Wehr, *Dictionary of Modern Written Arabic*, p. 1027 s.v. *haza'a*.
25 Izutsu, *Ethico-Religious Concepts*, pp. 152–153.
26 Q.15:94–96, trans. by Yusuf Ali, *Qur'an*, pp. 653–654; see Izutsu, *Ethico-Religious Concepts*, p. 153.
27 Izutsu, *Ethico-Religious Concepts*, pp. 4–5.

2

TEXT

> It is therefore an absolute principle of excavation, which allows of no exceptions at all, that the whole area must not be cleared simultaneously.
>
> Kenyon, *Beginning in Archaeology*, p. 77.

It is the intention of this Chapter to survey a number of books and films which have given rise to accusations of blasphemy in the East and the West. We propose, however, to ignore here the furore which arose in Egypt over the controversial work on pre-Islamic poetry written by Ṭāhā Ḥusayn (1889–1973); this has been exhaustively treated many times elsewhere.[1] Instead, we will survey here the *content* of: (a) the Nobel Prize-winning Egyptian novelist Najīb Maḥfūẓ's book *Awlād Ḥāratinā*, a title which translates literally as *The Children of Our Quarter* but has also been rendered in English as *Children of Gebelawi*[2]; (b) Salman Rushdie's novel *The Satanic Verses*[3]; and (c) the Greek novelist Nikos Kazantzakis' book *The Last Temptation*[4]. We will look too at the film of the latter directed by Martin Scorsese entitled *The Last Temptation of Christ*.[5] Some comparative reference will also be made in passing to the film by Jean-Luc Godard entitled *Je Vous Salue, Marie* (*Hail, Mary*)[6], when discussing the furore which arose over *The Last Temptation of Christ*.

Awlād Ḥāratinā (Children of Gebelawi) **by Najīb Maḥfūẓ [born 1911]**

This earlier novel by the distinguished Egyptian novelist Najīb Maḥfūẓ has had a chequered publishing history. It was first produced as a serial in the Egyptian newspaper *al-Ahrām* between 21st September–25th December 1959; the resulting uproar meant that the serialisation was only completed due to the friendship between the editor of *al-Ahrām*,

Muḥammad Haykal, and President Nasser.[7] *Awlād Ḥāratinā* has never been published in book form in Egypt but it appeared thus, in a slightly expurgated form, in Lebanon in 1967, published by Dār al-Ādāb of Beirut.[8] It has been claimed that the English translation of the book by Philip Stewart constitutes the most complete version of the work in book form now in print.[9]

After Najīb Maḥfūẓ was awarded the Nobel Prize for Literature in 1988 – and it is worth noting that *Awlād Ḥāratinā* was clearly referred to at the Nobel presentation in Stockholm[10] – the Egyptian evening paper *al-Masā'* attempted to serialise the novel again, without the author's permission, but this time it was stopped by Maḥfūẓ himself who, by now, took a wholly pragmatic view of the affair.[11] A similar pragmatism, even fatalism, imbued his attitude when he found himself, like Salman Rushdie, on the receiving end of a *fatwā*.[12] As Shyam Bhatia put it: 'For all his physical infirmities, his mind, uncluttered by age, is brilliantly clear. In an era that has seen the revival of Islamic extremism – which led to the banning of one of his books and the proclamation of at least one *fatwa* against him – *Mahfouz refuses to be intimidated.*'[13] Currently a new translation of *Awlād Ḥāratinā* is under way in the United States.

Like John Bunyan's *Pilgrim's Progress*, *Awlād Ḥāratinā* is an allegory. Indeed, it 'is one of the few allegorical novels in Arabic.'[14] Rasheed El-Enany has succintly characterised it as 'an allegorical lamentation on the failure of mankind to achieve social justice and to harness the potential of science for the service of man.'[15] Whether it is a good or a bad allegory, or merely an indifferent one, may be judged by the reader. However, a few remarks from some of the literary critics are appended to this descriptive section.

The novel may also be described as a satire and it has clearly been regarded as such by some writers: 'Within this allegorical treatment, which is only partially successful, *the social satire is as direct and bitter as in any of the works* . . . The Hara is unmistakably a quarter of old Cairo, in which people suffer from dirt and poverty, and are subject to the tyranny of organized bands of thugs. The lives of the people of the Hara are lived out in a context of violence, injustice and oppression.'[16]

Typical of the allegory, and perhaps indicative of the satire within, *Awlād Ḥāratinā* is divided into 114 chapters, a dramatic parallel to the structure of Islam's most sacred book, The Holy Qur'ān, which has the same number of *sūras* (chapters). Neither the professional modern literary critic[17] nor the Islamic fundamentalist[18] has been able to avoid noticing this parallelism.

Yet, while quite blatantly establishing links with Islamic sacred history – as Badawi puts it, 'Maḥfūẓ here is giving modern man's view of the stories of prophecy narrated in the Koran'[19] – the author also, from the very beginning, plugs his narrative into the wider secular stream of Arabic popular literature. His 'very fast-moving short *nouvelles*, held together by means of certain parallelisms and continuities and, of course, one unifying concept'[20], to cite Badawi again, have something in common, structurally at least, with *The Thousand and One Nights* corpus, though the overall themes and linking factor are, of course, very different.

Maḥfūẓ begins with a *Prologue* (*Iftitāḥiyya*):

> This is the story of our alley, [*ḥikāya ḥāratinā*] or these are its stories. I myself have lived only through the most recent events, but I have written down everything as it is told by our many professional storytellers who learnt them in the cafés or from their fathers.[21]

The first of the *nouvelles* is that of Adham. And in his introductory paragraph, Maḥfūẓ sets the scene and the tone for the rest of the entire novel:

> In the beginning the site of our alley [*makān ḥāratinā*] was part of the desert at the foot of the mountain Gebel Mukattam. Nothing stood in this desert save the Big House that Gebelawi had built in defiance of fear and barbarism and banditry. Its towering wall enclosed a garden to the west and the house with its three storeys to the east.[22]

The 114 chapters of the book are structured, after the *Prologue*, into five distinct major sections, each of which is called after the hero who figures prominently in that section. However, the Arabic names are transparent disguises for the leading prophets of Islam and, indeed, other religions too.[23] Thus Adham, the first major name, to which we have just referred, is, of course, the first prophet of Islamic history and God's *khalīfa* or deputy on earth,[24] Adam: his Arabic name Ādam is not exactly distant from Maḥfūẓ's Arabic Adham.[25] The other four figures are, respectively, Jabal (=Moses)[26], Rifā'a (=Jesus),[27] Qāsim (=Muḥammad),[28] and 'Arafa (=Scientific Man/Science).[29] Al-Jabalāwī, whose brooding presence pervades the novel from the beginning, is God himself.[30] A range of other characters, events and features in Maḥfūẓ's novel have also been identified with prominent figures, events and features from religious history and scripture.[31] The *Ḥāra*, or Quarter, identified as 'The World or Existence' (*al-'Ālam aw al-Kawn*)[32] is, in essence, a timeless portrait of Old Cairo;[33] and the area of this particular imaginary Quarter, called by the author the Jabalāwī Quarter, constitutes a primary frame for

Maḥfūẓ's novel.[34] Finally, it is clear from the allegory that the Big House, to which we referred earlier in our quotation,[35] represents Paradise itself.[36]

So much for the actual setting. The tale of *Awlād Ḥāratinā* may be summarised very briefly by concentrating on its five main sub-divisions which, though they tell very different stories, are united by the lurking presence and unseen existence of al-Jabalāwī Himself.

(i) Adham/Adam[37]

The story begins with the Master of the Big House (*al-Bayt al-Kabīr*), al-Jabalāwī, calling together his sons Idrīs, 'Abbās, Riḍwān, Jalīl and Adham. They are all clearly in great awe of their father. To their consternation he appoints Adham as the administrator of the estate owned by al-Jabalāwī. Adham's mother was black and this provokes the racist hostility of his brother Idrīs (=Iblīs). Moreover, Adham is the youngest of the brothers. He is thus singled out by the narrator of the story as very much a prototype Joseph or Benjamin. Idrīs's vociferous protests lead to his being physically expelled by his father from the House, cursed and disowned. When Adham marries Umayma, a relative of his mother, the wedding procession is temporarily interrupted by a furious Idrīs.

At first Adham is very happy in his marriage to Umayma. But the idyll cannot last. A seemingly reformed Idrīs tempts Adham to read his father's will which is kept hidden in a secret room off al-Jabalāwī's bedroom. Later Umayma also tempts Adham to do the same and learn their futures. Adham is discovered by al-Jabalawī in the secret room and expelled, with his wife, by the enraged father from the Big House. They build a hut to the west of this House: this is the beginning of the *Ḥāra*, or Quarter, of the novel.

Umayma gives birth to twin sons, Qadrī and Himām. When Himām is older he is told by al-Jabalāwī, his grandfather, that he will be allowed to live in the Big House. Qadrī later kills Himām. Before Adham and Umayma themselves die, Adham is visited by the great figure of al-Jabalāwī Himself: He has finally forgiven His son and come to tell him that the estate will be inherited by Adham's descendants, that is, the offspring of Qadrī and Qadrī's wife Hind (the daughter of the evil Idrīs). The blood lines of the Quarter are thus, from the very beginning, destined to be a mixture of the basically good (via Adham) and the intrinsically evil (via Idrīs).[38]

(ii) Jabal/Moses[39]

The Quarter has become degenerate with poverty widespread, and corruption, greed and extortion rife among those who administer, rule or achieve any power within that Quarter. The oppressed people appeal to the Trustee of that estate, Effendi, to help them in their afflictions but they only encounter hostility from him. Jabal, the foster son of Effendi, is much moved by their plight and he sides with the protestors, regarding himself, in essence, as one of them: this is where his real father and mother come from. Jabal becomes increasingly conscious of the tyranny the people are suffering. He kills a bully to save a man and eventually joins the oppressed people of the Quarter.

Jabal marries Shafiqa, the daughter of a snake charmer, and he becomes a snake charmer himself. He returns to the house of the Trustee, Effendi, and speaks on behalf of his people but he is treated with fury and disdain. However, snakes invade the Quarter, including the Trustee's house; Jabal is summoned to get rid of the snakes. Upon certain conditions he does so. However, Effendi, not a man of his word, agrees to an attack on Jabal and his people in revenge but the latter are victorious. Jabal confronts Effendi again. The defeated Trustee offers to make him Chief but Jabal demands only the rights of his people. They are finally granted by the Trustee. Jabal assumes a position of power over his sometimes fractious and greedy people, and he rules them with fairness, refusing to exploit them.

(iii) Rifā'a/Jesus[40]

A carpenter Shāfi'ī and his pregnant young wife 'Abda are driven into exile in the Sūq al-Muqaṭṭam. Shāfi'ī is at a loss to understand the reason: all he has done is talk of Jabal and his age. 'Abda reminds him of the virtue of patience: it has been said that al-Jabalāwī will one day return to save his people.

After some twenty years of exile (which Maḥfūẓ indicates by a mere chapter change), during the first part of which their son Rifā'a is born, they return to the Quarter. Their former persecutor is dead and another Chief has succeeded him. The family is welcomed by many of the townspeople but the new Chief Khunfis (more classically spelled Khunfus) is hostile from the start. Shāfi'ī resumes his trade as a carpenter. Rifā'a visits Jawād, the poet, and is stirred by seeing a picture of al-Jabalāwī in his house. Rifā'a asks if anyone has ever seen Him and is told that none of the present generation has. Later, Rifā'a's parents indicate that they would like him to marry ʻAysha, the daughter of Khunfis, but Rifāʻa objects vehemently and leaves home temporarily. Feeling the need to be alone he goes into the desert.

One day Rifāʻa claims to have heard al-Jabalāwī's voice. His father Shāfiʻī is appalled. Later a woman called Yāsmīna is discovered in compromising circumstances. Rifāʻa saves her with an offer of marriage which is duly undertaken. Rifāʻa's behaviour becomes even stranger in the eyes of the people when he begins to go round calling on them to trust him and to let him exorcise their evil spirits. A small band of former reprobates gathers round Rifāʻa and they become his followers. Meanwhile Rifāʻa's new wife Yāsmīna resumes an affair with her former lover, Bayūmī, the strong-man of the Quarter; during their meeting he intemperately announces that al-Jabalāwī is dead or might just as well be.

News of Rifāʻa's activities comes to the attention of the Trustee and Rifāʻa is summoned for questioning by the Chiefs. He proclaims that he only desires the people's happiness. Rifāʻa's wife Yāsmīna betrays his movements to Bayūmī; but during a 'last supper' Rifāʻa agrees to free his wife from the evil spirit which still possesses her. As Rifāʻa and his friends begin a projected escape, they are apprehended by Bayūmī and others. Bayūmī and Khunfis cudgel Rifāʻa to death and quickly bury him. His grief-stricken disciples exhume the body and rebury it in a proper tomb. They then go to live on the fringes of the desert.

After Rifāʻa's parents, ʻAbda and Shāfiʻī, have accused the Chiefs of their son's murder, the Chiefs search vainly for Rifāʻa's body in its first hasty grave but they find nothing. The day comes when Yāsmīna is chased into the desert by Bayūmī's former wife's people and she encounters Rifāʻa's disciples in a hut. One of them strangles her, enraged at her betrayal of Rifāʻa. Later, one of the Chiefs is discovered murdered and a persecution begins of Rifāʻa's disciples and their friends. The Trustee sends for one of the former called ʻAlī and reaches an agreement with him. ʻAlī is entrusted with the stewardship of part of the estate and Rifāʻa is exalted among the people in death in a way that he never achieved during his lifetime. Peace returns to the district but the disciples differ over the interpretation of the mission of Rifāʻa. For some of them his significance lay in his healing of the sick and contempt for rank and power. But ʻAlī married and prospered from the estate.

(iv) Qāsim/Muḥammad[41]

The first paragraph with which the section on Qāsim opens stresses the lack of change and the sense of timelessness in the Quarter. Poverty and hypocrisy remain. The Trustee of the day resembles his predecessors and the Chiefs are as brutal and corrupt as ever. Qāsim's parents have died and he lives with his uncle.

One day, taking advantage of a sleepy doorkeeper, Qāsim enters the Trustee's garden, eats the fruit and splashes in the fountain. He is chased out by an awakened and enraged gatekeeper. Later on, an older and wiser Qāsim prevents a nasty fight over lost or stolen money. The money is recovered and Qāsim wins the admiration of the people.

Despite his lack of money, Qāsim marries a widow, Qamar, and she bears them a daughter whom they call Iḥsān. But Qāsim now begins to act strangely and one night, Qamar, awakened by the crying baby, discovers that her husband is missing. He is found at Hind's Rock, unconscious. On recovering his senses Qāsim tells his wife what happened: she will be the first to hear the news. He has encountered Qandīl (more classically spelled Qindīl), the servant of al-Jabalāwī, at Hind's Rock in the desert during the night. Qandīl confirms that al-Jabalāwī is alive and well in the Big House, and aware of all that happens in the Quarter. Al-Jabalāwī has sent a message of great significance: all the people of the Quarter are His children equally and the tyranny of the Chiefs must end. Indeed, the Quarter is to become 'an extension of the Big House' (*imtidād li 'l-Bayt al-Kabīr*)[42] itself, a kind of Paradise on earth. They are all the heirs of the estate.

It is not surprising that the message conveyed to Qasīm via Qandīl generates intense controversy. Qāsim himself is later harangued by an infuriated Trustee. Worse, Qāsim's wife Qamar falls sick and eventually dies, to the great grief of Qāsim who is left to look after their daughter. Later Qāsim learns of a plot to kill him and he flees with his companions. A new Quarter on the mountain (*ḥāra jadīda fawq al-jabal*)[43] is formed and Qāsim hailed as the Chief, despite his protestations. For the time being, he, his friends and his daughter Iḥsān are safe. Qāsim remarries and finds renewed happiness with his new bride. A successful attack is mounted on a procession from their former Quarter and a counter-attack from that Quarter, enraged by Qāsim's first success, is repulsed after a fierce fight: eight of Qāsim's men are killed but ten of the enemy. The disaster worries the Trustee who tries to rally the Quarter and keep it united. But Qāsim and his men later arrive with cudgels and win the final battle for the Quarter. The victor enters the Trustee's dark and shuttered house and finds it deserted: the Trustee has fled with his family and retinue. Qāsim becomes the undisputed Chief of the Quarter and assumes the function of Trustee. A new and more peaceful age beckons.

The people of the Quarter enjoy an era of tranquillity and love under the benevolent rule of Qāsim.

(v) ‘Arafa/Scientific Man[44]

The names of the great figures from the past like Jabal, Rifā‘a and Qāsim have become embroidered in myth. Little has changed in the Quarter: ‘The eye sees only an alley sunk in darkness and storytellers singing of dreams’[45] One day ‘Arafa, the son of a woman called Jahsha, returns to the Quarter, having been away for a long time. The denizens of the Quarter mock the fact that his father is unknown. ‘Arafa claims that he is a sorcerer, a magician (*sāḥir*),[46] and he despises the legends of the past. Yet the novel, as El-Enany stresses, ‘establishes ‘Arafa as a recipient of revelation like his prophetic predecessors. What we have here is a gallant attempt by Mahfouz to bestow on science the spiritual power inherent in religion.’[47]

‘Arafa marries ‘Awāṭif and boasts to her of the power of his magic. It has the potential to end the harsh rule of the Chiefs and feed the hungry people of the Quarter. ‘Awāṭif wonders about her husband’s sanity.

One dark, scent-filled night, ‘Arafa breaks into al-Jabalāwī’s house, seeking the latter’s mysterious book which contains the terms of the endowment (*shurūṭ al-waqf*) together with magical spells (*āyāt al- siḥr*).[48] During his incursion he is forced to strangle a servant who wakes up. Later, ‘Arafa is amazed to learn that al-Jabalāwī Himself is dead. Apparently, on discovering the death of His servant, al-Jabalāwī has been carried off by shock and frailty and extreme old age. ‘Arafa’s crime is detected by the Trustee of the day who forces him into an alliance and makes use of ‘Arafa’s magic to build up his own power base. ‘Arafa falls first into adultery and then into deep despair. He tells his helper and follower Ḥanash:

> This prison no longer gives me anything but thoughts of death. The pleasure and wine and dancing girls are just the music of death. I seem to smell the grave in every pot of flowers.[49]

‘Arafa decides to run away, taking his estranged wife with him, but the Trustee captures them both. They are put into two sacks and buried alive in the desert. At first, the people of the Quarter are pleased by the news of ‘Arafa’s death because he precipitated, albeit indirectly, the death of the great Jabalāwī Himself. Later it is rumoured that Ḥanash, ‘Arafa’s friend, has gained possession of ‘Arafa’s own book of magic and disappeared. The people now exalt ‘Arafa’s memory and begin to yearn for the return of Ḥanash in the role of magician and saviour. On that depressing, unfinished and unsatisfying note, whose message is deeply pessimistic, Maḥfūẓ's allegory ends, with the people still hoping (vainly?) for miracles in the face of evil and injustice.

Awlād Ḥāratinā is one of Maḥfūẓ's earlier novels and it is by no means his best. Somekh notes:

> The great majority of the characters are black-and-white . . . the main protagonists of the five different sections are only portrayed in quick-moving sketches . . . The picture that emerges lacks the touch of life . . . The abundant dialogue in the book adds little to understanding of the inner selves of these people . . . The end at which Mahfuz aimed – namely blending a novel and an allegory – has therefore not been successfully attained. Consequently, we have to accept *Awlad* as basically a system of symbols . . .[50]

The allegory is also, perhaps, *too* obvious, as Maḥfūẓ later discovered to his cost when faced by individual critics and fundamentalist or establishment groups who condemned the novel. One Western newspaper, having referred to this novel as 'a book as remarkable as any he had written, which concluded with a vision of a man searching in a rubbish dump for clues about his salvation', noted of the book and its author:

> The book was serialised in Al-Ahram, Egypt's biggest national daily newspaper, but has never been published in book form in Egypt. *Naguib Mahfouz has his critics. The calm pursuit of a literary career under the very different administrations, shows a Dryden-like shrewdness at work. One commentator even called him a 'ratfink'.*[51]

Mustafa Badawi has neatly summed up some of the literary faults of *Awlād Ḥāratinā*:

> . . . Maḥfūẓ went on to write more, and much greater, novels after *The Children of Gebelawi*, which constitutes an impressive, though imperfect, landmark in the development of his art as a novelist . . . As a novel *The Children of Gebelawi* suffers from serious defects: it is too repetitive, too full of fighting, too fast-moving, too thickly populated to allow for convincing characterization and, for a work on man's religious quest, it is too explicitly prosaic and lacking in the poetic spirit. Its interest lies chiefly on the level of themes and ideas, although its message is

> not exactly redolent of hope. Yet its spiritual preoccupations, its existentialist terror of death, point forward to future works.[52]

Robin Ostle was rather kinder in his assessment, in which he stressed, as we saw above, the satirical elements of the allegory:

> Pessimism would also be the abiding impression for the reader of 'Awlad Haratna' (1959), which can be included in the category of [Maḥfūẓ's] Cairene novels, even though Mahfouz removes his beloved old Cairo out of specific historical time, and treats the story of its inhabitants as an allegory, using the context of the whole of human history and the stages of prophetic revelation to which mankind has been exposed. Within this allegorical treatment, which is only partially successful, *the social satire is as direct and bitter as in any of the works* . . . The Hara is unmistakably a quarter of old Cairo, in which people suffer from dirt and poverty, and are subject to the tyranny of organized bands of thugs. The lives of the people of the Hara are lived out in a context of violence, injustice and oppression.[53]

We will conclude this section with two final brief examples of relevant literary and cultural criticism, by way of illustrating the kind of reception which Maḥfūẓ's novel has had among the critics. Rasheed El-Enany holds that

> *Awlād Ḥāratinā* remains today Mahfouz's major and most lucid statement on the question of religion; he spelt out there what he had only half said before. He never ceased, however, to demonstrate in his later novels *the irrelevance of religion to the predicament of modern man*.[54]

El-Enany finds this theme powerfully pursued in Maḥfūẓ's later novels. For example, he notes that *al-Ṭarīq* (*The Search*, *The Way*), published in 1964, 'is again a powerful metaphor of the futility of mankind's search for God.'[55] This is a novel where 'the protagonist wastes his life looking for his father (i.e. God) whom he had never known. In the course of the search he is offered the chance of a self-reliant life, a job and a true love, but he relinquishes all that for the search and ends up in despair.'[56]

Somekh believes that 'never before in his works has the author been so sad'[57] as he is in *Awlād Ḥāratinā*. This scholar concludes that while '*Awlad* is an audacious departure from the author's familiar style . . . it loses much of its literary value because of the imbalance between the form and the content. The resort to allegory does not really lend any greater profundity to the ideas.'[58]

The Satanic Verses by Salman Rushdie [born 1947]

The Satanic Verses was published by Viking Penguin on 26th September 1988. Thereafter, slowly at first but with increasing rapidity, the publishing history of the book assumed a momentum of its own. Despite prior warnings from the publisher's editorial consultant,[59] the great furore which developed seems to have taken both author and publisher by surprise.

At the time of its publication Salman Rushdie had already gained a notable reputation, not only as an innovative writer but as a controversial one. For example, his first major novel, *Midnight's Children*,[60] which appeared in the UK in 1981 and won him the coveted Booker Prize award in that same year, also provoked the legal wrath of the late Prime Minister of India, Mrs. Indira Gandhi.[61] *Midnight's Children* is basically the story of one, Saleem Sinai, who was born at the midnight hour of 15th August 1947, together with 1001 others. The hour is particularly auspicious since at that exact moment India achieved its independence from Britain. Rushdie endows each of the children with particular magical powers. It was not this, however, which so infuriated Mrs. Gandhi but the suggestion 'that Mrs Gandhi was responsible for the death of her husband through neglect.'[62]

Another novel, *Shame*, published in 1984,[63] also provoked antagonism.[64] In this book '[Rushdie] took an aim on Pakistan, its political characters, its culture and its religion. Some you enjoyed, some you loathed and much you did not understand.'[65] Of this novel Timothy Brennan observed:

> *Shame* covers a central episode in Pakistan's internal life, which it portrays as a family squabble between Iskander Harappa (Zulfikar Ali Bhutto) and his successor and executioner Raza Hyder (Zia ul-Haq). History in *Shame* is a history filtered through the ambitious self-images of its protagonists . . . As though fearing reprisals, *Shame* does not present history openly but hides it in allusive references to the past which are buried in casual placenames and family titles and ironic reincarnations of figures from legend.[66]

That said, it has not been difficult to identify the protagonists. 'The Virgin Ironpants', for example, has been identified as Benazir Bhutto,[67] a Prime Minister of Pakistan.

Yet the annoyance provoked in certain quarters by *Midnight's Children* and *Shame* pales into insignificance when one examines the publishing history of *The Satanic Verses*. Speaking some four years after the publication of this novel, Salman Rushdie confessed to an interviewer: 'I expected a few mullahs would be offended, call me names, and then I could defend myself in public . . . *I honestly never expected anything like this*.'[68]

October 1988 saw a spate of letters and phone calls to Viking Penguin from angry Muslims, asking for the book to be withdrawn. At the beginning of the month the Indian government banned the work and in this action it was later followed by Bangladesh (November 1988), Sudan (November 1988), South Africa (November 1988), Sri Lanka (December 1988), Kenya (March 1989), Thailand (March 1989), Tanzania (March 1989), Indonesia (March 1989), Singapore (March 1989) and Venezuela (June 1989). Outrage and protests were expressed by many other countries and organisations, as well as leading individuals.[69] And the outrage was not restricted to Islam. For example, a French Roman Catholic Cardinal in February 1989 expressed his sorrow that, once more, the faith of believers had been transgressed.[70] By contrast, on 8th November 1988 a few months earlier, *The Satanic Verses* was awarded the literary Whitbread Prize.[71]

The whole affair reached a shattering climax in the first two months of 1989. The Muslims of Bradford in Yorkshire expressed their revulsion in a *symbolic and ritual* manner by publicly burning a copy of the book on 14th January 1989;[72] Muslim protesters in Islamabad, Srinagar in Kashmir, and Bombay expressed their anger in a more *physical* manner by demonstrating against the book and suffering many fatalities in consequence;[73] finally, the Ayatollah Khomeini added a *legal* voice, issuing his famous *fatwā* against Salman Rushdie on 14th February 1989, holding that the author should be executed.[74] Salman Rushdie went into hiding.

Thereafter, two distinct streams are identifiable in the publishing history of the book: on the one hand, worldwide Muslim protests and condemnations have continued, the resolution of the Organization of the Islamic Conference to ban the publications of Penguin throughout forty five Muslim countries, on 16th March 1989, being fairly typical.[75] On the other, Rushdie began to look forward to a paperback edition of his novel, though the road towards this was fraught with many pitfalls and his ambition encountered numerous obstacles.

By the beginning of February 1990 *The Satanic Verses* had already sold more than a million *hardback* copies.[76] On 24th December 1990 Salman Rushdie appeared to embrace Islam and he observed that he would not allow a paperback edition or translation 'while any risk of further offence exists.'[77] However, to cut a long story short, an anonymous consortium of publishers (anonymous to prevent individual identification and revenge attacks on individuals) banded together and the first US paperback edition appeared in 1992.[78]

At the time of writing the Muslim war on the book, and strong disgust felt against it, continue. The *fatwā* has not been cancelled.[79]

When Salman Rushdie met the British Prime Minister, John Major, together with Frances D'Souza (who directs Article 19, an organisation which campaigns on behalf of the author) in the House of Commons, Muslim reaction was hostile. Iqbal Sacranie, 'joint convenor of the UK Action Committee on Islamic Affairs' accused John Major of insensitivity and said that all Muslims worldwide would condemn the meeting. But opposition also came from those concerned about trade and good political relations with Iran. Peter Temple-Morris MP, 'chairman of the all-party Britain–Iran Parliamentary Group', also spoke in disparaging terms about the meeting.[80]

Rushdie's *Satanic Verses* has also been used as a tool to service a variety of fundamentalist agendas. For example, at the beginning of July 1993, Islamic fundamentalists set fire to the Madimak Hotel in Sivas, Turkey, which was hosting a Festival in honour of a sixteenth century heretical poet. One of the guests was a seventy-eight year old author, Aziz Nesin, who had published unauthorised Turkish translations from *The Satanic Verses*. Nesin escaped but perhaps as many as forty people were killed.[81] Rushdie condemned both the riot *and* the author: 'Nesin and his associates wished to use me, and my work, as cannon fodder in their struggle against the growth of religious zealotry in Turkey.'[82]

Rushdie continues to argue that 'the enemies of Islam are those who wish the culture to be frozen in time';[83] this is a statement which cuts little ice with his opponents like Dr. Kalim Siddiqui of The Muslim Institute in London who holds that 'the mistake Rushdie and others of his ilk make is to regard us as "frozen in time".' He goes on to stress that 'the fact is that the modern global Islamic movement is based on at least 200 years of intense intellectual activity . . . The global Islamic movement . . . is neither frozen nor blind. Its intellectual foundations include the reinterpretation of Islamic history, political mood, philosophy and a true and more profound understanding of Western civilisation.'[84]

If, as Professor Edward Said maintains, we may have an 'intellectual who, because of exile, cannot or, more to the point, will not make the adjustment, preferring instead to remain outside the mainstream, unaccommodated, unco-opted, resistant', then perhaps we might consider whether this is a role which Mr. Salman Rushdie has chosen to play with skill and passion.[85]

Turning now to the book itself, which has been described by Timothy Brennan as 'the most ambitious novel yet published to deal with the immigrant experience in Britain', setting out, as it does, 'to capture the immigrants' dream-like disorientation, their multiform, plural 'union-by-hybridization',' [86] it is clear from a careful reading that the book is fundamentally a study in *alienation*. Or, as Muhammad Mashuq ibn Ally has put it more elaborately:

> *The Satanic Verses* is about identity, alienation, rootlessness, brutality, compromise, and conformity. These concepts confront all migrants, disillusioned with both cultures: the one they are in and the one they join. Yet knowing they cannot live a life of anonymity, they mediate between them both. *The Satanic Verses* is a reflection of the author's dilemmas.[87]

In a very real sense, as Ally shows, *The Satanic Verses* is the, albeit surreal, record of its own author's continuing identity crisis. Born in Bombay, and first educated at a missionary school there, Rushdie attended Rugby School in England from the age of thirteen, and later, King's College, Cambridge.[88] Rushdie himself is on record as having claimed that his book was not about the Islamic faith 'but about migration, metamorphosis, divided selves, love, death, London and Bombay.'[89] Elsewhere, Rushdie said of this work: 'It's a novel which happens to contain a castigation of Western materialism. The tone is comic.'[90] Ally sees the author ultimately as a victim, 'the victim of nineteenth-century British colonialism.'[91]

The Satanic Verses is divided into nine Chapters or main sections: each will be surveyed here in turn. They are entitled: (i) The Angel Gibreel; (ii) Mahound; (iii) Ellowen Deeowen; (iv) Ayesha; (v) A City Visible but Unseen; (vi) Return to Jahilia; (vii) The Angel Azraeel; (viii) The Parting of the Arabian Sea; and (ix) A Wonderful Lamp.

(i) The Angel Gibreel[92]

The Satanic Verses may be likened to a bubbling cauldron whose principal ingredients are two people[93] and three places.[94] The two people are Gibreel Farishta and Saladin Chamcha. For anyone schooled in the study of Islam and Islamic history, the names which Rushdie has given to his two heroes are intensely stirring and evocative. The Arabic word for Gabriel, the great angel through whom the revelation of the Qur'ān was made to the Prophet Muḥammad, is *Jibrīl*, easily anglicised in transliteration to Gibreel. The Persian word for 'angel' is *firishta*. Saladin is, of course, the anglicised version of Ṣalāḥ al-Dīn: the most famous bearer of this name was the warrior hero of Islamic history (1138–1193) who defeated the Crusaders at one of Islam's most memorable battles, the Battle of Ḥaṭṭīn (1187), and captured Jerusalem.[95] Only the name Chamcha lacks a specifically Islamic resonance. He has been identified with the Bombay film star Amitabh Bachan[96] and N.T. Rama Rao, 'famous in Indian cinema for his portrayal of mythological beings.'[97] Ruthven draws our attention to the various meanings and overtones of *chamcha* including that of 'spoon' in Urdu.[98]

These, then, are Rushdie's pivotal protagonists but like so much in his novel, the characters have an evanescent quality. They have 'layers' of significance like the structure of the novel itself. As Brennan in his masterly analysis puts it: '[The] three identities – prophet, evil spirit and God's messenger – are assumed by Gibreel Farishta, who comes to London to blow the trumpet of doom in yet another incarnation: Azraeel, the exterminating Angel.'[99] Azraeel, Azrael, or, more properly transliterated, 'Izrā'īl, is the main Islamic angel of death who has a particularly fearsome reputation 'for toughness and ruthlessness.'[100] When a person dies, that 'individual's death is signalled by a leaf falling from the tree beneath God's throne on which the fated person's name appears. It is then 'Izrā'īl's task to separate that person's soul from his or her body.'[101]

Rushdie's three principal loci are soon dealt with. They are the (real) cities of London and Bombay, and the 'mythical' city of Jahilia. Rushdie has claimed in an interview that the three are 'really the same place.'[102] London and Bombay require no introduction; suffice it to repeat that the author is very familiar with both having been born in Bombay in 1947 and lived in London. Jahilia, however, needs a rather more extensive gloss for the non-Arabist. The Arabic word *Jāhiliyya* has a profound historical, cultural and linguistic baggage. It means primarily a 'state of ignorance; pre-Islamic paganism, pre-Islamic times'[103], in other words, that perceived dark age, by later Muslims, in Arabia before the coming of Islam. The word thus resonates with concepts of polytheism, inter-tribal fighting, darkness and superstition as well as the basic one of ignorance. *It is basically an abusive epithet.* We saw earlier how slippery the semantic field of a word may be and noted the cultural and temporal conditioning of many words. Rushdie makes use of this linguistic cliché in a particularly dramatic way: in *The Satanic Verses* the holy Islamic City of Mecca appears under the title of the City of Jahilia, thinly disguised.

We are now in a position to attempt a brief survey of the actual content of the first Chapter which, as we have seen, the author calls *The Angel Gibreel.* To appreciate and understand what is a highly complex

– sometimes obscure – novel written on several different levels, it is useful to bear in mind the preceding identifications or, perhaps better, resonances of the author's principal heroes and their given arenas of activity. Other individuals will be identified where necessary in what follows, and it would not be unfair to say that there is a kind of gnostic code in operation in the book to which only those knowledgeable about Islam, or skilled in Islamic History and Studies, have *real* access.[104]

Several commentators have drawn attention to the extraordinarily dramatic and unusual opening of *The Satanic Verses* in which Gibreel Farishta and Saladin Chamcha fall safely to earth, or by an English beach to be more precise, after their jumbo jet has been hijacked and then blown up by terrorists.[105] For Brennan 'the scene of course re-enacts Shaitan's fall.'[106] Rushdie describes how a great bang splits the aircraft and dramatically throws Gibreel and Saladin into the open thin air through which they hurtle earthwards in a confused and frightened welter of emotions and thoughts.

It is clear from the start that Rushdie's novel belongs to a broadly picaresque tradition which includes, for example, Cervantes' *Don Quixote*, and this is particularly evident in the way that the former frequently transcends time and space. The novel also has much in common with the allegorical tradition although one would hesitate to describe it, *in toto*, as an allegory after the manner of, say, Maḥfūẓ's *Awlād Ḥāratinā*. However, just as the hero of Bunyan's *Pilgrim's Progress* represents struggling man, so, initially at least, Rushdie's heroes Gibreel and Saladin represent incarnations of good and evil respectively, 'a symbolic angel and devil.'[107] (The allegorical aspect of the tale is later massively reinforced when Saladin, fallen to earth, finds he has grown hooves, horns and a huge penis. Gibreel, conversely, sports a halo.[108])

The two men come ashore on an English beach. Gibreel has been a famous, workaholic mega-star of the Indian cinema for fifteen years, specialising in a genre of religious films called 'theologicals' in which he has played a variety of gods from the vast Indian pantheon, beginning with Ganesh, the Elephant God, and going on to Hanuman, the Monkey King, and Krishna, as well as the great Mughal Akbar. Gibreel is notorious both for having been plagued by ill health which has threatened his career, and severe halitosis. His disappearance panics the Indian film industry in the form of seven distinct studios to which he is contracted, and which all depend on his presence. It also precipitates the suicide of a wealthy lover and neighbour, Rekha Merchant, who takes her children with her in death. (As he falls from the aircraft, Gibreel sees her adorned ghost astride a flying carpet). But great film stars can be forgotten and the hoardings in Bombay with the advertisements for his films begin to fade and decay. So do his films themselves. A question hangs in the air: is the plane disaster part of a course of retribution which has overtaken him because he has eaten pork after recovering from a mystery illness?

Saladin Chamcha shares Gibreel's profession, though his talents (or opportunities?) are rather more limited. He has just paid a visit home to his native City of Bombay for the first time after fifteen years, in the company of a troupe of actors called The Prospero Players. Saladin is the son of a wealthy businessman Changez Chamchawala. The son has been an ardent anglophile from his youth, educated in England from the age of thirteen (like Salman Rushdie himself[109]); his mother Nasreen has choked to death on a fishbone and his father has remarried another 'Nasreen', precipitating a rift between father and son. By the end of his University studies in England, Saladin is the proud possessor of a British passport and intent on becoming an actor. He marries a disturbed English girl, Pamela Lovelace. However, when he embarks with The Prospero Players to India, to put on George Bernard Shaw's *The Millionairess* – the trip which precedes the air disaster – he is unfaithful to his wife with an Indian girl whom he has known in his youth called Zeeny Vakil. She insists that he has surrendered totally to the culture and mores of his adopted country, England, and become *alienated* both from his own country and himself. She laughs at the commercial radio and TV work which he does and which employs to the full his talent for mimicry and changing voices.

However, it becomes clear that the real reason for Saladin's return to India with the troupe of actors is not so much to act in his native land as to seek forgiveness from (or give forgiveness to?) his now aged and ascetical father. Their meeting is not a success. *The Millionairess* ends its tour and Saladin ends his relationship with Zeeny Vakil. He catches the ill-fated 747 aeroplane for London, Flight A1-420, the *Bostan*.

Rushdie's name for his terror aircraft is significant and deeply ironical. *Bustān* is one of the words used in Arabic and Persian for 'garden'. The author specifically notes that the aircraft is so-called after one of the (seven) famous Gardens of the Islamic Paradise.[110] Adam, the first man and first prophet in Islam, initially found his Garden Paradise a place of security before his traumatic expulsion. Saladin's journey follows a similar paradigm: his 'Garden' aircraft, the *Bostan*, is at first a place of security, and indeed escape, from the personal traumas of Bombay.[111] Later, with the terrorist hijack and subsequent explosion, the 'Garden' turns into a nightmare of cataclysmic proportions. This does not happen, however, before Rushdie has brought his two protagonists together and Gibreel Farishta has had the opportunity to explain to Saladin Chamcha his infatuation with a female mountaineer called Alleluia Cone.

In sum, then, this first Chapter has, as its main function, the setting of the whole cosmic scene. We are introduced to the two principal players and the Chapter employs a fairly realistic narrative voice, although there is a certain movement and fluidity between the characters, their backgrounds and the hijack frame story as Rushdie's heroes are fleshed out and endowed with fundamental characteristics and histories. Over all hangs the brooding presence of the *real* Archangel Gabriel; this is particularly the case when, during the long days of the hijack, Gibreel begins to dream endlessly that he has really become that angel.

(ii) Mahound[112]

By contrast with the 'realism' of the first Chapter, commentators agree that the second, notorious, one constitutes a kind of 'dream sequence', as does Chapter Six.[113] For the non-Islamicist, the name Mahound needs some explanation. This demonic name was applied as a term of virulent abuse by mediaeval Europe to Muḥammad, the founder Prophet of Islam, and it derived from the mediaeval *chansons de geste*.[114] Brennan stresses that the early Islamic Mecca portrayed in this Chapter is not intended as 'an historical flashback' but rather 'the (imagined? dreamed?) contemporary set of a popular religious film being directed by Gibreel, whose career has floundered after coming to England and who is trying to make a comeback.'[115] From a structural point of view then, we can immediately identify at this point two distinct registers in Rushdie's novel: 'the 'realistic' and what might be termed here the 'imaginative'. The one acts as a contrast or a counterpoint for the other. However, it would be unwise to restrict our analysis simply to these twin registers. Like *Midnight's Children*, Rushdie's *Satanic Verses* works in many layers, or on many levels, and the 'realistic' and 'imaginative' registers must also be assessed through the shifting lens of time and space. Characters appear in more than one temporal or spatial dimension. The novel is often a surreal quicksand and demands careful reading. Not least of the contrasts are the Bombay English vernacular and its sounds, into which Saladin hates to lapse, and the standard English towards which he aspires.[116]

The reader is certainly jolted in Chapter Two to find the focus so changed and suddenly discover a Sixth-Seventh Century world remote indeed from the Cities of London and Bombay. Or, as Salman Rushdie might have asked, is it? Here we have instead the City of Jahilia.

By contrast with Chapter One, Chapter Two is short, being less than half the length of the former. It opens with the image of the human Gibreel falling asleep, remembering (significantly?) how his mother used to call him Shaitan (Satan) in maternal exasperation at his childish pranks. He dreams of his angelic namesake, the great Islamic angel and vehicle of the revelation of the Qur'ān from God to Muḥammad. All that follows in this Chapter is a barely hidden account of early Islamic history from its origins to the *hijra* (migration) from Mecca to Medina in the year 622. Indeed, the fabric of the text here is utterly soaked in Islam.

The angel is shown uncovering the waters of Zamzam for Hagar and Ismā'īl in the pre-Islamic, Abrahamic era. Later we see Mahound (who represents Muḥammad in Rushdie's text) climbing Mount Cone, a name clearly intended to mirror the Mount Ḥirā' north east of Mecca where Muḥammad received his first revelation, but also uneasily echoing a female mountaineer Alleluia Cone with whom Gibreel Farishta has become infatuated and who has already appeared briefly in Chapter One. We are introduced in passing to the House of the Black Stone (=the Ka'ba) and its idols, as well as a water carrier named Khalid; the latter's role here, however, is fictional. In actual Islamic history Khālid b. al-Walīd (who died in 641) was one of the great early *generals* of Islam, fighting in many of the major battles like 'Aqrabā', Ajnādayn and Yarmūk.[117]

The tribe of the City of Jahilia is called Shark, and this comes as no surprise to the Arabist: the English word is simply a translation of the Arabic *Quraysh* which was the name of the dominant tribe in Mecca at the time of Muḥammad and the one to which the Prophet himself belonged via his clan of Hāshim.[118] In this Chapter we meet one of the great lords of Jahilia, who bears the name Karim Abu Simbel. His identification as the historical Abū Sufyān (who died in about 653), a long time opponent of Muḥammad,[119] is made easier by the fact that the historical Hind,[120] Abū Sufyān's wife, preserves her own name in Rushdie's fiction. Sardar and Davies surmise that Abū Sufyān is given the name of a Pharaonic monument, Abu Simbel, in an effort to underline the tyranny of the historical Abū Sufyān; for the Qur'ānic Pharaoh is also a tyrant.[121] In Rusdie's narrative we also meet Muḥammad's famous uncle Hamza,[122] like Hind bearing his own name, and two other names much revered in Islam: Salman and Bilal.

Salman, whom the novel characterises as 'some sort of bum from

Persia',[123] and whose fictional portrait, according to one author, has had 'considerable liberties' taken with it,[124] is Salmān al-Fārisī,[125] an early Persian convert to the Islamic faith. Bilal, or to give him his full name, Bilāl b. Rabāḥ (died *circa* 641),[126] was a freed Abyssinian slave and the first muezzin used by Muḥammad. Finally, by way of setting the scene, Rushdie refers to some of the notable Meccan deities: Allah, Uzza, Manat and Al-Lat.[127]

The story line in Chapter Two of *The Satanic Verses* starts properly with the satirical poet Baal being assaulted by Abu Simbel having demanded that the former write some scurrilous verses about Mahound.[128] Mahound then comes to tell his followers that Abu Simbel, who fears Mahound, wants a deal: toleration of the latter's message in return for some acknowledgement of the three deities Lat, Uzza and Manat. Mahound seems interested but his followers are appalled. His uncle Hamza advises him to consult the angel Gibreel. Mahound returns from a difficult session with the angel and acknowledges, in the presence of Abu Simbel and others, the desirability of intercession via the three deities. Abu Simbel and the surrounding throng are delighted: the City of Jahilia gives itself up to festivity and fighting on this, the last night of a festival in honour of the prophet Ibrahim. Bilal, Salman and Khalid, now drunk, are attacked, only to be rescued by Hamza. Two of Hind's brothers lie dead.

Mahound awakes in Hind's bedroom. He has been brought there unconscious having fainted the previous night during the feasting. Later, having wrestled with the Archangel Gibreel on the mountain, he comes to believe that his acceptance of the three deities has really been inspired by Satan. *But Gibreel, unstable composite of film director and Archangel, acknowledges that he has been responsible for both the initial statement of acceptance and the later denial.*[129] This is of crucial significance in any assessment of the theology of *The Satanic Verses*. Mahound goes to the Ka'ba and repudiates the verses he has previously recited in support of Lat, Uzza and Manat.

A persecution of the new religion called *Submission* (=Islam) now begins. Mahound's followers, and eventually Mahound himself, travel north to the oasis of Yathrib (=Medina) in what is clearly a mirror account, albeit much abbreviated, of the famous migration of Muḥammad and his followers from Mecca to Medina in 622. In the novel Gibreel watches them depart from the top of Mount Cone. He is attacked at night by three creatures with wings and claws: Lat, Uzza and Manat.

(iii) Ellowen Deeowen[130]

With Chapter Three we return to the major frame story and the 'reality', or narrative proper, of Rushdie's fiction. The story of the two main protagonists, Gibreel Farishta and Saladin Chamcha, who have left their aircraft so precipitately, is resumed. Ellowen Deeowen is, of course, L-O-N-D-O-N, the name of London spelled out letter by letter. We are already familiar with the words Ellowen Deeowen from Chapter One, having been told that, as a child, Saladin Chamcha incorporated them 'like a mantra' into his game of grandmother's footsteps: L-O-N-D-O-N/ Ellowen Deeowen is Saladin's 'dream-city'.[131]

At the beginning of Chapter Three we are introduced to an eighty-eight year old former expatriate woman named Rosa Diamond. She sees ghosts with her gift of second sight and broods over a South American past. She has 'seen' the Battle of Hastings in her youth, or so she thinks. To her astonishment she sees Gibreel Farishta and his companion come ashore on a snow-covered beach. She goes down to them and already seems to detect the beginnings of a halo over Gibreel's head and Saladin Chamcha's horns. Having taken them into her house, she is disturbed by police. Chamcha is arrested as an illegal immigrant. Soon afterwards he grows two full horns while a proper halo appears behind Gibreel's head. The latter makes an attempt to prevent Saladin's arrest, but stays on for a while with Rosa Diamond. However, the latter dies, dramatically conjuring up various versions or visions of her South American past.

Meanwhile the anglophile Saladin is being roughly disabused of his romantic view of the British. He is debagged in the police van and shown to have broad hairy thighs and a huge erect penis, in addition to his horns. Not surprisingly, Saladin begins to wonder if this really is the England of his dreams and even if he is really alive. He defecates, goat-like, in the van and is forced by his sadistic police captors to eat his own excrement. However, he is then identified by the Police National Computer as a British Citizen and rendered unconscious by his now frightened captors. Waking up in hospital, Saladin is ministered to for pneumonia by a kindly physiotherapist. He finds to his dismay that all his goat-like attributes remain, including his hooves and horns. It is with some relief that he manages to escape from the hospital.

Meanwhile, in a brief intermezzo section, Rusdie shows us Pamela Chamcha, née Lovelace, Saladin's 'widow', being consoled in bed by her lover Jumpy Joshi who learns, however, in a phone call, that Saladin *is* still very much alive. Jumpy eventually tells Pamela who refuses to believe him. She is nearly killed in a road crash, driving too quickly.

Revelling in a born-again feeling, Pamela mentally frees herself from the burden of her upsetting past and the memory of her 'former' husband. But an unkind nemesis awaits! After a seven day orgy of love-making, Pamela and Jumpy are startled and appalled one night by the terrifying return of Saladin Chamcha, arrayed in his new hooves, horns and hairiness.

Gibreel, meantime, has begun to fear that *he* may be turning into his namesake, the Archangel Gibreel himself. Gibreel is recognised on an Eastbourne–Victoria train for what he is, Gibreel Farishta, Movie Star, by a boring, universalist religious fanatic by the name of John Maslama. The latter is later cowed into respect and terror by the sight of Gibreel's halo.

Almost by way of contrast, Rushdie now portrays for us here a visiting guest speaker, Alleluia Cone (Gibreel Farishta's love), speaking of her adventures to a classroom full of teenage girls. The two are clearly destined to meet again.

Gibreel Farishta arrives at Victoria Station in London. He has begun to have visions of the dead Rekha Merchant who pursues him through London as he explores the underground system. Finally, he is found by Alleluia Cone by pure chance.

(iv) Ayesha[132]

Chapter Four of *The Satanic Verses* bears the same evocative and resonant name as that of a particularly famous figure in early Islamic history. 'Ā'isha, easily anglicised from the Arabic into Ayesha, was the third wife of the Prophet Muḥammad and his favourite. Her full name was 'Ā'isha bint Abī Bakr. The Prophet died and was buried in her bedchamber. Later she was unsuccessful in battle with 'Alī b. Abī Ṭālib at the famous Battle of the Camel in 656. She died in 678.[133] Of 'Ā'isha it has been written:

> She has always remained a sacred personage to the majority of the Muslims . . . 'Ā'isha occupies a prominent place amongst the most distinguished traditionists. 1,210 traditions are recorded as having been reported by her direct from the mouth of the Prophet. She was often consulted on theological and juridical subjects. She is praised for her talents. She had learnt to read, and knew several poems by heart. Some writers assert that she possessed a special copy of the Ḳur'ān.[134]

It is clear from all this, then, that the name 'Ā'isha in Islamic circles is immensely evocative of early Islam and inspires huge respect, not least because of the respect, love and affection which was accorded her by the Prophet Muḥammad himself. This is beautifully illustrated in the following anecdote cited by Watt:

> [Muḥammad] was able to enter into the spirit of childish games and had many friends among children. 'Ā'isha was still a child when he married her, and she continued to play with her toys. He would ask her what they were. 'Solomon's horses', she replied, and Muḥammad smiled.[135]

It is in the light of all this that one must read Akhtar's remarks: 'The chapters 4 and 8 entitled 'Ayesha' and 'The Parting of the Arabian Sea' deal with a superstitious peasant girl in Rushdie's India who plans a pilgrimage, through the Arabian Sea, to Mecca. Given that Ayesha was, in real life, the Arabian Prophet's young wife, and that a character by the same name appears in a brothel scene set in Muhammad's Mecca (p. 384 ff.) we cannot assume that these two chapters are irrelevant to Muslim reservations about the novel.'[136] Sardar and Davies draw attention also to the fact that a certain Empress Ayesha is later identified as the pagan goddess Al-Lat.[137]

Chapter Four thus begins with a fresh theme. The focus switches from Saladin Chamcha and Gibreel Farishta for a while and studies instead, the strange history of Rushdie's Ayesha. Gibreel Farishta is not, however, totally neglected, for the Chapter *begins* with him and his 'serial visions'.[138] Dream and reality achieve an equal tangibility.

The dream reveals an exiled Imam (Khomeini during his period of exile?) who hangs on his wall the picture of an arch-enemy, the Empress Ayesha, Empress of Desh which is his homeland. The Imam keenly feels his alienation from the Kensington suburb of London in which he temporarily resides. He keeps his curtains drawn, and the radiators turned up. His son, who brings water to the Imam, is called Khalid and one of the guards rejoices in the name of Salman Farsi. An American convert named Bilal broadcasts on a transmitter. He is the voice of the Imam to the latter's homeland of Desh. Rushdie actually refers to him as 'Bilal the muezzin'.[139] He has been chosen by the Imam because he has a beautiful voice.[140] He is also called Bilal X at one point.[141] Now all these names given by the author to his protagonists are immensely evocative: we have already encountered Khalid, Salman and Bilal at another time, in another place, in Chapter Two. There also, Khalid was a 'water carrier'. The name Bilal in *this* Chapter, by bearing the added epithet X, has an additional resonance and evokes the black American leader Malcolm X (1925–1965).[142] By keeping these names, with only small or subtle shifts in their characterisation, Rushdie deliberately emphasises that his heroes transcend the boundaries of time and place and have a universal relevance or applicability in his fiction.

The Imam summons the Archangel Gibreel whose *alter ego* is Gibreel Farishta, and, in a parody of the famous Night Journey to Jerusalem undertaken by Muḥammad,[143] they fly through the night to the city of the Empress who surely symbolises the Shāh of Iran. In the city they see large numbers of people allowing themselves to be machine-gunned to a martyr's death in front of her palace gates. But the Empress Ayesha is overthrown and her 'shell' is seen to spawn the goddess Al-Lat who joins battle with Gibreel: the latter finally wins. The Imam lies at the gates and swallows the marching people. Thus Rushdie graphically portrays what he considers to be the overthrow of one tyrant by another, using Gibreel as the Imam's proxy warrior. All this, however, is, as it were, a prelude to the main action in Chapter Four which is the substance of Gibreel Farishta's *next* dream.

Mirza Saeed Akhtar and his wife Mishal live in a region infested with butterflies. On his fortieth birthday Mirza is filled with renewed love for his still-sleeping wife, but also with lust for a young woman whom he sees first breakfast on the ubiquitous butterflies and then suffer an epileptic fit. He and Mishal bring the sick girl to their own bedroom to recover.

The girl's name is Ayesha and she has an admirer, a former untouchable who has converted to Islam, called Osman. Osman is, of course, a variant of 'Uthmān. 'Uthmān b. 'Affān (*reg.* 644–656)[144] was the third of the Rightly-Guided Caliphs who ruled over the Islamic community after Muḥammad's death. It is not, however, clear from Rushdie's text whether his fictional Osman in Chapter Four is intended to mirror the historical 'Uthmān. More easily identifiable is the village headman's tactless wife who rejoices in the same name as that of the Prophet Muḥammad's first wife, Khadīja.

Ayesha not only claims to have seen Gibreel but to have been told by the Archangel that Mishal has breast cancer. Medical examination confirms the Archangel's diagnosis and Mishal is given, at most, six months to live. Ayesha then disappears for a week and, on her return, she brings a message that everyone in the village is to make a pilgrimage to Mecca. Ayesha also promises that after the 200 mile march to the sea, the latter will part and they will be able to walk to Mecca across the seabed, like latter-day Israelites led by Moses.

The villagers make their preparations for the journey and Mishal is given to understand that her cancer will be cured when she has undertaken the required pilgrimage. An irate Mirza Saeed tries to prevent the whole enterprise but, at last, he reluctantly joins the villagers.

(v) A City Visible but Unseen[145]

With this Chapter we are introduced to a new character, the emigré and former schoolteacher from Dhaka, Muhammad Sufyan, who is now the proprietor of the Shaandaar Café in London and landlord of the boarding house above it. The Chapter resumes where part of Chapter Three finished. Jumpy Joshi arrives at the Café with the horned Saladin Chamcha to the surprise of Sufyan's family. Sufyan's wife is called Hind and thus, again, we note how Rusdie attempts to recreate the past in the present through the medium of the names which he uses: in early Islamic history, of course, as we have noted, Hind was the wife of Abū Sufyān (died *circa* 653), one of the Meccan notables who, after much opposition to the Prophet Muḥammad, finally converted to Islam.[146] In Rushdie's novel, the Café proprietor has two daughters, one of whom is named Mishal. The reader will not fail to remember that in the preceding Chapter, the wife of Mirza Saeed Akhtar is also called Mishal. With such devices does Rushdie play games with time, space and place.

Saladin is allowed by Sufyan to occupy an attic room and we are now briefly introduced to the name of Billy Battuta who has managed to turn a holiday firm (Battuta's Travels) into a wealthy shipping empire. Most readers 'in the know' will find this intensely amusing since the magnate's name immediately evokes that of Ibn Baṭṭūṭa (1304–1368/9 or 1377), the great North African traveller and author of a famous travelogue who is frequently compared to Marco Polo.[147]

Saladin flies into a rage on reading a report in a cinema magazine that Gibreel Farishta is not only alive but is about to make a new 'theological' film; he claims that he missed the plane which was blown up. Meanwhile, his friend Jumpy Joshi is sleeping with Pamela, Saladin's wife, and she becomes pregnant.

Saladin has continued to grow and become even more goat-like, reaching a height of over eight feet. He leaves the attic finally in the back of a van, visits an empty night club and then, after a traumatic but inexplicable metamorphosis, he regains his normal size and shape, throwing off his animal features and *persona*.

With this sudden change, Rushdie shifts the story back to Alleluia Cone and Gibreel Farishta, taking up where he left off at the end of Chapter Three. The two celebrate their reunion in bed and Gibreel moves in with Alleluia for three weeks only to find himself asked to leave at the end of that time. Gibreel begins to feel more and more that he really is the Archangel whose name he bears. He sees, and converses with, the ghost of the suicide Rekha Merchant on her carpet, whom the reader last encountered towards the end of Chapter Three.

Wandering around the City of London, Gibreel makes an over-literal, or over-enthusiastic, attempt to persuade the busy London traffic to notice him, and he arrives back on Alleluia Cone's doorstep severely bruised, having been knocked down by a film producer, S.S. Sisodia. The latter begins to try and fatten Gibreel up, buying food from the Shaandaar Café among other places. Although Gibreel is also receiving psychiatric medical help, Sisodia is instrumental in having Gibreel signed up to play the role of his Archangelic namesake in a series of films. Gibreel moves out of Alleluia's flat again and a grand re-entry into Show Biz is planned during a spectacle at Earls Court, put on by a company owned by Billy Battuta. However, the audience riots when it recognises him, Gibreel escapes and lands up again on the doorstep of Alleluia Cone's house.

(vi) Return to Jahilia[148]

As with Chapter Two, this Chapter returns the reader to the land of dream[149] inhabited by that earlier Chapter. We meet Baal the poet again, this time a witness to a blood-coloured teardrop flowing from the eye of the statue of the goddess Al-Lat. Baal believes that this betokens Mahound's return. Baal has aged but Hind, also encountered in Chapter Two, has not. The City of Jahilia has become a dangerous place.

In conversation with Baal, a disillusioned Salman *admits to altering the revelations deliberately as he recorded what Mahound dictated.* Hind learns that her husband Abu Simbel (=Abū Sufyān) has surrendered the City to Mahound and embraced the new religion himself. A furious Hind tries unsuccessfully to persuade the crowd to assault her husband. Khalid cleanses what is clearly the Ka'ba of its idols at Mahound's request and we see Hind, too, convert to Islam. The scribe Salman the Persian only just escapes execution.

A fruitless search is made for Baal who takes refuge in a popular Jahilia brothel called *The Curtain.* Here the prostitutes assume the names of Mahound's wives which increases the revenues dramatically. The prostitutes are married off to Baal who becomes a kind of 'mirror' of Mahound. Later, however, the brothel is closed and its Madam commits suicide. The Vice Squad officer who has raided the brothel is called 'Umar and the careful, or knowledgeable, reader will, of course, be aware that this was the name borne by the second of the Rightly-Guided Caliphs who succeeded Muḥammad, 'Umar b. al-Khattāb (*circa* 591–644).[150] Later still, Baal himself is seized after singing verses outside the City jail to the now imprisoned prostitutes. The latter are condemned to death, as is Baal by Mahound himself. The goddess Al-Lat attends Mahound's own death. She tells him that the fatal sickness he suffers is her revenge on him. Mahound thanks her for her gift.

(vii) The Angel Azraeel[151]

As we noted earlier, Azraeel is an anglicised form of the Arabic 'Izrā'īl, the principal Islamic Angel of Death.[152] The last Chapter concluded at the deathbed of Mahound where he asked if it were Azraeel who was there in attendance on him, and learned that it was Al-Lat instead. Chapter Seven takes up again the saga of Saladin Chamcha and Gibreel Farishta, the latter having been last encountered at the end of Chapter Five on Alleluia Cone's doorstep.

Chamcha visits Pamela, pregnant by his friend Jumpy Joshi. He realises he no longer loves her or wants her back but, nonetheless, announces that he will move back into part of their house, to the utter chagrin of Jumpy. Saladin sees Mishal Sufyan at a meeting and, somehow recognising her as the harbinger of his death, faints. Later, Saladin encounters Gibreel again, but it is a Gibreel now diagnosed as a paranoid schizophrenic, and drugged to control the symptoms.

Alleluia Cone invites Saladin to stay with her at a retreat in Scotland and later, the two men meet again in London. They visit the Shaandaar Café. Gibreel splits up with Alleluia Cone, after a spate of anonymous obscene telephone calls to both (made in fact by Saladin) but also after vandalising her climbing mementoes. Alleluia vows she will never have him back. He goes on to buy a trumpet from a music shop owned by Mr. John Maslama (see above Chapter Three) who recognises him as the Archangel and attempts, unsuccessfully, to *give* him the trumpet. Gibreel names his new trumpet Azraeel! The shop attendants seem to see a halo round Gibreel's head; and Alleluia merges in his mind with the figure of the goddess Al-Lat.

Visiting the environs of Kings Cross and St. Pancras station, Gibreel finds the prostitutes there appearing to take on the *personae* of those twelve prostitutes in the Meccan brothel who adopted the names of the Prophet's wives (see above Chapter Six). He blows the trumpet and fire comes out (so he believes) which destroys the approaching pimps. Now he *knows* he really is the Archangel Gibreel. Walking into a riot he seems to blow more fire. The Shaandaar Café is ablaze, Sufyan and his wife on the floor unconscious from the smoke.

Saladin Chamcha, having just spent an evening with Alleluia Cone, also arrives at the Café which he enters shouting for Mishal, Sufyan and Hind, and intent on their rescue. Good momentarily triumphs over evil. Saladin suffers a heart attack. However, Gibreel follows him into the Café, finds the fallen Saladin and carries him outside, miraculously seeming to part the fire and smoke 'like the red sea' with his breath. Gibreel too, has given in to the impulse of good, and in the eternal battle waged between Good and Evil, represented at various times by the conflict and enmity between Gibreel and Saladin, good appears to be in the ascendant. The two men represent a drama on a cosmic scale throughout the novel. As the dust-jacket puts it: 'Gibreel and Saladin have been chosen . . . as protagonists in the eternal wrestling match between Good and Evil. But which is which? Can demons be angelic? Can angels be devils in disguise?'. Here, at least, Good has triumphed. The Chapter ends with the two men being taken away in an ambulance.

(viii) The Parting of the Arabian Sea[153]

The title of this Chapter is clearly intended to parallel and echo, in another place, time and dimension, what has just taken place in Gibreel's rescue of Saladin: Gibreel's breath has acted like a latter-day Moses in the fire-stricken Café. Chapter Eight also constitutes a continuation of one of the dream sequences in Rushdie's multi-layered novel[154] and takes up another of the narrative threads of the text, that which tells the story of Ayesha, which we left at the end of Chapter Four. Of this Ayesha pilgrimage story Malise Ruthven has noted:

> For most readers outside the Indian subcontinent the episode (also occurring in one of Gibreel's extended dreams) in which Ayesha persuades her followers to walk across the sea to Mecca would appear as surrealistic fantasy . . . Yet the story of Ayesha is based on an actual episode that occurred at Hawkes Bay in Karachi in February 1983, when thirty-eight people, all of them Shi'a, entered the sea in the expectation that a path would open enabling them to walk, via Basra, to the Shi'a holy city of Kerbala in Iraq.[155]

Eighteen were drowned in this episode.[156]

Rushdie's eighth Chapter opens with an unlikely pilgrim, Srinivas the toy merchant, joining the pilgrimage led by Ayesha. He notices with interest that she has the same face as that of the goddess depicted in a calendar hanging on his factory wall.

An agitated Mirza Saeed follows the procession. Khadija, wife of the Sarpanch, Muhammad Din, sees Azraeel in a dream: here Rushdie gives us a dream within a dream! The next day she lies down in a ruined inn and dies. Ayesha assures the bereaved husband that anyone who dies on the pilgrimage has a guaranteed place in Paradise. However, the Sarpanch becomes as sceptical about the whole enterprise as Mirza Saeed and joins the latter in his car and follows the procession.

Osman's bullock also dies and is shrouded with the ubiquitous butterflies. More *people* begin to die too and Mirza's Mercedes becomes the focal point of those who are discontented on the march; but his cancer-striken wife Mishal becomes Ayesha's most ardent devotee.

The procession towards the Arabian Sea continues, triumphing over all obstacles, including man-made barricades, but flooding causes Mirza to abandon his car. After a baby is stoned to death, the tired pilgrims mutiny and refuse to continue the pilgrimage, despite the exhortations of Ayesha. Mirza tries to do a deal with Ayesha to halt the march completely; Ayesha is tempted but in the end refuses his offer of an *air* pilgrimage to Mecca for herself, Mishal and twelve selected villagers.It is not clear if the number twelve is meant to be significant here: Rushdie refers earlier to the twelve wives of the Prophet, and twelve prostitutes in the Meccan brothel as well as in the environs of Kings Cross and St. Pancras.

Finally all the pilgrims reach the Arabian Sea and they enter it behind Ayesha, wading out of their depth. Ayesha, Mishal and the credulous villagers appear to be drowned. However, those few who have survived the expedition – like the Sarpanch, Osman, Sri Srinivas – give testimony afterwards that at the very last moment the Sea did indeed part for the pilgrims. The sorrowful Zamindar Mirza Saeed Akhtar, who alone has not witnessed this miracle, returns home to his mansion *Peristan* in the now empty and drought-afflicted, village of Titlipur. He starves himself to death: at the end he finds himself in the water with Ayesha. His heart and body finally 'open' to the truth of her message and he too sees the waters open and part to enable them all to walk on pilgrimage across the seabed to the City of their dreams, Mecca.

(ix) A Wonderful Lamp[157]

The title of this Chapter, the last of Rushdie's novel, evokes the fabled Aladdin and *his* lamp. With it the author concludes the major narrative of Saladin Chamcha and Gibreel Farishta which has constituted the main frame story within which – or, at least, within the *light* of which – all the other stories have been articulated across place, time and space. We resume where Chapter Seven stopped.

Eighteen months have passed and Saladin Chamcha flies home to his estranged[158] father who is in the terminal stage of cancer. Saladin finds to his horror that the name of his Air India 747 is *Gulistan*, the name, Rushdie stresses, of a garden in Paradise, as was *Bostan*, the name of the aircraft which blew up and hurtled him earthwards on a previous flight. He finds the producer Sisodia (see Chapter Five) has caught the same plane. Indeed, in this final Chapter, Rushdie deliberately brings many of his principal characters together in Bombay for a final dénouement. It is also here that we learn that *The Parting of the Arabian Sea* and *Mahound*, the names of the Chapters commentators have considered to be dream sequences, were also the names of films starring Gibreel Farishta which flopped. Were they *firstly*, *primarily*, Gibreel's dreams, nightmares, before they were translated onto celluloid? Rushdie does not tell us but there are many indications in the text to support such an interpretation: the author frequently talks of 'the dreamer', 'dreaming' and 'dreams'.[159] Indeed, the dream is a primary motif in the novel and a major instrument for shifting between reality and fantasy, as well as the different dimensions of time, place and space.

Chapter Nine is a tale of 'return to one's roots', to Bombay, a counter to the *alienation* perceived and felt so powerfully in such other Cities as London. Thus we are party to much introspection on the part of Saladin as he flies home. On arrival, he finds his father near to death and makes his peace with him. The father's study contains a copper and brass lamp which is supposed to be able to grant wishes if rubbed but it has never been tested. Saladin does not test it either.

He helps his father through his last dying days in the house and is present at his final deathbed in the hospital. Returning from the funeral, Saladin enters his father's study and rubs the lamp three times. Zeenat Vakil (see Chapter One) comes in. Saladin tells her he loves her. He has adopted his full name of Salahuddin rather than the anglicised Saladin which he has borne for so many years. He has, indeed, in this as in other things, returned to his roots.

With the death of his father, Saladin is compared by Rushdie to the orphaned founder of Islam, Muḥammad, thus subtly linking him to previous Chapters. The difference, of course, is that the Prophet of Islam was orphaned at a very early age, whereas Saladin's own orphaning is a product of middle age.

Saladin inherits a large fortune and one might have thought that he would now be allowed to rest and enjoy his return home. But the past returns to haunt him. Gibreel Farishta has also come back from London to Bombay, and is working on a modern-dress film of the Ramayana epic, funded by himself, since the two films (mentioned above) have flopped. Accusations of 'blasphemy' are in the air over the production of the Ramayana epic.[160] Not only, then, do we have in Rushdie's novel dreams within dreams but – irony of ironies in the light of the reception of *The Satanic Verses* by the Islamic world – references to a fictional film regarded by some as blasphemous within a real work of fiction regarded by many Muslims as blasphemous!

Apparently Gibreel still has a mental health problem and it becomes clear to Saladin that the love and forgiveness, born in, and forged from, the Shaandaar Café fire (see Chapter Seven) have proved somewhat fragile.

Alleluia Cone also arrives in Bombay with a mountaineering team and Saladin begins to feel 'haunted'. Later the body of the film producer, S.S. Sisodia, is discovered murdered in Gibreel Farishta's flat while Alleluia Cone is killed falling from the self-same skyscraper from which Rekha Merchant had committed suicide two years before. Gibreel, suspected of the two crimes, disappears but turns up at Saladin's father's house. In a confused narrative, Gibreel recites or echoes to Saladin, *inter alia*, some of the verses which Saladin has earlier used on the telephone, anonymously, to help engineer the breakup of the relationship between Gibreel and Alleluia Cone.[161] The past has indeed come to haunt the present and the wrongs of the past have their share in precipitating the evils of the present. Gibreel removes the lid of the prime symbol in this Chapter, the lamp, and rubs it with his hand three times. A gun appears in his other hand. He puts the gun to his mouth and kills himself.

This long picaresque novel of Rushdie's does, however, end on a note of tranquillity. Saladin gazes out at the Arabian Sea from his childhood home. The link with the dream/film of *The Parting of the Arabian Sea* is intentional: Rushdie tells us that the moon seems to make a silver path 'like a parting' on the water. Zeenat Vakil summons Saladin from his reverie to leave and come to *her* house.

Despite all his sins, Saladin, initial representative or incarnation of the forces of *Evil*, is given a second chance. But Gibreel, the incarnation of *Good* and mirror of the great Archangel, has despaired and committed suicide. It is not so much here a question of the final triumph of evil over good as the capacity for the one to metamorphose into the other. And *that* perhaps is the principal theme of the novel and the message which Rushdie wishes to leave with his reader. *Alienation*, of course, is a key tool or *ground* in the execution of such metamorphoses and the prime *locus* as well for man's inhumanity to man.

The Satanic Verses has received mixed reviews and comments. The novelist Angela Carter described the work as 'an epic into which holes have been punched to let in visions.'[162] For her it was an 'exhilarating novel'[163] and she urged the reader to appreciate a book which is 'populous, loquacious, sometimes hilarious, extraordinary, contemporary.'[164] Nisha Puri in a glowing review found the work 'a magnificent puzzle.'[165] The readers 'surge forward on an irresistible tide of delighted bafflement'[166] and this reviewer proclaimed *The Satanic Verses* as 'the giant novel of (Rushdie's) maturity.'[167] However, the review was, perhaps, slightly optimistic when, after referring to the difficulties inherent in reading Joyce's *Ulysses*, it claimed that 'Rushdie remains buoyantly accessible to anyone who responds to all that is good and living in the supreme fictions offered by literary genius.'[168] As my survey above shows, *The Satanic Verses* is only 'buoyantly accessible' to a reader steeped in early Islamic history! Puri's somewhat purple prose concludes by lauding this work as possessing 'the consuming beauty which in life as in art speaks of imperishable truths.'[169]

The Iranian literary newspaper *Kayhan Farangi* took a rather different line: 'The truth of the matter is that Rushdie's artistic and moral degradation is so immense that he even makes ridiculous comments about how Prophet Mohamed released Balal Habashi, which was a demonstration of Islam's compassionate face . . . Rushdie has fallen from the grace as a writer with a good knowledge of Islam to something like total moral degradation.'[170]

Professor Dr. Syed Ali Ashraf, Director General of the Islamic Academy in Cambridge, England, tended to agree. He challenged the novel's merits from both a religious and a literary perspective:[171] 'There is . . . no relief in this novel. It is mentally disturbing, almost paranoic, in its love of a corrupt society.'[172] Hugh Trevor-Roper was also less than sympathetic: 'If an expert entomologist deliberately pokes a stick into a hornets' nest, he has only himself to blame for the result.'[173] Trevor-Roper concluded: 'The social offence of Mr. Rushdie is that, by his brutal and vulgar manners, he played into the hands of the fanatics.'[174]

The debate over the merits or otherwise of *The Satanic Verses* has taken place, as the above quotations show, on many planes: literary, religious, cultural, political and social. It is a book which has already inspired some to the peaks of admiration, and infuriated others beyond endurance. Like the events in the novel itself, the debate has frequently transcended, or at least disturbed, the boundaries of time and space, for the novel's supporters and detractors have both sometimes felt the need to evoke other times and other places to justify or condemn, and confer legitimacy on their own views. It is a debate which has focussed attention, powerfully and profoundly, on a key literary issue, that of *artistic licence versus artistic responsibility*. Who sets the limits? Should there, indeed, be authorial limits? To what extent can any work of fiction or text constitute a blasphemy?

On this last issue Salman Rushdie is quite clear in his own mind: 'If there is a god, I don't think that he's very bothered by The Satanic Verses, because he wouldn't be much of a god if he could be rocked on his throne by a book. Then again, if there isn't a god, he certainly isn't bothered either.'[175]

The attitude expressed here has profound literary, religious, cultural, political and social implications. It will be our task in what follows to survey and elaborate some of these.

The Last Temptation by Nikos Kazantzakis [1883–1957]

P.A. Bien describes *The Last Temptation* as 'the summation of the thought and experience of a man whose entire life was spent in the battle between spirit and flesh.'[176] The novel was published in Greek in December 1955 by Dífros in Athens. An earlier novel, *Christ Recrucified*,[177] had created a massive stir in Greece and nearly led to Kazantzakis' excommunication;[178] the Holy Synod described this book as 'impious.'[179] Bien notes that '*The Last Temptation* fanned the inquisitorial flames all the more . . .'[180] The novel was 'either condemned or praised according to religious bias' for its detractors believed that the author 'ought to have followed the Gospels in every respect.'[181]

So the book was condemned by the Greek Orthodox clergy and unsuccessful attempts were made to have Kazantzakis' books banned.[182] The Roman Catholic magisterium placed the German text of the book on the *Index of Forbidden Books* in 1954;[183] like the Orthodox Church, the Catholic Church regarded Kazantzakis as dangerous.[184] So did the Protestants: and a campaign was mounted by American Protestant fundamentalists 'who campaigned to have the work removed from libraries (transforming it into a best seller).'[185] In Ashland, Wisconsin, a Roman Catholic priest told his parishioners that they were not to read Kazantzakis' *Last Temptation* under pain of mortal sin, and the book was withdrawn from Ashland Public Library.[186] Greek critics regarded it as simple blasphemy.[187] The reaction in France was mixed;[188] and generally, the religion dominant in a country dictated the reaction: because of the strength of the Catholic and Orthodox Churches in France and Greece, *greater* offence was taken at the book than in the more liberal Protestant USA and UK.[189]

Kazantzakis' English translator, Bien, notes that, at the time of Kazantzakis' death, the Greek Orthodox Archbishop refused permission for the body to be given a lying-in-state in an Orthodox church in Athens.[190] The stir and controversy over the novel were resuscitated worldwide in 1988 with Scorsese's production of a film version of the book, under the title *The Last Temptation of Christ*. This film will also be considered when we have surveyed the original novel.

The publishing history of Kazantzakis' *The Last Temptation* shows that both author and book have distinct affinities with Maḥfūẓ and Rushdie and *their* works which we have delineated above; each of these three authors has produced a work or works, which have hurt the religious susceptibilities of believers of various faiths. However, the three authors are also linked by their preoccupation with religious 'history' and some of its most sublime figures, and an attempt to re-articulate this in a totally different mode from that of either orthodox theology or scriptural exegesis. We will thus return to examine the intertextual relationship of the three principal novels under discussion in this book in a later chapter.

Structurally, *The Last Temptation* has *thirty three* distinct Chapters. We have already noted that Maḥfūẓ's *Awlād Ḥāratinā* has 114 chapters, 'modelled' after the 114 Qur'ānic *sūras*. Does Kazantzakis here, consciously or unconsciously, attempt to draw attention to the approximate span of Christ's earthly life as popularly perceived by religious commentators,[191] by this division into thirty three? It seems at least highly probable since Kazantzakis at one point in his text acknowledges Christ's age as thirty three.[192] Whatever the case, our survey here will be divided into five *artificial* sections imposed by me, since the text lacks the neat, authorial fivefold division of *Awlād Ḥāratinā* or ninefold one of *The Satanic Verses*.

(i) Author's Prologue[193]

The author's preoccupation is with the age-old clash between body and soul. The humanity of Christ helps us to know and love him 'and to pursue his Passion as though it were our own.'[194] The last temptation of the book's title occurs upon the cross itself: what if Christ had married and become a father? What if he had chosen to escape the terrors of the cross? However, he does not, in the end, yield to this final seductive temptation. Kazantzakis tells us that he wrote his book because he 'wanted to offer a supreme model to the man who struggles.'[195]

(ii) Chapters One-Eleven: Setting the Scene[196]

A young man lies dreaming a dream in Nazareth, which articulates in various forms the ancient longing for the Messiah. He awakes but is aware of having had a bad dream. For him God and the Devil can 'exchange faces.'[197] (There are parallels here with the roles of Gibreel and Saladin in *The Satanic Verses*). For him 'God sometimes becomes all darkness, the devil all light – and the mind of man is left in a muddle.'[198]

A red-bearded giant of a man, Judas, visits him in the early morning. The young man has been making a cross for a Zealot awaiting crucifixion; the red-beard urges rebellion, urges that the Zealot be saved from the Romans. After all, he may be the Messiah! But the young man tells the red-beard that 'the Messiah will not come in this way.'[199] Judas has a sudden premonition that *the young man* is the Messiah.

This young man is one pursued by God. He has nearly married the Rabbi's daughter Magdalene but has been prevented by the 'powers' which pursue him. Magdalene, we learn, has become a prostitute in consequence. We learn now that the young man's name is Jesus and that his mother Mary is bitterly disappointed with her strange dreamy son.

Jesus drags the cross for the crucifixion of the Zealot up the hill, to the disgust of the crowd. There is a profound, and surely intentional, irony here in Kazantzakis' presentation of Jesus as a cross-maker and now, as a prototype Simon of Cyrene. Growing tired, he is helped in turn by Peter the fisherman. As the Zealot is crucified, the crowd hopes for the miracle which will reveal the condemned man as the Messiah, but it is not to be. The Zealot's mother, present at the crucifixion of her son, curses Jesus who has helped to crucify him, and wishes the same on Jesus.

After the event, Simeon the Rabbi announces that the Messiah will indeed come very soon. He visits Mary in her house and asks Jesus, quietly, how long he will resist God. Jesus replies that he will do so until death. Later Jesus leaves the family house and heads for a monastery of pious men. It is clear from all that has happened thus far that he is still uncertain about his own identity.[200] He thinks of himself simply as a *man* pursued by God. Later he muses over whether he might in fact have been sent by the devil.[201] What we have, then, in Kazantzakis' narrative is a very *Arian* Christ. On one occasion he screams that he is Lucifer.[202]

A woman who feeds Jesus on his way to the monastery tells him that the real God is to be found in men's homes, not monasteries. On the journey he goes down to Magdala and visits Magdalene in a brothel, seeking forgiveness. Arriving at the monastery, he finds that the Abbot is dying. The latter recognises Jesus and dies. Judas has also come to the monastery and awaits Jesus, whom he regards as a traitor, with a knife.

In the monastery a very upset Jesus unburdens himself of his thoughts and dreams to his uncle Simeon, the Rabbi, but the latter has no cure for what possesses his nephew, Jesus. The latter, however, after his confession, feels a sublime exaltation. After talking with Jesus, Judas decides not to kill him after all.

(iii) Chapters Twelve-Twenty Four: Earthly Ministry[203]

Later, near the Lake of Gennasaret, as Magdalene is about to be lynched by a mob, Jesus appears dressed in white like the monks in the monastery, followed by a great body of people. He tells the enraged crowd that the one among them who is without sin should throw the first stone. Climbing a hill, he is followed by the mob to whom he narrates the parable of the sower. He tells them to love one another and enumerates the beatitudes. Later still, he tells the parable of the rich man and Lazarus to the wealthy but the ending diverges from the scriptural version. Kazantzakis' Jesus ends *his* parable with God sending Lazarus to bring the rich man out of the flames of Hell to drink at the fountains of Heaven for all eternity.[204]

The fishermen Peter and Jacob are recruited and added to the throng of Jesus' disciples whom he summons to become, 'fishers of men.'[205] Pausing in the course of a long journey, Jesus tells a Samaritan woman by a well that he who drinks of the water he gives will never thirst again.[206] He visits John the Baptist who recognises him and confirms his mission by baptizing him. As this happens, the waters of the Jordan cease to flow and a white bird descends, seeming to proclaim Jesus' new name. Jesus spends three days in solitary converse with the Baptist and the typological analogy of Christ's three days in the tomb cannot have been far from Kazantzakis' mind. All this annoys Judas who believes that violence, and revolt against the Romans, is the way to Israel's redemption.[207] Jesus then leaves his disciples with John to be baptized while he goes into the desert where he is severely tempted.

Returning to Bethany, Jesus is welcomed by Martha and Mary. While in their house, their brother Lazarus brings news that John the Baptist has been executed. Jesus returns to his waiting disciples and all head back towards Galilee. After being assaulted in Nazareth, he leaves for Cana where he cures a Roman centurion's paralysed daughter. This is the first really overt miracle worked in Kazantzakis' text by Jesus; previously, when challenged by the people[208] to perform miracles, he has declined.

Matthew, the repentant publican and tax gatherer, joins Jesus and begins to write his Gospel. Arriving in Magdala with the disciples, they are greeted by a joyful Magdalene. Pressed on all sides by the multitude demanding cures and miracles, Jesus leaves but this time he takes Magdalene in his entourage. She has become his disciple. Later, *in a dream*, Peter sees Jesus walk to him on the water during a storm. (As in *The Satanic Verses*, the device of the dream plays a significant role in the fabric of the narrative. Here it is used to 'explain' the New Testament account of Jesus and Peter walking on the water[209]). In Kazantzakis' account Peter too, when challenged, walks on the water but, becoming afraid, begins to sink. He is rescued by Jesus.

Peter awakes and relates the dream to Matthew *with some embroidery*. Matthew's attitude, both here and elsewhere, to the recording of events and the compilation of scripture is instructive and bears comparison with that of Salman in Chapter Six of *The Satanic Verses*. Salman is guilty of altering the revelation narrative as dictated by Mahound from Gibreel; Matthew in *The Last Temptation* 'matches' prophecies to events and, as we shall see, is sometimes forced by an angel to record what he believes to be untrue.

Matthew records what Peter tells him mentally and vows to write it down in the morning. When he is asked whether Jesus really came in the night and took him out to sea, Matthew tells Peter that this was *not* a dream and that 'this miracle definitely took place.'[210] Matthew, however, ponders how to record the dream for he himself is confused about its reality: he is not sure whether he *is* dealing with a dream or a real event. In a sense it is both, a miraculous occurrence which he cannot situate in earthly space but whose true locale he cannot identify either.[211] This is a highly significant passage in any attempt to assess the author's own attitude towards the Gospel miracles.

The disciples, now apostles, go forth to spread the Good News. Jesus performs many miracles and everything is recorded by Matthew. Once again, it is a doubting, even inventive, evangelist whom Kazantzakis places before us. Matthew notices that what Jesus says and does matches the earlier proclamations of the Old Testament prophets. Any apparent mismatch denoted a fault in human understanding. But sometimes it was necessary to *twist* the text to make a forcible match between prophecy and life. This was forgivable and Matthew consoles himself with the thought that he wrote at the dictate of an angel.[212]

In this passage Kazantzakis shows himself well aware that 'the kingdom of God (of 'the Heavens' in Matthew) is the reassertion that the Law and prophets are 'fulfilled' – a phrase which means that their hopes have been not only realised but also perfected . . . Matthew is not the only one of the three synoptists to make use of arguments from the Old Testament, but he relies so heavily on this argument that he has made it one of the chief characteristics of his Gospel.'[213] Other Biblical scholars, too, have commented on Matthew's 'special use' of the Old Testament.[214] For example, he has a 'characteristic habit of frequently noting how *Jesus fulfills Old Testament prophecy* [which] underscores his insight into the religious meaning of the events of Jesus' career.'[215] Indeed, 'Matthew is preoccupied with the demonstration of how *Old Testament prophecy has been realized* with divine perfection and completeness in Jesus.'[216]

However, Kazantzakis, in the passage to which we have referred above, introduces a note of doubt, even fraud, into his account and, here again, we may make comparisons between the figure of Salman in Rushdie's *Satanic Verses* and the Greek author's evangelist. When the angel reminds Matthew to record that 'Mary was a virgin',[217] after the prophet Isaiah, and that Jesus' birthplace was Bethlehem, not Nazareth, after the prophet Micah,[218] Matthew growls at the dictating angel, 'It's not true. I don't want to write and I won't.'[219] But a voice asks how he can possibly understand what the truth, which has seven levels, is. For the highest level is that of God which has no resemblance to man's truth.[220] Matthew is forced to record despite himself.

Thus does Kazantzakis play, not just with a possible twisting or fabrication of the truth by his evangelist, but with the very nature of truth itself, its different levels, especially in Biblical exegesis,[221] and the possible interchangeability of truth and falsehood. Does the author also, like a latter-day European Averroist, hint at a species of 'double-truth' doctrine where, in this case, what is true on one level is false on another?

In the novel, Jesus now climbs a hill above the Lake of Gennasaret. Often his discourse to the following multitude echoes the New Testament. At other times, Kazantzakis puts words into Jesus' mouth. For example, he portrays Jesus announcing that He sees the whole Universe pass in front of Him, and He has a choice between all those who have overindulged, on the one hand, and the hungry and oppressed on the other. Jesus states that He chooses the latter and from them He will build His New Jerusalem.[222]

Here, Kazantzakis gives us a Third World Christ, champion of the poor and the downtrodden.

While Jesus is at supper one evening with his disciples in Capernaum, he is visited by the old Rabbi of Nazareth, Simeon. The latter has suffered recently from insomnia but when he finally falls asleep he has a disturbing, recurring dream. Awaking, he climbs to the summit of Mount Carmel and sees three men in shining white garments with radiant faces: Jesus is in the centre, with Elijah on his left and Moses on his right. Thus Kazantzakis, in his inimitable way, represents another major episode from the Gospel accounts of Christ, the Transfiguration,[223] subtly changing it so that the sole witness of *this* Transfiguration is the old Rabbi of Nazareth, rather than the three apostles Peter, James and John. Indeed, Kazantzakis relates the episode almost as if it were a continuation of the recurring dream which has afflicted the old Rabbi, or a waking dream. How is the reader intended to take it? Is it a real 'vision'?[224]

(iv) Chapters Twenty Five–Twenty Nine: Pre-Passion and Passion[225]

Jesus journeys from Capernaum to Jerusalem and goes each day to the Temple. He tells his disciples that he will destroy it in three days and build a new one in three days. Melchizedek brings news that Jesus has raised Lazarus from the dead. Jesus returns from Bethany surrounded by children with palm branches. This is still an Arian Jesus, one still unsure of his own mission: 'He still could not believe it, nor did he want to: was the power of the soul so great? . . . Could it tear apart the earth and bring forth the dead . . .?'[226] Again, 'this resurrected man [Lazarus] still tottered between life and death. God had not yet been able to conquer the rottenness within him.'[227] With Lazarus, then, we have a very grudging, half-resurrection,[228] with much doubt cast on both God's powers and those of Jesus.

The latter is brought to Pontius Pilate for an audience by Rufus, the centurion whose daughter he has cured. Jesus tells Pilate that his kingdom is not of this world.[229] The Roman Governor bids Jesus to return to Galilee. Afterwards the latter confesses to Judas that he *is* the Messiah but also that he will die to save the world. Later he will come in glory as the judge of the living and the dead.[230] Judas is much disappointed.

Jesus reads what Matthew has been writing and becomes very angry, crying that the Messiah has no need of miracles. He tells Matthew that his real birthplace was Nazareth, not Bethlehem, he has no recollection of the Magi, he never visited Egypt and that the words of the dove at his baptism ('This is my beloved son') were unclear even to him, Jesus.[231] A shaken Matthew tells him that this was all revealed to him by 'the angel'. Jesus wonders to himself whether what man calls truth, God calls lies. Did all that Matthew mentioned happen on the 'highest level of truth'? Jesus tells Matthew to go on writing but it is clear from the text that he has cast doubt on the 'truth' (at some human level) of the evangelist's Gospel.

Later, Jesus rides into Jerusalem seated on an ass, and is greeted by a palm-waving crowd. The classical story of the Passion begins to unfold. He goes to the Temple and whips the buyers and the sellers out of that holy building. Jesus seems to connive with Judas in his forthcoming betrayal and death: 'It is necessary for me to be killed and for you to betray me. *We two must save the world.*'[232]

The Last Supper takes place. Jesus gives bread and wine to his disciples telling them that it is his body and blood. He also tells his astonished followers that he is the lamb for the slaughter of whom Isaiah spoke, but that he will rise again after three days and send them the Comforter.

In Gethsemane Jesus' agony begins and he pleads with the Father for the cup he must drink to pass him by. An angel appears to him with a silver chalice which the apparition touches to his lips. Here the angel is a messenger not of comfort or prophecy but of stern duty. Jesus is seized by the mob led by Judas, and taken, first before Caiphas and then before Pilate. After being scourged and crowned with thorns, Jesus is led out to be crucified. Simon the Cyrenian helps him.

As Jesus is crucified there is an eclipse of the sun. The Cyrenian lifts his eyes and sees angels from Heaven nail Jesus to the cross. Simon murmurs that 'God himself, God himself is crucifying him!' Jesus cries 'Eli . . . Eli' and then faints.[233] *Here begins the last temptation of the title.*

(v) Chapters Thirty–Thirty Three: The Last Temptation[234]

Jesus finds himself leaning against a huge flowering tree. An angel, who tells him that he is his guardian angel, comes to him. The angel says that the entire Passion has been a dream, albeit one which has physically marked his body with the marks of five wounds.[235] The *leitmotiv* of the dream here is as important as in the work of Rushdie.

Jesus is led by the angel to a wedding with Mary Magdalene. He sleeps with her but later he dreams that she is stoned to death. The angel tells him that it was God who killed her, when he awakes. In this section of the narrative there are dreams within dreams. Jesus fears at one point that 'he might wake himself up.'[236]

In Mary and Martha's house he takes on the features of Lazarus, their finally dead brother. Jesus makes love to Mary. She bears his child nine months later.[237] Martha, too, makes love to Jesus and bears his children. One day, Mary, very upset, comes to Jesus. She has had a dream that the whole of her waking 'reality' is really a dream. One cannot but note here the complex fashion in which both Rushdie and Kazantzakis play with the motif of the dream, and the dream within a dream.[238]

A half-drunk traveller, Simon of Cyrene, brings news that Pilate has been crucified on Golgotha. Saul, now called Paul, a large but youthful hunchback, also seeks out Jesus. Paul says he will save the world. He confesses that before his conversion he was the murderer of Mary Magdalene. Now he preaches the passion, death and resurrection of Jesus *to Jesus*! The latter denies it all and identifies himself to Paul. He proclaims: 'I am not the son of God, I am the son of man – like everyone else. What blasphemies you utter!'[239] There is considerable irony for the reader in the last statement, in view of the way that the whole text of *The Last Temptation* was considered to be blasphemous. Jesus tells Paul that he has lived for years under another name.

However, in a passage highly significant both for the theology of Kazantzakis' novel and the idea put forward by some scholars that Christianity is a *Pauline* invention,[240] Paul says that he does not care whether the message he preaches is really true or not. He proclaims: 'I create the truth, create it out of obstinacy and longing and faith.'[241] He tells Jesus that it is essential for the world's salvation for Jesus to be crucified and resurrected and that he, Paul, will crucify and resurrect Jesus 'like it or not.'[242] Once again Kazantzakis is playing with the whole nature and reality of truth and clearly saying here that Paul, not Jesus, is the real founder of Christianity: 'I shall construct you and your life and your teachings and your crucifixion and resurrection just as I wish. Joseph the carpenter of Nazareth did not beget you; I begot you – I, Paul the scribe from Tarsus in Cilicia.'[243] Paul, for Kazantzakis, is the *creator* of Christ in a very real sense if we accept that this passage mirrors the author's own views.[244] Paul's attitude to truth as presented here bears interesting comparison with that of Kazantzakis' Matthew treated above.

In the novel, at the end of their meeting, Paul rushes off towards Jerusalem. Jesus falls ill.

Many years pass. At the beginning of Chapter Thirty Three, the last in the book, we encounter a white-bearded Jesus sitting under an old vine arbour on Passover Day. Jesus falls out with his guardian angel (as always in the form of a negro) who leaves. Jesus and his family receive news that Jerusalem has fallen to the Romans. Although Kazantzakis does not say so, this must be a reference to the fall of Jerusalem to the Romans in AD 70.[245] The Jesus of Kazantzakis' novel must, therefore, be in his early to mid-seventies. God has abandoned his holy City Jerusalem in the same way that Jesus' guardian angel has finally abandoned him.

A group of old men, Jesus' former disciples, visit Jesus. The latter finally recognises Peter and, in a commentary, perhaps, on the contemporary church, and in particular the papacy, Jesus says: 'Peter! Are you the rock on which, once upon a time in the folly of my youth, I wanted to build my church? How you've degenerated, son of Jonah! No longer a rock, but a sponge full of holes!'[246]

All have failed, all are disillusioned. Judas accuses Jesus of treachery and cowardice: 'You changed your face and your name, you fake Lazarus, to save yourself . . . As he faced the cross this fake Messiah went dizzy and fainted. Then the ladies got hold of him and installed him to manufacture children for them.'[247] Jesus' wounds begin to bleed anew as he is abused by Judas. Jesus begs his forgiveness and admits that he should have been crucified. But the disciples cannot forgive him. Matthew, in particular, laments that his whole work is fruitless: 'How masterfully I matched your words and deeds with the prophets!'[248] Only Thomas remains faithful.

The disciples leave, shouting their disillusioned accusations. The house, village and everything disappear in front of Jesus' eyes. (It is clear that the faint, or dream, ends here[249]). He finds a vinegar soaked sponge pressed against his lips and yells 'Lama Sabacthani.' *He is on the cross*!

He realises that he *has* undergone the Passion after all and that his disciples' accusations are baseless. When he cried 'Eli, Eli' and fainted 'temptation had captured him for a split-second and led him astray. The joys, marriages and children were lies . . .'[250]

The well-known scholar, critic and translator of Kazantzakis, Peter Bien, believes, as we saw, that '*The Last Temptation* is the summation of the thought and experience of a man whose entire life was spent in the battle between spirit and flesh.'[251] Anthonakes finds that, despite Kazantzakis' own intentions, the Christ of his novel is, *essentially*, a highly orthodox one.[252] *The Sunday Telegraph* wrote of 'this magnificent novel

. . . [which] brings to its spiritual theme the vivid details of a Brueghel painting.'[253] But perhaps it is not surprising that the religious establishment was perturbed. Bien notes: 'For Kazantzakis . . . it is paramount that Jesus be constantly tempted by evil in such a way that he feel its attractiveness and *even succumb to it*, for only in this way can his ultimate rejection of temptation have meaning. *This is heresy*.'[254]

Elsewhere, Bien observes that a 'loving and yet distanced relationship to his materials is carried forward in the final novels and especially in *Christ Recrucified* and *The Last Temptation* . . .'[255] He believes, furthermore, 'that novels like *Zorba*, *Christ Recrucified* and *The Last Temptation* succeed all-in-all because in them we feel a unified and consistent flavour that in turn comes from a successful marriage of language to content.'[256]

Yet the same critic also asks whether Kazantzakis is 'a universal genius or the most overrated and atrocious writer of our times?'[257] He is unable to answer his own question but, for our purposes, that does not really matter. Kazantzakis stands as yet one more author whose artistic achievement has been characterised as 'blasphemy' by an outraged 'orthodoxy'.

The Last Temptation of Christ directed by Martin Scorsese [born 1942]

The film of Kazantzakis' novel, which was given the slightly extended title of *The Last Temptation of Christ*, appeared in 1988. Directed by the American Martin Scorsese, it was 163 minutes in length and received its premier at the 1988 Venice International Film Festival. William Defoe starred in the role of Jesus, Harvey Keitel played Judas, Barbara Hershey was Mary Magdalene and Verna Bloom was Mary, the mother of Jesus.[258]

The furore[259] which greeted the film was not entirely surprising or unexpected. There were demonstrations and protests against the film and even an offer to buy the film rights so that all the copies could be burned.[260] During one demonstration, an actor 'pretended to drive nails through Jesus' hands into a wooden cross.'[261] None of this should have surprised, given the troubled production history of the film. Scorsese had attempted to direct Kazantzakis' novel as early as 1983 and been forced, *inter alia*, by rising budgets, religious protests and the threat of a theatre chain not showing the film, to cancel the project.[262] 'I think it became like a hot coal, and people just didn't want to go near it.'[263]

When the film did finally open in 1988, it was the theology of the film, rather than the sex scenes or 'the erroneous idea that Jesus was to be portrayed as a homosexual',[264] which perceptive critics realised would cause most offence to religious 'orthodoxies'. Pam Cook, for example, observed: 'Those who, sight unseen, cry blasphemy have nevertheless got it right. Scorsese and Paul Schrader [the film writer] have produced a deeply transgressive view of religion which at the very least opens it up for general discussion *beyond the protective confines of the Church*, and at the most unmasks the perverse and contradictory impulses at the heart of Christian faith. *In theological terms, the film decisively breaks with dogma in both form and content*.'[265] The critic here, then, clearly sees the film as both an assault on what is perceived to be a narrow clerical guardianship of religious truth and authority (that is, on religious hierarchical *power*), and on dogmatic theology itself.

It is instructive to note here, and compare, the words of Eleni Kazantzakis, the novelist's wife: 'When the book appeared, many said that it was a masterpiece, the best novel that had ever been written about Christ. So often those who said the book was blasphemous had not read it. It was the same with the film.'[266]

Other commentators have refused to see the parallel which is usually drawn between *The Satanic Verses* and the film *The Last Temptation of Christ*.[267] It is true that both have provoked outrage but Ali Mazrui, for example, believes that the film regards Christ as both holy and good.[268] And the debate over whether the film is indeed blasphemous has continued long after the film was withdrawn from general release and confined, in the main, to a circulation in video form. When the BBC bought the film a large number of complaints were received 'about the possibility of the film being shown, according to the BSC [Broadcasting Standards Council] annual report. "This is a record number of complaints and people are concerned about blasphemy but there's nothing we can do unless it is shown," the BSC said.'[269]

In 1992 the film critic Michael Medved launched a ferocious attack on Hollywood: '[Universal's woeful experience with] *The Last Temptation of Christ*,' he said, 'typifies the pervasive and self-destructive hostility to religion that has taken root in Hollywood.'[270]

Richard Corliss agrees that 'born-again Christians may not agree that *The Last Temptation* has therapeutic value. Their God is as pure as H.B. Warner in *King of Kings* . . . But surely a sinless man needs sinners, and a backdrop dark with whores and moneychangers, political oppression and religious fanaticism, against which to shine.'[271] Corliss believes, furthermore, that Scorsese knows far more than many of his detractors about his subject.[272] The former concludes that 'the final proof of *The*

Last Temptation's message is that it has greater numbers of the non-religious thinking and arguing seriously about Jesus than a snake-shaking fundamentalist could dream of. It's a Billy Graham Crusade for the lapsed Christian.'[273]

In the light of the quotations which we have cited above, that last statement will clearly be questioned by many, not least, or especially, by those who refuse to view the film. And it is to the film itself that we will now turn.

The film critic David Thompson was absolutely correct when he noted that the film followed the 'narrative path' of the novel 'with utter fidelity.'[274] Since this is the case, the film's story will not be outlined here in view of its adherence to the structure and narrative sequence of the text of the novel. However, it is inevitable that in any screenplay there will be, at least minor, omissions and some changes. These we will refer to. It may be noted in passing that a preliminary reading of the novel certainly facilitates comprehension of the film, whose narrative without such a textual reading may occasionally appear confusing.

Perhaps the principal omission in the film is the major role which the novel gives to the apostle Matthew. There is a consequent cinematic loss of the whole of Kazantzakis's debate about truth and the levels of scriptural truth. Matthew nowhere appears in the film as a major contemporary recorder of the events which are played out.

Secondly, unlike the novel, there are no winged angels to be seen: indeed, there are no *explicitly* supernatural beings in the film at all. The angel in the novel provides a vivid *leitmotiv* of the divine. That role is lost on the screen. The story of the centurion's daughter is also omitted.

All that said however, we may note that the Jesus of the film is as doubtful about his own role, as Arian, as the Jesus of the novel. The cinematic portrayal of the character of Jesus is also somewhat banal and tame and never seems to achieve the emotional intensity of the protagonist of the novel. This is in vivid contrast to the fiery Jesus of Pier Paolo Pasolini's *The Gospel According to St. Matthew* which was released in the US in 1966.[275]

The other differences between film and book are of a more minor nature: in the latter, the three temptations are represented by a snake, a lion and a dazzling archangel (Lucifer). In the film, the last becomes a blazing column of fire. (One film critic rather aptly notes that 'Christ's temptations in the desert are shown with a worrying literalness that some will read more as Disney silliness than Pasolinian simplicity.'[276]) At

Jesus' baptism in the Jordan no sound is heard in the film nor bird seen. Lazarus in the film is finally murdered *outside a house* rather than on a mountain slope. The angel in Gethsemane who comes to Jesus with a cup or bowl takes the form of a very human bearded man, quite unlike the stern, pale angel of the novel. On the screen the 'guardian angel' in the final temptation of the title is an adolescent girl with a yellow robe, golden hair and an English accent who maintains this shape throughout. In the novel, by contrast, the 'guardian angel' is at first a beautiful male with two green wings who later adopts the almost permanent disguise of a little negro boy. Scorsese felt that to portray the guardian angel on the screen in this way was inappropriate: '. . . I felt that brought connotations and we'd have difficulties. People would get upset and it would get in the way of what the film's really about. So then we decided it should be an old man . . . but that concept didn't seem right. So we went with a little girl, even though we couldn't get away from Pasolini's use of a young girl as an angel, whose face is so extraordinary, like Botticelli.'[277]

Another feature which is not in the novel is that this cinematic angel tells Jesus soon after meeting him, and having drawn out the nails of the cross, that he is *not* the Messiah. Again, unique to the cinema portrait of Jesus is his discovery of the dead Mary Magdalene. 'God killed her,' says the angel. In the novel, of course, the reader will recall that Mary Magdalene is stoned to death.

There a few final disparities between film and book which are worth mentioning here, and which occur towards the end of the film. Jesus' 'guardian Angel' turns into the same pillar of fire that Jesus saw in the (cinematic) representation of the last of the temptations in the desert. The 'angel' is thus revealed as Satan or Lucifer. In the book, of course, Jesus simply falls out and quarrels with the angel who, with profound irony given the rebellion of Lucifer in Heaven, characterises Jesus as 'Rebel!'[278] Later, after the meeting in the book between Jesus and his querulous disciples, 'the negro boy had disappeared.'[279]

The final transition between the dream of the last temptation and the reality of the cross is handled differently in the book and the film. In the book everything begins to disappear as the frustrated disciples harangue their former master, and Jesus is back on the cross within a few lines.[280] In the film we see Jesus slowly climbing the wall of a building (the Temple?) in Jerusalem which is burning in the background, the result, presumably, of the Roman assault. We hear Jesus say that he wants to be crucified and rise again and be the Messiah. *Then* we see him back on the cross and his final words 'It is accomplished' are articulated in both the film and the book.

As we have noted, the film seems to have caused offence on two main counts, theology, and presentation and direction. Not only is the *theology* of the film, like that of the book, thoroughly Arian but Kazantzakis' inventions about the life of Jesus are replicated on screen. Some were also offended by *the presentation and direction*, that is, the sex scenes and the nudity, although an examination of both shows that these do not, in fact, amount to very much. Indeed, one critic observed that 'the objections on the grounds of sex are clearly a red herring. Whatever else this Jesus may be after, it is not sex.'[281] It may be argued that the sex scenes are not very explicit and that the nudity *is* historically accurate: the Zealot is crucified naked; some of John's converts by the River Jordan are perceived naked, shaking and wailing ecstatically. Jesus is scourged and beaten naked and finally crucified naked. Scorsese himself had no doubts about what he was doing. For him this was a quite legitimate attempt at verisimilitude: 'After the film was first cancelled around 1983, I subscribed to the *Biblical Archeology Review* . . . One whole issue dealt with the only archaeological evidence of a crucifixion, a young Jew in his twenties in about AD 100. Sure enough, he was crucified naked . . .'[282]

The film critics and others have varied in their reactions to the film. Thompson, for example, admits that the film has its faults like the temptation scenes to which we referred above. His final verdict, however, is that 'Scorsese has succeeded magnificently in bringing a Christ to the screen who lives as a man of *this* world. And the conclusion could hardly be more affirmative, the spiritual journey more intense.'[283]

Richard Corliss held that 'Scorsese's film is plenty acute, and in its way reverent, as an exploration of the Jesus legend.' He found it a 'severe, coherent, passionate, and beautifully made film.'[284]

Kauffmann, however, notes that 'the angel who takes Jesus from the cross tells him that one woman is much like another, they are all one woman with different faces.' He makes the acute point that much controversy has focussed on the sexual scenes in the film but 'no one has mentioned its sexism.'[285]

Others have been frankly appalled by the film. We have referred above to Michael Medved's comments. He clearly did not enjoy watching the film: 'I found the entire experience as uplifting and rewarding as two hours and forty-four minutes in the dentist's chair.'[286] Medved slated both the direction and the acting. He concluded: 'It is the height of irony that all this controversy should be generated by a film that turns out to be so breathtakingly bad, so unbearably boring. In my opinion, the controversy about this picture is a lot more interesting than the film itself.'[287]

By way of highlighting that controversy, it is useful, and serves as a neat conclusion to this Chapter, to examine briefly another film whose content and direction, not to mention nudity, aroused a similar furore. The film is sometimes spoken of in the same breath as Scorsese's *Last Temptation of Christ*:[288] it is Jean-Luc Godard's 1984 *Je Vous Salue, Marie* (*Hail, Mary*).

The theological theme of this film, that of the Incarnation itself, was a worthy one. What appalled the religious establishment was the direction and presentation: for Godard's film, denounced by the Pope,[289] presents a modern Incarnation which, nonetheless 'keeps to the main essentials of the New Testament story.'[290]

Mary is a basketball-playing student and occasional petrol-pump attendant. Joseph, her boyfriend, drives a taxi. Mary is visited by 'Uncle Gabriel', who tells Mary that she will give birth to a child; Joseph is instructed by Gabriel to do his duty by Mary and, becoming finally convinced that she is still a virgin, he marries the now pregnant Mary who insists on her chastity and virginity. The child is born and later Gabriel greets Mary in the street with the words 'Je vous Salue, Marie.' There is a sub-plot as well which need not concern us here.[291]

For the critic Derek Elley

> the crunch comes at the end, after the baby 'Jesus' has been born: Marie and Joseph are now a comfortable, bored upper-middle-class family, with Marie the housewife and Joseph demanding his breakfast before setting off for the office. The man has still not penetrated the mystery of his wife, the mystery of creation, and for their son (as he explores his mother's naked body and receives poetic answers to his questions) the mystery is only just beginning.[292]

While the views of Catholic orthodoxy on the film, particularly in France, were hardly a surprise, the physical articulation of those views was perhaps more unexpected: in Versailles a cinema was invaded and two reels of the film, which was characterised as 'shocking and profoundly blasphemous', were damaged. Unsuccessful attempts were made at having a national ban imposed.[293] It is clear that many were offended by the nudity of Myriem Roussel who played the lead role of Mary; this was a feature also commented on by many critics.[294] The latter have been divided, or ambivalent, in their assessment of the film.

Elley noted bluntly: 'On first glance, *Hail, Mary* may strike many as yet another example of Godard hogwash'; but he went on to observe: '[The film] is spectacular both to look at and listen to.'[295] Dieckmann found it 'meditative, serene' and 'an extraordinarily soulful film.'[296] Elaina Henderson was less enthusiastic: '*Hail, Mary* is packed in the way that we have come to expect of a Godard movie, but, unfortunately, this one does not carry its luggage very lightly. The heaviness stems from a confusion in how we respond to Mary. Beautifully played by Myriem Roussel, she remains steelily remote throughout the film, and the weight of philosophical speculation placed on her fragile shoulders makes her characterization shaky at best.'[297]

We may conclude by asking what the two films, *The Last Temptation of Christ* and *Je Vous Salue, Marie*, have in common. Both deal with New Testament themes in an original way. Both roused the wrath of the religious establishment, and especially the Christian fundamentalist wing of that establishment, to a high degree. Both were directed by men deeply interested in religion, especially the Catholic faith;[298] yet they were not afraid to risk offending the religious susceptibilities of religious people. Both films regard nudity as an artistic requisite.

From the point of view of *direction and presentation* then, there is much in both films which might cause those so disposed to cry 'blasphemy'. From the point of view of *theology*, however, the two films are somewhat different. *The Last Temptation of Christ* presents an Arian, doubting Messiah figure who undergoes a totally unscriptural 'last temptation.' The figures in the modern Incarnation presented to us in *Je Vous Salue, Marie*, however, act out their strange lives according to the fundamental orthodox New Testament paradigm of the Incarnation and the Virgin Birth. The modern setting and nudity may be grossly offensive to many but there is no doubt that Godard is a more orthodox, or scriptural, cinematic exegete than Scorsese. The latter, of course, could 'blame' Kazantzakis to whose novel he is exceptionally faithful.

NOTES

1 See, for example, Pierre Cachia, *Ṭāhā Ḥusayn: His Place in the Egyptian Literary Renaissance*, (London: Luzac, 1956), pp. 143–166; M.M. Badawi, *Modern Arabic Literature and the West*, (London: Ithaca Press, 1985), pp. 181–182.

2 For the Arabic text see *Awlād Ḥāratinā*, (Beirut: Dār al-Ādāb, 1967; 5th imp. 1986) [hereafter referred to as *AH*]; trans. into English by Philip Stewart, *Children of Gebelawi*, Arab Authors 15, (London: Heinemann, 1981) [hereafter referred to as *CG*].

3 *The Satanic Verses*, (London & New York: Viking Penguin, 1988) [hereafter referred to as *SV*].

4 *The Last Temptation*, trans. P.A. Bien, (London: Faber & Faber, 1991) [hereafter referred to as *LT*].

5 *The Last Temptation of Christ* (1988); see Tom Milne (ed.), *The Time Out Film Guide*, 2nd edn., (London/Harmondsworth: Penguin Books Ltd., 1991), p. 372.

6 *Je Vous Salue, Marie* (1984); see Milne (ed.), *Time Out Film Guide*, pp. 275–276.

7 See 'Translator's Introduction' in Stewart (trans.), *CG*, p. vii; Lisa Appignanesi & Sara Maitland (eds), *The Rushdie File*, (London: Fourth Estate, 1989), p. 204.

8 Ibid.

9 See Muḥammad Yaḥyā & Mu'tazz Shukrī, *al-Ṭarīq ilā Nūbil 1988: 'Abra Ḥāra Najīb Maḥfūẓ*, (Cairo: Umma Press li 'l-Ṭibā'a wa 'l-Nashr, 1989), p. 6; see also the back of the paperback edition of the Stewart translation cited above n. 2.

10 See Yaḥyā & Shukrī, *al-Ṭarīq*, p. 6. I am indebted to Dr. Rasheed El-Enany for drawing my attention to this and other facts concerning the career of Najīb Maḥfūẓ.

11 See Yaḥyā & Shukrī, *al-Ṭarīq*, p. 106. One might compare Maḥfūẓ's pragmatism here with Salman Rushdie's insistence on a paperback edition of *SV*.

12 See Malise Ruthven, *A Satanic Affair: Salman Rushdie and the Rage of Islam*, (London: Chatto & Windus, 1990), pp. 116, 123, 153.

13 Shyam Bhatia, 'Broad Path, Courageous heart', *The Observer*, 8th March 1992, p. 62 (my italics). See also the interview with Maḥfūẓ in *Ākhir Sā'a* (Egyptian Weekly Magazine), 10th May 1989.

14 Badawi, *Modern Arabic Literature and the West*, p. 169; idem., 'Microcosms of Old Cairo' in Younes A. El-Batrik (ed.), *The World of Naguib Mahfouz*, (London: Egyptian Education Bureau, 1989), p. 29. See also S. Somekh, 'The Sad Millenarian: An Examination of Awlad Haratina' in Trevor Le Gassick (ed.), *Critical Perspectives on Naguib Mahfouz*, (Washington: Three Continents Press, 1991), p. 101. Somekh also calls it 'a philosophical tale in its purest form' (ibid., p. 102), and also notes that 'on one occasion [Maḥfūẓ] draws a comparison between his work and *Gulliver's Travels*' (ibid., p. 104).

15 Rasheed El-Enany, *Naguib Mahfouz: The Pursuit of Meaning*, Arabic Thought and Culture Series, (London & New York: Routledge, 1993), p. 25.

16 Robin Ostle, 'Urban Form, Literary Form: Conflict and Polarity in the Work of Naguib Mahfouz' in El-Batrik (ed.), *The World of Naguib Mahfouz*, p. 23 (my italics).

17 See Badawi, *Modern Arabic Literature and the West*, p. 169; idem., 'Microcosms of Old Cairo' in El-Batrik (ed.), *The World of Naguib Mahfouz*, p. 29.

18 See Yaḥyā & Shukrī, *al-Ṭarīq*, p. 99.

19 See Badawi, *Modern Arabic Literature and the West*, p. 169; idem., 'Microcosms of Old Cairo' in El-Batrik (ed.), *The World of Naguib Mahfouz*, p. 29.

20 Ibid.

21 *AH*, p. 5 trans. by Stewart, *CG*, p. 1.

22 *AH*, p. 11 trans. by Stewart, *CG*, p. 5.

23 Badawi, *Modern Arabic Literature and the West*, p. 169; idem., 'Microcosms of Old Cairo' in El-Batrik (ed.), *The World of Naguib Mahfouz*, p. 29.

24 See Q.2: 30.
25 *AH*, pp. 9 ff; *CG*, pp. 5 ff; Yaḥyā & Shukrī, *al-Ṭarīq*, p. 34.
26 *AH*, pp. 113 ff; *CG*, pp. 73 ff; Yaḥyā & Shukrī, *al-Ṭarīq*, p. 35.
27 *AH*, pp. 211 ff; *CG*, pp. 137 ff; Yaḥyā & Shukrī, *al-Ṭarīq*, p. 36
28 *AH*, pp. 307 ff; *CG*, pp. 199 ff, Yaḥyā & Shukrī, *al-Ṭarīq*, p. 38.
29 *AH*, pp. 445 ff; *CG*, pp. 287 ff; Badawi, *Modern Arabic Literature and the West*, p. 169; idem., 'Microcosms of Old Cairo' in El-Batrik (ed.), *The World of Naguib Mahfouz*, p. 29; Rasheed El-Enany, 'Naguib Mahfouz' in ibid., p. 36; see also Yaḥyā & Shukrī, *al-Ṭarīq*, p. 40 for whom 'Arafa is *al-shuyūʿī al-mulḥid* (the heretical communist).
30 See Badawi, *Modern Arabic Literature and the West*, p. 169; idem., 'Microcosms of Old Cairo' in El-Batrik (ed.), *The World of Naguib Mahfouz*, p. 29; Yaḥyā & Shukrī, *al-Ṭarīq*, p. 34.
31 See, for example, the survey in Yaḥyā & Shukrī, *al-Ṭarīq*, pp. 34–40.
32 See ibid., p. 34.
33 Badawi, *Modern Arabic Literature and the West*, p. 169; idem., 'Microcosms of Old Cairo' in El-Batrik (ed.), *The World of Naguib Mahfouz*, p. 29; see also Francis Xavier Paz, *The Novels of Najīb Maḥfūẓ*, PhD Thesis, University of Columbia, 1972, p. 148, and Mattityahu Peled, *Religion My Own: A Study of the Literary Works of Najîb Maḥfûẓ*, PhD Thesis, University of California, Los Angeles, 1971, pp. 271–272.
34 Paz, *Novels of Najīb Maḥfūẓ*, p. 148.
35 See n. 22 above.
36 See Yaḥyā & Shukrī, *al-Ṭarīq*, p. 34.
37 *AH*, pp. 9–112; *CG*, pp. 5–72; see also Peled, *Religion My Own*, pp. 273 ff.
38 See Peled, *Religion My Own*, p. 274.
39 *AH*, pp. 113–210; *CG*, pp. 73–136; see also Peled, *Religion My Own*, p. 275.
40 *AH*, pp. 211–306; *CG*, pp. 137–198; see also Peled, *Religion My Own*, p. 275.
41 *AH*, pp. 307–443; *CG*, pp. 199–286; see also Peled, *Religion My Own*, p. 275.
42 *AH*, p. 353 trans. by Stewart, *CG*, p. 228.
43 *AH*, p. 406.
44 *AH*, pp. 445–552; *CG*, pp. 287–355; see also Peled, *Religion My Own*, pp. 275–279.
45 *AH*, p. 447 trans. by Stewart, *CG*, p. 287.
46 *AH*, p. 453; *CG*, p. 291.
47 El-Enany, *Naguib Mahfouz: The Pursuit of Meaning*, p. 143, see also p. 21.
48 *AH*, p. 493; *CG*, p. 316.
49 *AH*, p. 541 trans. by Stewart, *CG*, p. 347.
50 Somekh, 'The Sad Millenarian', pp. 105, 107, 108. The symbols of *Awlād Ḥāratinā* and other works are discussed in Chapter Four of this present monograph.
51 *The Independent*, 15th October 1988 (my italics) cited in El-Batrik (ed.), *The World of Naguib Mahfouz*, p. 56.
52 Badawi, *Modern Arabic Literature and the West*, p. 170; idem., 'Microcosms of Old Cairo' in El-Batrik (ed.), *The World of Naguib Mahfouz*, p. 30.
53 Ostle, 'Urban Form, Literary Form' in El-Batrik (ed.), *The World of Naguib Mahfouz*, p. 23 (my italics).
54 R. El-Enany, 'Religion in the Novels of Naguib Mahfouz', *British Society for Middle Eastern Studies Bulletin*, vol. 15, nos. 1–2 (1988), p. 26 (my italics).

55 Ibid., p. 27.
56 Ibid.
57 Somekh, 'The Sad Millenarian', p. 112.
58 Ibid.
59 M.M. Ahsan & A.R. Kidwai (eds.), *Sacrilege Versus Civility: Muslim Perspectives on The Satanic Verses Affair*, (Leicester: The Islamic Foundation, 1991), p. 11.
60 Salman Rushdie, *Midnight's Children*, (London: Jonathan Cape, 1981).
61 See Ahsan & Kidwai (eds.), *Sacrilege Versus Civility*, pp. 67, 166. In a letter to *The Independent* (19th January 1989), the five judges who awarded Salman Rushdie the Booker Prize for *Midnight's Children* in 1981, wrote that this work was 'a major novel whose subsequent worldwide success endorsed our judgement. We consider Rushdie to be an outstanding novelist of great artistic and intellectual integrity.' (Reprinted in Jørgen S. Nielson (ed.), *The "Rushdie Affair" – A Documentation*, Muslims in Europe Research Papers Series, no. 42 (June 1989), (Birmingham: Selly Oak Colleges, CSIC, 1989), p. 3.
62 See Ahsan & Kidwai (eds.), *Sacrilege Versus Civility*, p. 166.
63 Salman Rushdie, *Shame*, (New York: Vintage/Aventura, 1984).
64 See Ahsan & Kidwai (eds.), *Sacrilege Versus Civility*, pp. 62, 67.
65 Ibid., p. 67
66 Timothy Brennan, *Salman Rushdie and the Third World: Myths of the Nation*, (London: Macmillan, 1989), p. 119.
67 See ibid., p. 126.
68 'The Hunter Davies Interview', *The Independent*, 11th February 1993, p. 12 (my italics).
69 See Ahsan & Kidwai (eds.), *Sacrilege Versus Civility*, pp. 11–24 for a full and very thorough chronology; for a briefer chronological outline see Nielson (ed.), *The "Rushdie Affair" – A Documentation*, p. 2.
70 See Ahsan & Kidwai (eds.), *Sacrilege Versus Civility*, p. 14.
71 Nielson (ed.), *The "Rushdie Affair" – A Documentation*, p. 2.
72 Ibid.; see also Ahsan & Kidwai (eds.), *Sacrilege Versus Civility*, p. 13 and Neal Robinson, 'Reflections on the Rushdie Affair – 18 April 1989' in David G. Bowen (ed.), *The Satanic Verses: Bradford Responds*, (Bradford: Bradford and Ilkley Community College, 1992), esp. p. 39.
73 See Ahsan & Kidwai (eds.), *Sacrilege Versus Civility*, pp. 13–14.
74 Ibid., p. 14; Nielson (ed.), *The "Rushdie Affair" – A Documentation*, p. 2.
75 Ahsan & Kidwai (eds.), *Sacrilege Versus Civility*, p. 15.
76 Ibid., p. 19.
77 Ibid., p. 21.
78 Salman Rushdie, *The Satanic Verses*, 1st US paperback edn., (Dover, De.: The Consortium, Inc., 1992).
79 For a survey by Salman Rushdie of his predicament, four years after the *fatwā*, see his article 'Out of the Shadows', *The Sunday Times Magazine*, 7th February 1993, pp. 16–21.
80 *The Independent*, 12th May 1993, p. 6.
81 *The Independent on Sunday*, 4th July 1993, p. 15; *The Sunday Times*, 4th July 1993, p. 15.
82 Salman Rushdie, 'Pawn in a Wider Game', *The Observer*, 4th July 1993, p. 23.

83 Letter to *The Independent* from Salman Rushdie, 7th July 1993.
84 Letter to *The Independent* from Kalim Siddiqui, 8th July 1993.
85 Edward Said, 'Intellectual exile: expatriates and marginals', [Edited text of one of his 1993 Reith Lectures], *The Independent*, 8th July 1993, p. 16.
86 Brennan, *Salman Rushdie and the Third World*, p. 149.
87 Muhammad Mashuq ibn Ally, 'Stranger Exiled from Home' in Dan Cohn-Sherbok (ed.), *The Salman Rushdie Controversy in Interreligious Perspective*, Symposium Series, vol. 27, (Lewiston/Queenston/Lampeter: The Edwin Mellen Press, 1990), p. 135.
88 Ibid., pp. 131–149, esp. p. 132.
89 Ibid.
90 'The Hunter Davies Interview', *The Independent*, 11th February 1993, p. 12.
91 Mashuq ibn Ally, 'Stranger Exiled from Home', pp. 131–149, esp. p. 132.
92 *SV*, pp. 1–87.
93 See Brennan, *Salman Rushdie and the Third World*, p. 157.
94 See Shabbir Akhtar, 'Art or Literary Terrorism?' in Cohn-Sherbok (ed.), *The Salman Rushdie Controversy*, p. 3.
95 See 'Ṣalāḥ al-Dīn' in Ian Richard Netton, *A Popular Dictionary of Islam*, (London: Curzon Press/Atlantic Highlands: Humanities Press, 1992), p. 222. See also Ruthven, *A Satanic Affair*, p. 16.
96 Brennan, *Salman Rushdie and the Third World*, p. 153; Akhtar, 'Art or Literary terrorism?', p. 3 (who spells the name Bachchan).
97 Ruthven, *A Satanic Affair*, p. 16.
98 Ibid.
99 Brennan, *Salman Rushdie and the Third World*, p. 155.
100 ''Izrā'īl' in Netton, *Popular Dictionary of Islam*, p. 131.
101 Ibid., p. 132.
102 See Akhtar, 'Art or Literary Terrorism?', p. 3.
103 Wehr, *Dictionary of Modern Written Arabic*, p. 144 s.v. *jāhilīya*.
104 For other identifications, see Ziauddin Sardar & Merryl Wyn Davies, *Distorted Imagination: Lessons from the Rushdie Affair*, (London: Grey Seal, 1990), pp. 158–159 ff.
105 Brennan, *Salman Rushdie and the Third World*, pp. 153–154; Akhtar, 'Art or Literary Terrorism?', p. 2; Ruthven, *A Satanic Affair*, p. 17.
106 Brennan, *Salman Rushdie and the Third World*, p. 154; see also Ruthven, *A Satanic Affair*, p. 17.
107 Akhtar, 'Art or Literary Terrorism?', p. 2.
108 Ibid.; see also Brennan, *Salman Rushdie and the Third World*, p. 156; Ruthven, *A Satanic Affair*, p. 17.
109 Ruthven, *A Satanic Affair*, p. 20.
110 *SV*, p. 31; see also 'al-Janna' in Netton, *Popular Dictionary of Islam*, pp. 134–135.
111 See *SV*, pp. 35, 73, 74, also pp. 40–41.
112 Ibid., pp. 89–126.
113 See Akhtar, 'Art or Literary Terrorism?', p. 3; see also Brennan, *Salman Rushdie and the Third World*, p. 157.
114 Sardar & Davies, *Distorted Imagination*, p. 37; see also Ruthven, *A Satanic Affair*, p. 35; Rana Kabbani, *Letter to Christendom*, (London:

Virago Press, 1989), p. 6; W. Montgomery Watt, *Muhammad, Prophet and Statesman*, (London: Oxford University Press, 1967), pp. 2, 231.

115 Brennan, *Salman Rushdie and the Third World*, p. 157; see *SV*, p. 108.

116 See *SV*, pp. 33, 53.

117 See 'Khālid b. al-Walīd' in Netton, *Popular Dictionary of Islam*, p. 143.

118 See 'Quraysh' in ibid., pp. 207–208.

119 See 'Abū Sufyān' in ibid., p. 18.

120 See 'Hind' in ibid., p. 103.

121 Sardar & Davies, *Distorted Imagination*, p. 158.

122 See 'Ḥamza' in Netton, *Popular Dictionary of Islam*, p. 95.

123 *SV*, p. 101.

124 Akhtar, 'Art or Literary Terrorism?', p. 10; see also Sardar & Davies, *Distorted Imagination*, p. 162.

125 See 'Salmān al-Fārisī' in Netton, *Popular Dictionary of Islam*, pp. 223–224.

126 See 'Bilāl b. Rabāḥ' in ibid., p. 57.

127 Netton, *Popular Dictionary of Islam*, pp. 151, 161, 255 s.v. 'al-Lāt', 'Manāt', 'al-'Uzzā'.

128 See *SV*, pp. 98, 106.

129 See ibid., p. 123.

130 Ibid., pp. 127–202.

131 Ibid., p. 37.

132 Ibid., pp. 203–240.

133 See ''Ā'isha bint Abī Bakr' in Netton, *Popular Dictionary of Islam*, p. 25. For a slightly more extensive treatment, see W. Montgomery Watt, ''Ā'isha Bint Abī Bakr', *EI*[2], vol. 1, pp. 307–308. See also Nabia Abbott, *Aishah, the Beloved of Mohammed*, The Middle East Collection, (New York: Arno Press, 1973, repr. of University of Chicago Press, 1942 edn.).

134 M. Seligsohn, ''Ā'isha Bint Abī Bakr' in H.A.R. Gibb & J.H. Kramers (eds.), *EIS*, (Leiden: E.J. Brill/London: Luzac, 1961), pp. 25–26; see also Abbott, *Aishah*, p. 218.

135 W. Montgomery Watt, *Muhammad at Medina*, (Oxford: Clarendon Press, repr. 1968), p. 323; see also Abbott, *Aishah*, pp. 7–8.

136 Akhtar, 'Art or Literary Terrorism?', p. 3. See also Ruthven, *A Satanic Affair*, pp. 44–47.

137 Sardar & Davies, *Distorted Imagination*, p. 167; see *SV*, p. 214.

138 *SV*, p. 205.

139 Ibid., p. 210

140 Ibid., p. 211.

141 See ibid.

142 See Alex Haley, *The Autobiography of Malcolm X*, (New York: Ballantine Books, 1964).

143 See 'al-Burāq' and 'Isrā'' in Netton, *Popular Dictionary of Islam*, pp. 59, 128.

144 See ''Uthmān b. 'Affān' in ibid., pp. 254–255.

145 *SV*, pp. 241–356.

146 See 'Abū Sufyān' and 'Hind' in Netton, *Popular Dictionary of Islam*, pp. 18, 103.

147 See 'Ibn Baṭṭūṭa' in ibid., p. 111.

148 *SV*, pp. 357–394.

149 See Akhtar, 'Art or Literary Terrorism?', p. 3; Brennan, *Salman Rushdie and the Third World*, p. 157.
150 See ''Umar b. al-Khaṭṭāb' in Netton, *Popular Dictionary of Islam*, p. 252.
151 *SV*, pp. 395–469.
152 See ''Izrā'īl' in Netton, *Popular Dictionary of Islam*, pp. 131–132.
153 *SV*, pp. 471–507.
154 See Ruthven, *A Satanic Affair*, pp. 44–47.
155 Ibid., pp. 44–45.
156 Ibid., p. 46.
157 *SV*, pp. 509–547.
158 See ibid., Chapter One.
159 See, for example, *SV*, pp. 73, 92, 108, 226, 363. There are many other examples.
160 Ibid., p. 539.
161 See ibid., Chapter Seven.
162 *The Guardian*, 23rd September 1988, cited in Appignanesi & Maitland (eds.), *The Rushdie File*, p. 10.
163 Ibid.
164 Ibid., p. 12.
165 *Indian Post* (Bombay), 2nd October 1988, cited in ibid., p. 13.
166 Ibid.
167 Ibid.
168 Ibid.
169 Ibid., p. 15.
170 Cited in ibid., p. 24 from *The Independent's* (21st February 1989) edited reprint of the *Kayhan Farangi* review.
171 *Impact International*, 28th October–10th November 1988, cited in Appignanesi & Maitland (eds.), *The Rushdie File*, pp. 25–26.
172 Ibid., p. 27.
173 *The Independent Magazine*, 10th June 1989, p. 14.
174 Ibid.
175 'Out of the Shadows', *The Sunday Times Magazine*, 7th February 1993, p. 16.
176 P.A. Bien, 'Translator's Note on the Author and His Language', *LT*, p. 509.
177 2nd edn., (Athens: Dífros, 1955).
178 Bien, 'Translator's Note on the Author and His Language', *LT*, p. 516.
179 Michael A. Anthonakes, *Christ, Freedom and Kazantzakis*, PhD Thesis, University of New York, 1965, p. 135.
180 Bien, 'Translator's Note on the Author and His Language', *LT*, p. 516.
181 Peter Bien, *Nikos Kazantzakis, Novelist*, Studies in Modern Greek, (Bristol: Bristol Classical Press/New Rochelle: Aristide D. Caratzas, 1989), p. 66. See also Anthonakes, *Christ, Freedom and Kazantzakis*, p. 2 (abstract).
182 See Anthonakes, *Christ, Freedom and Kazantzakis*, esp. pp. xv, 134, 135–136, 138, 142.
183 Bien, *Nikos Kazantzakis, Novelist*, p. 66; Martin P. Levitt, *The Cretan Glance*, (Columbus: Ohio State University Press, 1980), p. 61. The Vatican, in fact, placed *LT* on the Index in December 1953 but the Decree which put it on the Index was dated 12th January 1954 (Anthonakes, *Christ, Freedom and Kazantzakis*, pp. 132, 134).

184 See Anthonakes, *Christ, Freedom and Kazantzakis*, p. 158.
185 Bien, *Nikos Kazantzakis, Novelist*, p. 66; see Levitt, *The Cretan Glance*, p. 61
186 Anthonakes, *Christ, Freedom and Kazantzakis*, p. 186.
187 Levitt, *The Cretan Glance*, p. 61.
188 Anthonakes, *Christ, Freedom and Kazantzakis*, pp. 167–171.
189 See ibid., p. 190.
190 Bien, 'Translator's Note on the Author and His Language', *LT*, p. 518; see Anthonakes, *Christ, Freedom and Kazantzakis*, pp. 155–156.
191 See E.P. Sanders, *The Historical Figure of Jesus*, (London: Allen Lane, The Penguin Press, 1993), pp. 10–11, 290.
192 See *LT*, p. 454.
193 Ibid., pp. 7–10.
194 Ibid., p. 8.
195 Ibid., p. 9.
196 Ibid., pp. 11–164.
197 Ibid., p. 21.
198 Ibid.
199 Ibid., p. 23.
200 See also ibid., p. 231.
201 Ibid., p. 126.
202 Ibid., p. 151.
203 Ibid., pp. 165–371.
204 Ibid., p. 207; compare *Luke* 16: 19–31.
205 *LT*, p. 214.
206 Ibid., p. 227.
207 Ibid., pp. 208–209.
208 See especially ibid., p. 315.
209 See *Matthew* 14: 22–33.
210 *LT*, p. 351.
211 Ibid.
212 Ibid., p. 357.
213 *The New Jerusalem Bible*, p. 1606.
214 Benedict T. Viviano, 'The Gospel According to Matthew' in Raymond E. Brown, Joseph A. Fitzmyer & Roland E. Murphy (eds.), *The New Jerome Biblical Commentary*, (London: Geoffrey Chapman, 1989), p. 632.
215 David M. Stanley, *The Gospel of St. Matthew*, 2nd rev. edn., New Testament Reading Guide, no. 4, (Collegeville, Minnesota: Liturgical Press, 1963), p. 12.
216 Ibid., p. 13.
217 *LT*, p. 357.
218 Ibid.
219 Ibid., p. 358.
220 Ibid.
221 See Henry Wace & Philip Schaff (eds.), *A Select Library of Nicene and Post-Nicene Fathers of the Christian Church, Second Series, Volume XI: Sulpitius Severus, Vincent of Lerins, John Cassian*, (Oxford: James Parker & Co./New York: The Christian Literature Company, 1894), esp. pp. 435–445 (= Cassian's Conferences: XIV The First Conference of

Abbot Nesteros: *On Spiritual Knowledge*). I am indebted to the late Dom Sylvester Houédard OSB for drawing this work to my attention. See p. 437 n. 2 which refers to 'the four senses of scripture, viz., the historical, tropological, allegorical and analogical.'

222 *LT*, p. 362.
223 See *Matthew* 17: 1–8.
224 *LT*, pp. 366, 368.
225 Ibid., pp. 372–453.
226 Ibid., p. 379.
227 Ibid., p. 400.
228 See also ibid., p. 423 which draws attention to the 'unreality' of Lazarus' flesh: Lazarus' hair, scalp and arm come away in the would-be assassin Barabbas' hand, and Barabbas seems unable to kill Lazarus with a knife.
229 *LT*, p. 390.
230 Ibid., p. 396.
231 Ibid., p. 401.
232 Ibid., pp. 430–431 (my italics).
233 Ibid., p. 453.
234 Ibid., pp. 454–507.
235 Ibid., p. 455.
236 Ibid., p. 468.
237 See ibid., p. 476.
238 For Biblical and Qur'ānic antecedents for the use of the dream in sacred literature, see the Joseph story in *Genesis* and *Sūra* 12 of the Qur'ān. See also 'Yūsuf (2)' in Netton, *Popular Dictionary of Islam*, pp. 261–262.
239 *LT*, p. 487.
240 See, for example, the work of Geza Vermes, *The Religion of Jesus the Jew*, (London: SCM, 1993) esp. pp. 207, 210, 212. See also Karen Armstrong, *A History of God*, (London: Mandarin, Reed Consumer Books, 1994), p. 103.
241 *LT*, p. 488.
242 Ibid.
243 Ibid., p. 489.
244 Ibid., p. 490.
245 See Flavius Josephus, *The Destruction of the Jews*, trans. by G.A. Williamson, (London: Folio Society, 1971, repr. from Penguin edn. of 1959).
246 *LT*, p. 496.
247 Ibid., p. 502.
248 Ibid., p. 505.
249 Bien (*Nikos Kazantzakis, Novelist*, p. 73) characterises Chapters 30–33 as a 'dream sequence'. Compare the several extended dream sequences in *SV*.
250 *LT*, p. 507.
251 'Translator's Note on the Author and His Language', *LT*, p. 509.
252 See Anthonakes, *Christ, Freedom and Kazantzakis*, pp. 194–195.
253 Back cover of *LT* (paperback).
254 *LT*, p. 517 (my italics).
255 Peter Bien, *Nikos Kazantzakis*, Columbia Essays on Modern Writers 62, (New York & London: Columbia University Press, 1972), p. 40.
256 Idem., *Kazantzakis and the Linguistic Revolution in Greek Literature*,

Princeton Essays in European and Comparative Literature, no. 6, (Princeton: Princeton University Press, 1972), p. 254.

257 Idem., *Nikos Kazantzakis*, p. 41.

258 Mary Pat Kelly, *Martin Scorsese: A Journey*, (London: Secker & Warburg, 1991–92), pp. 302–303, 3–14; Pam Cook, [Review of] 'The Last Temptation of Christ', *Monthly Film Bulletin*, vol. 55, no. 657 (October 1988), pp. 287–288; see also Milne (ed.), *Time Out Film Guide*, p. 372; Leonard Maltin (ed.), *Movie and Video Guide, 1993 Edition*, (London/ Harmondsworth/New York: Signet, Penguin, 1992), p. 685; Geoff Andrew, *The Film Handbook*, (Harlow: Longman, 1989), pp. 260–262.

259 See David Thompson, [Review of] 'The Last Temptation of Christ', *Films and Filming*, no. 409 (October 1988), pp. 37–38; [Mid Section] 'For Christ's Sake', *Film Comment*, vol. 24, no. 5 (September–October 1988), pp. 31–43; 'L"Affaire" Scorsese', *Positif*, no. 333 (November 1988), p. 2.

260 See Kelly, *Martin Scorsese*, pp. 235–241, and inside front of dust-jacket.

261 Ibid., p. 241.

262 See 'For Christ's Sake', *Film Comment*, p. 38; Kelly, [Chapter Six] 'Almost the Last Temptation', *Martin Scorsese*, pp. 161–180; see also Steve Jenkins, 'From the Pit of Hell', *Monthly Film Bulletin*, vol. 55, no. 659 (December 1988), pp. 352–353.

263 Kelly, *Martin Scorsese*, p. 180.

264 Jenkins, 'From the Pit of Hell', p. 353; Cook, [Review of] 'The Last Temptation of Christ', p. 288.

265 Cook, [Review of] 'The Last Temptation of Christ', p. 288 (my italics).

266 Kelly, *Martin Scorsese*, p. 239.

267 For example, by Billy Graham. See 'Graham Backs Muslims on Verses', *The Guardian*, 2nd June 1989, cited in Ahsan & Kidwai (eds.), *Sacrilege Versus Civility*, p. 128.

268 Ali Mazrui, *Ithaca Times*, 2nd–8th March 1989 cited in Shabbir Akhtar, 'Art or Literary Terrorism?', p. 14; Ali Mazrui, 'Novelist's Freedom vs Worshippers' Dignity' in Ahsan & Kidwai (eds.), *Sacrilege Versus Civility*, p. 217. See also Ruthven, *A Satanic Affair*, p. 47.

269 'Unscreened film draws complaints', *The Independent*, 8th July 1992.

270 John Davison, 'The family man who told Hollywood "your soul is sick"', *The Sunday Times*, 7th February 1993, p. 1; see Michael Medved, *Hollywood Vs. America: Popular Culture and the War on Traditional Values*, (New York: Harper Collins, 1992), esp. pp. 50, 37–49.

271 [Interview of Martin Scorsese by Richard Corliss in] 'For Christ's Sake', *Film Comment*, p. 42, see also pp. 36–43.

272 Ibid., p. 42.

273 Ibid., p. 43.

274 Thompson, [Review of] 'The Last Temptation of Christ', p. 37.

275 Michael Singer, 'Cinema Saviour', *Film Comment*, vol. 24, no. 5 (September–October 1988), pp. 46, 48. For some comparisons between Pasolini's and Scorsese's films, see the article by Stanley Kauffman, 'Stanley Kauffmann on Films: A Mission' [A Review of *The Last Temptation of Christ*], *The New Republic*, 12th–19th September 1988, p. 28. Here Kauffmann describes the book on which Scorsese's film is based as 'an overheated rendering of a sophomorically daring idea.'

276 Thompson, [Review of] 'The Last Temptation of Christ', p. 38.
277 David Thompson and Ian Christie (eds.), *Scorsese on Scorsese*, (London: Faber & Faber, 1990), p. 143.
278 *LT*, p. 494.
279 Ibid., p. 505.
280 Ibid., p. 506.
281 Cook, [Review of] 'The Last Temptation of Christ', p. 288.
282 Thompson & Christie (eds.), *Scorsese on Scorsese*, p. 138.
283 Thompson, [Review of] 'The Last Temptation of Christ', p. 38.
284 Richard Corliss, 'Body . . .' in 'For Christ's Sake', *Film Comment*, p. 34.
285 'Stanley Kauffmann on Films: A Mission', p. 29.
286 Medved, *Hollywood Vs. America*, p. 46.
287 Ibid., pp. 46–47.
288 For example, see Paul Pawlikowski, 'The Greatest Story Never Made?', *Stills*, no. 18 (April 1985), p. 13; Thompson & Christie (eds.), *Scorsese on Scorsese*, p. 122.
289 Thompson & Christie (eds.), *Scorsese on Scorsese*, p. 122.
290 Derek Elley, [Review of] 'Hail Mary', *Films and Filming*, no. 372 (September 1985), p. 42.
291 See Robert Brown, [Review of] 'Je Vous Salue, Marie (Hail Mary)', *Monthly Film Bulletin*, vol. 52, no. 620 (September 1985), pp. 267–268; Elaina Henderson, 'Sympathy for the Virgin: Hail Mary', *Stills*, no. 21 (October 1985), p. 42; Susan Barrowclough, 'Godard's Marie: The Virgin Birth and a Flurry of Protest . . .', *Sight and Sound*, vol. 54, no. 2 (Spring 1985), p. 80; Clancy Sigal, 'Hail Storm', *The Listener*, 17th October 1985, p. 40.
292 Elley, [Review of] 'Hail Mary', p. 42.
293 Barrowclough, 'Godard's Marie', p. 80. See also Jacques Bauvy, 'Dans l'Affaire "Je Vous Salue Marie"', *FILMéchange*, no. 32 (1985), pp. 63–68.
294 For example, see Hervé Le Roux, 'Le Trou de la Vierge ou Marie telle que Jeannot la Peint', *Cahiers du Cinema*, no. 367 (Janvier 1985), p. 12; Sigal, 'Hail Storm', p. 40; Katherine Dieckmann, 'Godard in His "Fifth Period": An Interview', *Film Quarterly*, vol. 39, no. 2 (Winter 1985–86), p. 3; Jean-Luc Douin, 'Jésus superstar, Certains préfèrent l'invisible', *Cinémation*, 49 (October 1988), pp. 33–42, esp. p. 39.
295 Elley, [Review of] 'Hail Mary', p. 42.
296 Dieckmann, 'Godard in His "Fifth Period"', p. 2.
297 Henderson, 'Sympathy for the Virgin', p. 42.
298 See Dieckmann, 'Godard in His "Fifth Period"', p. 3; Kelly, *Martin Scorsese*, esp. pp. 9–14.

3

CONTEXT

> The occupation debris will contain the objects lost or broken during the use of the structure.
>
> Kenyon, *Beginning in Archaeology*, p. 71.

In the previous Chapters brief references have been made to various historical figures of the past and to Christian heresies such as Arianism. However, little attempt was made to pursue such figures and doctrines because this was not the purpose of those earlier Chapters. Now however, having surveyed the concept of blasphemy and delineated the *content* of some of those literary and cinematic works which groups of believers have characterised as blasphemous, it is time to go more deeply into the *background* of what we have surveyed. This Chapter, therefore, by examining the past and present religious milieux of the works under discussion, will attempt to locate them in the precise historical and religious contexts of which they are the products.

In effect the same question will be asked in two ways: what is it about the religious past and present, in which the text is embedded, which has precipitated the charge of blasphemy in our own age? Alternatively, what aspects of the past and the present are embedded in, or behind, each text which have given rise to such charges?

For Maḥfūẓ's novel, we will look at the past Qur'ānic view of prophethood, with Muḥammad venerated as the seal of the prophets,[1] and the concept of God's eternity. Both doctrines, of course, are held in the present as well. However, specifically for the present, we will examine the rise of Islamic fundamentalism in the Middle East, with reference to many different examples for comparative purposes, and also the 'God is Dead' climate which swept Western theology.

For Rushdie's novel, we will survey the original Satanic Verses and, with special reference to Iran in the present, look too at how a revolutionary agenda, or internal turmoil, can easily foster an attitude of hostility to all that opposes, or seems to oppose, one of the main engines of the revolution, when that engine is Islam itself. Khomeini was not only the *Father* of a famous revolution; he was also the *product* of a preceding revolutionary climate, as was his *fatwā*.

Finally, regarding Kazantzakis' novel and Scorsese's film, we will examine the heresy of Arianism and Neo-Arianism in the past, and the drive towards an imposed religious orthodoxy, or, alternatively, fundamentalism, which sometimes characterises some of the Christian Churches today. The climate of religious hostility towards the film *The Last Temptation of Christ* had already, in the immediate past, been prepared by that whipped up against *Je Vous Salue, Marie*, and, in the more distant past, by the use of such instruments as the *Index of Forbidden Books*.

It should be noted about the methodology employed here in this Chapter that the past and present strata adumbrated to illuminate the context of a particular text, are not intended to be viewed as rigidly *confined* to that text, or, indeed, film. Each *may* be applicable to one of our other texts or films as well.

Maḥfūẓ's *Awlād Ḥāratinā*: (i) The Stratum of the Past

If one looks at the cover of the critique of Maḥfūẓ entitled *al-Ṭarīq ilā Nūbil 1988* (*The Road to the 1988 Nobel Prize*) by Muḥammad Yaḥyā and Mu'tazz Shukrī, published in Cairo in 1989, one is confronted with a colour picture of Najīb Maḥfūẓ wearing his customary sunglasses; but it is a face with a difference. Ghastly cracks rend the skull, neck, cheek and front of the face. It looks like a well-worn and much loved bust suddenly breaking open. In a small square at the top right-hand side of the cover, appears a small picture of Philip Stewart's English translation of *Awlād Ḥāratinā*, published by Heinemann under the title of *Children of Gebelawi*. It is covered by a large black X.

The cover of *al-Ṭarīq*, in sum, is a wordless, but hate-filled, articulation of one view of Maḥfūẓ's most notorious novel. The authors of *al-Ṭarīq* note: '[*Awlād Ḥāratinā*] is a symbolic tale in which the symbols are only hidden behind a thin veil of social material . . . *it is a tale which portrays God and the prophets and the divine messages in an irreligious fashion* . . . the story makes fast the principles of scientific socialism and heretical [or blasphemous] [*mulḥida*] Marxism as a substitute for religion [*dīn*] and divinity and revelation.'[2] The dedication (*ihdā'*) of Yaḥyā and Shukrī's book reads:

> To every monotheist [*muwaḥḥid*] . . . In the presence of every freethinker [*ibāḥī*] and apostate [or heretic] [*mulḥid*]: "Say: 'God.' Then leave them alone, playing their game of plunging."[3]

Al-Ṭarıq concludes by drawing the reader's attention to the ban placed on Maḥfūẓ's *Awlād Ḥāratinā* by al-Azhar in 1968.[4]

Yaḥyā and Shukrī were by no means the only people to find Maḥfūẓ's novel deeply offensive. Writing in *The Guardian* in 1989, Karim Alrawi reported that 'the main religious weekly, *Al-Noor*' had 'kept up an attack on Naguib Mahfouz, Egypt's Nobel Prize laureate. Whether through cartoons depicting Mahfouz burning in hell or reports of attempts by Egyptian publishers and distributors to get the ban on his novel, *Gebalawi's Children* [*Awlād Ḥāratinā*], lifted, *Al-Noor*'s message is clear: *Mahfouz is a blasphemer* and must be punished . . . there are plans to convene a conference at Mecca later this year at which both Naguib Mahfouz and Salman Rushdie will be denounced as *blasphemers* and possibly even apostates . . .'[5]

In the eyes of the religious establishment, then, Maḥfūẓ's offences appear to be manifold. However, we may identify here three areas which, because of their roots in the Qur'ānic stratum of the past, have been viewed as particularly heinous by that establishment.

The *first* was readily seized upon by the authors of *al-Ṭarīq ilā Nūbil 1988*. They held that Maḥfūẓ's novel could easily be construed as an attempt to produce 'a new Qur'ān',[6] an alternative sacred text! This was a new text, moreover, which encapsulated, dramatised and dwelled upon the concept of 'the death of God.'[7] While it is clear from the briefest acquaintance with the text that it was not Maḥfūẓ's intention to produce a rival Qur'ān, one can see how he played into the hands of his enemies to some extent by giving *his* work a parallel structure to that of the holy book of Islam.[8]

It is a cliché of Qur'ānic theology that the sacred text is inimitable. Any idea that it can be paralleled, duplicated or surpassed, either in content or style, is anathema to the Muslim. In three places in the Qur'ān man is challenged to produce a text like it. For example:

> And if ye are in doubt
> As to what We have revealed
> From time to time to Our Servant,
> Then produce a Sūra
> Like thereunto;
> And call your witnesses or helpers
> (If there are any) besides God,

If your (doubts) are true.
But if ye cannot –
And of a surety ye cannot –
Then fear the Fire
Whose fuel is Men and Stones –
Which is prepared for those
Who reject faith.[9]

The technical term used in Arabic to render the concept of Qur'ānic inimitability is *i'jāz*. This means 'literally "the rendering incapable, powerless"' and 'since the second half of the 3rd/9th century' it has been the 'technical term for the inimitability or uniqueness of the Ḳur'ān in content and form.'[10] Von Grunebaum notes that 'two factors combined to make the uniqueness of the Ḳur'ān crucial within the never fully systematized dogmatics of Islam: the necessity to prove the mission of the Prophet and the necessity to secure an incontrovertible authority for Muslim doctrine, law and mores. These interlocking needs could, in the atmosphere of the period, be met only by establishing the transcendental or miraculous character of the document of revelation and the singularity or miraculousness of the historical Muḥammad b. 'Abd Allāh revealing it.'[11] It is hardly surprising, in view of all this, that the Qur'ān assumed a central role in Islam 'as the focal point and justification of grammatical and literary studies' which was rarely challenged.[12] Nor is it surprising that the faintest perception, in the mediaeval or modern age, of any attempt to 'duplicate' the sacred text or produce a 'new Qur'ān' would produce a wrathful response.

A *second* area which seems to have caused offence in Maḥfūẓ's *Awlād Ḥāratinā* is the author's allegory of the prophets. Not only was such allegorisation intensely disliked but it is clear that, contrary to Islamic doctrine, the figure 'playing the role' of Muḥammad (Qāsim) in this novel is not the last of the prophets! He is succeeded in the novel by another 'prophet', 'Arafa, Scientific Man. The latter is established 'as a recipient of revelation like his prophetic predecessors.'[13] Of 'Arafa and his mission, El-Enany writes: 'What we have here is a gallant attempt by Mahfouz to bestow on science the spiritual power inherent in religion.'[14] Maḥfūẓ's 'crime' here, then, in his dealings with the prophets is not just his allegorisation of them and his refusal to allow Muḥammad/Qāsim to be the seal of the prophets, but 'his endeavour to establish science as the legitimate heir of religion' as El-Enany neatly puts it.[15] Here, in a very real sense, Science or Scientific Man is 'the Seal of the Prophets'. It is clear that Maḥfūẓ's text, and indeed his theology and prophetology (if such can be said to exist here in his work), have the capacity to be read on several different levels; the Islamic fundamentalist will leave his text with a quite different perception of the author's intention from that of the Western literary critic, for example.

Islam reveres many prophets, twenty eight of whom are mentioned in the Qur'ān.[16] Muḥammad, according to mainstream belief, is the last, the Seal of the Prophets.[17] The latter is so fervent an article of belief that heterodox Islamic groups like the Ahmadiyya, who appear to accept the existence of other prophets *after* Muḥammad, are frequently reviled by mainstream Islam.[18] 'Arafa, or Scientific Man, as the final successor of religious man, of the prophets, will not impress the Islamic fundamentalist; neither will Maḥfūẓ's allegorisation of Adam, Moses, Jesus, and Muḥammad. For by this literary device, commonplace though it is, Maḥfūẓ lays himself open to accusations of distorting the fundamentalist perception of the Qur'ānic prophets and their messages, and 'altering' the sacred Ur-Text, the Qur'ān, itself.

A *third* area which seems to have caused offence in Maḥfūẓ's novel finds its roots in the classical Islamic and Qur'ānic doctrine of the eternity of God. As we have already seen, *Awlād Ḥāratinā* concludes with the bold idea that the great Jabalāwī (=God) has died! Yet again and again, the Islamic Faith, basing itself on the Qur'ān, insists on the dogma of God's eternity: *al-Bāqī* (The Eternal) is one of the Ninety Nine Most Beautiful Names of God.[19] Another is *al-Qayyūm* which may be rendered both as 'The Self-Subsisting'[20] and 'The Eternal'.[21] The Qur'ān stresses that all things will perish except God's own face.[22] God's sempiternity, timelessness or infinite pre-existence (*qidam*)[23], or simply eternity,[24] is one of His essential (*dhātī* or *nafsī*) classical attributes,[25] as is His 'permanence' (*baqā'*).[26]

In the light of all this, the horrified preoccupation of such fundamentalist writers as Yaḥyā and Shukrī with Maḥfūẓ's delineation of themes like 'the death of God'[27] becomes at least explicable. The stratum of the past, here as elsewhere, reveals a weighty vein of theological material which chains the present and seeks to bind the future.

Maḥfūẓ's *Awlād Ḥāratinā*: (ii) The Stratum of the Present

Recent history has demonstrated with great clarity that authors like Maḥfūẓ, Rushdie and Kazantzakis, and film directors like Scorsese, are regarded as problematical by the religious establishments by which they are encircled. However, perhaps a major difference between East and West with regard to the wrath aroused lies in the way that that wrath is articulated, both by the religious establishment and the ordinary, but often equally sensitive, lay populaces who form the various constituencies of the religious leaders. Thus, while a potentially lethal *fatwā* wings its way from Khomeini to Rushdie, the Pope, whatever his disgust, does not direct a life-threatening edict towards either Jean-Luc Godard or Scorsese.

In other words, the *reaction in the West* seems, in modern times at least, to be rather more muted than the *reaction in the East*, if one might be allowed here, for the sake of simplicity, a monolithic characterisation. The disparity in reaction is partly because the days and the attitudes of the Inquisition in the West are long over; and partly because there has been an undeniable diminution in the sense of the Sacred here as well. Perhaps the main reason, however, is that a recognised tradition or phenomenon of religious dissent and theological heterodoxy has developed in the Twentieth Century West which feels totally *unconstrained* by those bonds of church or state which might have operated in the past.

Most notable of all the heterodox theological streams, or syndromes, which have developed in this century – and of which Maḥfūẓ must surely have been informed[28] – is that which has been characterised as 'God is dead' or 'Death of God' theology.[29] This mode of thought sparked considerable theological debate in the 1960s and it has a theological heir in that literary mode of criticism which is today called deconstruction. Of the latter Carl A. Raschke noted: 'Deconstruction, which must be considered the interior drive of twentieth-century theology rather than an alien agenda, is in the final analysis *the death of God put into writing*, the subsumption of the 'Word' by the 'flesh', the deluge of immanence.'[30] The *Dictionary of the Ecumenical Movement* refers to 'the *theological* concept of atheism which distances itself critically from traditional theism in order to be able to "believe in God atheistically" (the "God is dead" school).'[31]

Essentially, this 'death of God' theology has its origins in the thought of Friedrich Nietzsche (1844–1900), though it predates even him. In Section Two of 'Zarathustra's Prologue' in Nietzsche's *Thus Spoke Zarathustra*, the death of God is actually announced: Zarathustra meets 'the Saint' again:

> But when Zarathustra was alone, he spoke thus to his heart: 'Could it be possible! This old saint has not yet heard in his forest that *God is dead*!'[32]

John Llewelyn summarises this event and its aftermath:

> In the forest on the lower slopes he [Zarathustra] meets again the hermit who saw him go up, who continues to worship a transcendent God, and is quite incapable of understanding Zarathustra's news. Moving on to the nearby town, Zarathustra preaches in the market place that sin, which was once sin against a God beyond this world, is now sin against this world. It is now not with a Supraterrestrial Divinity, but with the earth that we are called to keep faith . . . However, for the people in the market place also Zarathustra's message comes too soon . . . although they may acknowledge that they have murdered God, they think they have therefore become God in His place.[33]

Llewelyn goes on to explain that 'Nietzsche's teachings expose his readers to other forms of disillusionment. When Zarathustra declares that God is dead he speaks not only of the God of religion, but of the absolutes of traditional metaphysics and morals. He is denying that existence moves towards some goal.'[34]

Roger Scruton reminds us, however, that 'the famous apothegm 'God is dead'' is older, even, than Nietzsche and received its first, really philosophical articulation by the "Young Hegelian" Max Stirner (1806–1856).[35] What Nietzsche did with the concept was striking and ensured its survival in the centre rather than on the fringes of modern thought. J.P. Stern believes that Nietzsche reversed the structures of real theology. For him, Christian theology is removed and in its place appears 'the penitential theology of a God-less universe.'[36]

In the late 1950s and 1960s the 'death of God' theological syndrome became fashionable again. It recognised a concept whose theological and cultural baggage had formerly denoted that which was anti-Christian and which now denoted that which was post-Christian.[37] Vahanian identified our era as 'post-Christian' because 'Christianity has sunk into religiosity . . . because modern culture is gradually losing the marks of that Christianity which brought it into being and shaped it . . . because tolerance has become religious syncretism, an amalgam of beliefs and attitudes without content or backbone.'[38] The same author, in the following paragraph, has neatly encapsulated the ethos of 'God is dead' theology:

> Modern man is the legatee of the Christian as well as of the atheist. He agrees with the Christian that all is grace. He agrees also with the atheist that God is dead. His argument is: All is grace, therefore God is dead. For if life is meaningless, then there must be no God. But, if it is meaningful – and it must be, or else it contradicts itself – it is meaningful by virtue of some kind of immanent grace;

therefore God does not exist. If all is grace, then God is dead. Or: All is grace because God is dead.[39]

Aspects of this stream or type of thinking have continued to appear in more recent decades. We earlier cited Carl A. Raschke who believes that deconstruction is '*the death of God put into writing*.'[40] Raschke characterises Nietzsche as 'our major prophet of modernity.'[41] Although it has rightly been stressed that 'death of God' theology was 'a movement which flourished in the U.S.A. during the 1960s', it 'essentially did not die' since it was 'continued in a different form through the influence of, e.g., Don Cupitt's books and broadcasts in England in the 1980s.'[42] Cupitt, born in 1934, noted, for example, that it was difficult for people to appreciate that the God of Christianity was the creation of power for the sake of power, who had exercised a repressive influence down the ages in the development of Christianity.[43] Much of Western religion, for Cupitt, resembles the worship of a God who is dead.[44]

Every so often a book appears, to the evident delight of the media and the chagrin of orthodox church authorities, which appears to peddle the same kind of 'God is dead' theology which we have been surveying. The volume entitled *God in Us: A Case for Christian Humanism*,[45] by the Rev. Anthony Freeman, Priest-in-Charge of St. Mark's Church in Staplefield, West Sussex, England, is an excellent example. Freeman proclaims a conversion from an oppressive Christianity to 'one which brought a glorious sense of freedom and joy. This freedom came when I accepted that I did not believe in God as traditionally understood.'[46] He was removed by his bishop from a training post because of this book.[47]

The domain of literature, as well as that of theology, has been touched by the 'God is dead' theological movement. We have seen this, notably, in Maḥfūẓ's novel. Glicksberg, furthermore, believes that 'on the whole, modern literature illustrates not the presence but the absence of God, not the triumph but the defeat of faith.'[48]

The stratum of the present, which we have adumbrated thus far, with its emphasis on 'God is dead' theology, assumes a considerable significance when one notes that Maḥfūẓ studied philosophy for his BA degree at what is now Cairo University and started to study for an MA in philosophy after graduating in 1934.[49] It was surely in these studies that he absorbed the knowledge of Nietzsche which informs, or at least acts as intellectual backdrop to, the novel *Awlād Ḥāratinā*.[50]

Of course, the 'death of God' school of thought was not the only aspect of the Western liberal tradition of religious dissent to which we referred above, even though it was probably the most striking and provoking. An associated vein, or theology, of religious *scepticism* was, and is, also characteristic of late Twentieth Century theological and religious writing. Recent examples range from the utterances of Dr David Jenkins, formerly Bishop of Durham,[51] ('We must face the issue of God – or the issue of the absence of God'[52]), through A.N. Wilson's biography of Jesus Christ, entitled simply *Jesus*,[53] to Barbara Thiering's *Jesus the Man: A New Interpretation from the Dead Sea Scrolls*.[54] Wilson's book perhaps tells us more about the author than his subject.[55] Reviewing the two books by Wilson and Thiering, Humphrey Carpenter concluded: 'Wilson's book belongs to one class of writings about Jesus: those that attempt to extract a historical figure from the accepted body of New Testament writings. Another approach is to take some more outré text, generally these days the Dead Sea Scrolls, and argue that the "real" Jesus is to be found there. Barbara Thiering's *Jesus the Man* is a more than averagely silly example of this genre.'[56] Both books, in their very different ways, are typical of a certain kind of 'liberal' religious writing prevalent in the West today. Perhaps the major difference is that, while some of the critics did have *some* kind things to say about Wilson's work,[57] Thiering's came in for a substantial barrage of hostile scholarly criticism.[58] Both too, built on a liberal 'unorthodoxy' which established itself in the 1960s and 1970s, aside from the 'death of God' theological movement.

This 'unorthodoxy' was articulated in such very different books as the seminal work edited by John Harwood Hick (born 1922) entitled *The Myth of God Incarnate*,[59] and the extraordinary book by John Allegro called *The Sacred Mushroom and the Cross*,[60] a work of truly bizarre scholarship. In the latter the author, who had done much valuable and scholarly work on the Dead Sea Scrolls,[61] decided that Christianity really originated as a sacred mushroom-worshipping fertility cult! Hugh Montefiore believes that Allegro's work was ultimately damaging to the kind of radical theology being done in Cambridge and Woolwich where theologians tried to make Christianity more comprehensible for mid-Twentieth Century man. He concluded that 'Allegro's mushroom book persuaded theologians of the hard right that Sixties theological liberalism had overreached itself.'[62]

The fact of the modern, pluralistic religious environment of the West which we have just sampled, however, does not mean that no sanctions at all were deployed by a sometimes outraged religious orthodoxy or hierarchy. As we noted before, the main difference between the Western and the Eastern reactions is that the former was – and is – generally *milder* than the latter. The penalties and sanctions handed down by Western religious authorities in the Twentieth Century may have been 'career' threatening; they were never life threatening in the sense of an Ayatollah's *fatwā*. No one was sentenced to death by the Vatican or the Eastern Orthodox Churches for religious dissent or blasphemy. The outrage felt might have been just as great; the sanctions available were rather slighter, and sometimes ignored.

Thus, the Greek Orthodox Church reacted angrily to the publication of Kazantzakis' *Last Temptation*, an anger which lasted beyond the author's physical death itself. The Vatican placed the book on the *Index*. And attempts were made, by the Roman Catholic Church especially, to silence dissident theologians. Teilhard de Chardin (1881–1955), for example, author of the famous *Phenomenon of Man*,[63] was banned from teaching at the Institut Catholique in Paris, effectively 'exiled' to China, and not allowed to write philosophy, among many other academic vexations in a life of turbulent scholarship.[64] Hans Küng (born 1928), author of a controversial work entitled *Infallible? An Enquiry*,[65] had his *missio canonica* (Roman Catholic teaching authority) withdrawn by Pope John Paul II; he was forced to vacate his Catholic Chair of Theology and move to a new Chair in the independent Institute for Ecumenical Research at Tübingen University.[66] The Dominican Edward Schillebeeckx (born 1914) with his book *Jesus: An Experiment in Christology*,[67] won 'acclaim by the wider public and the theological world and disapproval from the Vatican.'[68] He was summoned to Rome in December 1979.[69] A fellow Dominican, Matthew Fox (born 1940), with his book *Original Blessing*[70] and his original theological stance, was dismissed from the Dominican Order in 1993. Finally, we might note the dismay of the Jesuits, albeit temporary, in 1981, when Pope John Paul II (*reg.* from 1978) imposed upon that Order a personal delegate and temporary Superior General, an aged priest nearly eighty years old by the name of Fr. Paolo Dezza.[71] This was rather less severe than the possible liquidation or winding-up of the Order, possibly contemplated by Pope John Paul I, (*reg.* 1978)[72] – a disaster which had already overtaken the Order once in its long history, in 1773 under Pope Clement XIV[73] – but it indicated once again, in no uncertain fashion, that a Western religious orthodoxy and hierarchy might not be prepared to tolerate either a body of rivals or 'doctrinal deviations' in teachings and writings which might 'cause confusion among the faithful.'[74]

All that said however, it is clear that the sanctions which were deployed fell far short of the deadly. They included a prohibition on teaching and writing, the withdrawal of a licence to teach, a theological investigation, dismissal from one's religious family (i.e. Order), and the imposition of an unwelcome authority.

If, however, we now turn to the modern reaction in the East to such matters as blasphemy, heresy or perceived attacks on orthodox religion, especially Islamic or Hindu, it is clear that the responses are articulated in a much severer, more vehement and, often, bloodier, manner. We have already noted that many died in the demonstrations on the Indian sub-continent, precipitated by Rushdie's *Satanic Verses*. The famous *fatwā* issued by the Ayatollah Khomeini constitutes a perpetual sentence of death for the author. This is not to say, however, that there has never been a tradition of theological or religious dissent in the Islamic world. There has. Its articulation, though, *could* be extremely dangerous. Deviation, or theological innovation (*bid'a*) could frequently mean death.

Three very different examples, with very different consequences, will be surveyed here to illustrate this clearly yet briefly. In 922 in Baghdad the famous mystic al-Ḥusayn b. Manṣūr al-Ḥallāj was brutally executed for a mixture of religious and political reasons. Among his utterances was the notorious phrase 'I am the [Divine] Truth (*Anā 'l-Ḥaqq*]' which was interpreted by some as a claim to divinity by al-Ḥallāj.[75] A very different case is to be seen in the writings of the great blind Syrian poet Abū 'l-'Alā' al-Ma'arrī (973–1057) whose sceptical attitudes towards religion aroused considerable suspicions. One of his most notorious writings was the prose work *Risālat al-Ghufrān* (*The Epistle of Pardon*). In this he envisaged, among other things, visits to Hell and to Paradise, much in the style of Alighieri Dante, portraying Paradise as populated by many of the famous heathen poets of the pre-Islamic age: their sins have been forgiven and they are enjoying Paradise.[76] Of this *Risālat al-Ghufrān*, R.A. Nicholson wrote:

> [It] contains, in addition to many anecdotes of the *zindíqs* and blasphemous quotations from their poetry, a burlesque description of Paradise, where in the manner of Lucian he depicts the pre-Islamic heathen bards revelling and quarrelling and taking part in a literary causerie. Although some persons upheld his orthodoxy, the mask was thin and might not have availed him, if the state of Syria during his lifetime had left the authorities at leisure to deal with offences of this kind. As it was, he ran no great risk. The Fāṭimids were indulgent, and the Mirdásids indifferent, to religious scepticism, which indeed found plenty of support both amongst the learned classes and men of the world.[77]

Al-Ma'arrī was probably not anti-religion *per se* but against its organisation and ritualised aspects.[78] He sought truth but objected strongly to that truth being encapsulated in rigid formulae. The *Risālat al-Ghufrān* shows that al-Ma'arrī believed that the means of salvation were much more diverse than orthodox theology might teach and that those who would be saved would sometimes be other than those envisaged by religious orthodoxy. Whatever else it may be, the *Risālat al-Ghufrān* is *not* an attack on the Islamic faith.[79] It is clear that al-Ma'arrī would have been an ardent Islamic opponent of the mediaeval Christian dictum *extra ecclesiam nulla salus* as popularly interpreted,[80] had that latter phrase been pronounced by a Muslim in a Muslim context.

From the foregoing it will come as no surprise to learn that the *Risālat al-Ghufrān* and its author aroused profound suspicions and that al-Ma'arrī was regarded as a free-thinker. The Bohemian description of Paradise and what appears to be a send-up of Qur'anic terminology, for example, in that *Epistle*, not to mention the poet's own attempt to write a rival Qur'ān,[81] must have led many a casual reader to a similar conclusion.

In our own age, however, the great Egyptian author Ṭāhā Ḥusayn (1889–1973), who himself had considerable admiration for the works of al-Ma'arrī,[82] *did* incur the censure of the religious authorities because of his own writings. In 1926 he published a book entitled *Fī 'l-Shi'r al-Jāhilī* (*On Pre-Islamic Poetry*)[83] which outraged the Islamic orthodoxy of the day. The reason for this was that he concluded that much of the poetry believed to have been produced in the period which pre-dated the rise of Islam, was in fact the forgery of a later age. The Islamic scholars regarded Ṭāhā Ḥusayn's views as being 'in some way an attack on the language of the Qur'ān itself and its much-vaunted superiority over pre-Islamic antecedents. Ḥusayn's book was withdrawn, revised and published anew in 1927 under a modified title.'[84] Cachia reminds us that in *Fī 'l-Shi'r al-Jāhilī* Ḥusayn had 'not only made out that religious motives had contributed to the forging of so-called pre-Islamic poems, but also spoke of the Qur'anic stories of Ibrāhīm and Ismā'īl as myths. Such a challenge could not be ignored.'[85] He was accordingly declared an apostate by al-Azhar University in Cairo.[86] Cachia, however, believes that the whole affair did little real harm to Ḥusayn. The author's offer to resign from his University was refused, on the grounds of academic freedom, and 'he never recanted'[87] yet 'never again did he display defiance to the actual wording of the Qur'ān.'[88]

The affair, however, has cast a long shadow over the history of publishing in Egypt, as Maḥfūẓ, and others whom we shall mention below, have found to their cost. It is an affair which forms part of a never wholly-submerged folk-memory of publication followed by repression and prohibition. This lurking paradigm, particularly when an Islamic issue is involved, becomes of particular significance and danger for the author in our own age, especially when it is paralleled by the rise of a new Islamic fundamentalism in the Near and Middle East.

In an interview with the Egyptian weekly magazine *Ākhir Sā'a*, Najīb Maḥfūẓ referred directly to al-Ma'arrī's *Risālat al-Ghufrān*[89] and he was clearly very familiar with the work of that literary giant.[90] Yet poets and writers, as well as utterers of mystical sayings, are subject to the political and religious milieux in which they live. Al-Ḥallāj was killed; under another regime al-Ma'arrī survived. Ṭāhā Ḥusayn, too, survived, perhaps slightly bloodied. But the Eastern reaction to Maḥfūẓ's *Awlād Ḥāratinā*, in both its pre-Nobel and post-Nobel aspects, has been altogether more dangerous, from both a literary and personal point of view, than was the case with Ḥusayn's book. Not only was publication of the novel *as a book* banned in Egypt; the blind Shaykh 'Umar 'Abd al-Raḥmān issued a *fatwā* against Maḥfūẓ: 'If such an edict had been published years ago, said the Sheikh, when Mahfouz's *Children of Gebelawi* came out, Rushdie would never have dared to publish his blasphemies.'[91]

Thus, in any analysis or excavation of the stratum of the present, we have to take account also of the steady rise of that complex phenomenon loosely called Islamic fundamentalism,[92] in Egypt and elsewhere. Terrorist attacks on tourists and leading politicians in Egypt,[93] and the growing impact there of such groups as *al-Jamā'a al-Islāmiyya*, constitute one feature of that stratum. The other is the censorship of those literary works or films which might displease an establishment either imbued with fundamentalist ideals itself, or, as in the case of Egypt, frightened by Islamic fundamentalism.

In the Middle East the strength of the pen has often been regarded as just as dangerous as that of the sword. Examples of this are to be found all over the Arab world and not only in Egypt. The pen of the Palestinian cartoonist Nājī al-'Alī was clearly regarded by those who assassinated him in London in 1987 as too savage. (Later a romanticised film version of his life, which was shown at the Cairo International Film Festival, was considered to be insulting to Egypt and was criticised for its distortion of history. Calls were made for the film to be censored.[94]). A documentary film on Tuscany, made by the Italian Franco Zeffirelli, which showed the famous Botticelli painting *The Birth of Venus*, was banned in October 1991 by the Saudi Arabian authorities.[95] One of the Arab world's major novelists, 'Abd al-Raḥmān Munīf (born 1933), who was born in Saudi Arabia, and is best known in the West by the English translation of one of his nine novels *Mudun al-Milḥ* (*Cities of Salt*),[96] has been in exile for a large part of his life. El-Enany explains why: 'Cities of Salt . . . documents the evolution of the Kingdom of Saudi Arabia (albeit under a fictitious name) from pre-oil times to virtually the present day. Apart from its literary value, it is an unparalleled piece of social history, whose candidness spares neither prince nor pauper, and whose message is a prophecy of doom. It is no wonder that the author is exiled and his work banned in his homeland.'[97]

In the above examples, the censorship attempted or deployed was for a variety of reasons, by no means all religious. However, they are recorded here in our excavation of the stratum of the present as illustrations of the environment within which the contemporary Arab writer or film maker must work. Three further examples will now be reviewed, this time with a more religious orientation. From these it will be clear that Maḥfūẓ, recipient of a *fatwā* like Rushdie, is by no means alone in present-day Egypt in having roused the wrath of an entrenched religious orthodoxy and the new fundamentalism.

In 1988 an obscure Egyptian author by the name of 'Alā' Ḥāmid, who had worked in taxation, became rather more famous than he might otherwise have done, with the publication of a somewhat inferior novel entitled *Masāfa fī 'Aql Rajul* (*A Distance in a Man's Mind*), which ran to some 239 pages and went on sale with a cover price of 300 piastres.[98] After writing this novel Ḥāmid was given the epithet 'the Egyptian Salman Rushdie'[99] and a number of death threats were made against him.[100] The author was subjected to a complicated legal process, in which the outraged al-Azhar was heavily involved,[101] and finally sentenced to eight years in prison, together with his publisher and printer, on 25th December 1991.[102] At the time of the making of the BBC2 documentary on the author and his book[103] in March 1992, this sentence had not yet been implemented.

'Alā' Ḥāmid's offence was to have written a kind of Dantesque *Divine Comedy*,[104] what Adel Darwish characterises as 'a work of science fiction'[105] and what was, in fact, a rather badly written novel, 'in which the main character's dreams take him to heaven, then hell, where he reviews divine methods of torture.'[106] This was considered to be blasphemous and an insult to religion.[107] A very senior figure of the Azhar gave it as his view that the book contained language which was abusive, insulted religion and attacked all the prophets, holy books and angels.[108] A phrase which appeared in the Arab press more than once to explain or characterise what 'Alā' Ḥāmid had done was 'blaspheming [or reviling or cursing] the Prophets [*sabb al-anbiyā'*]';[109] it will be recalled that there was some discussion of the Arabic word *sabb* in Chapter One of this book.

Speaking in his own defence, 'Alā' Ḥāmid expressed the view that he was being used by the fundamentalists as a test case to discover their own weaknesses and strengths.[110] Another commentator surmised that the Saudi government had put pressure on Egypt to have the book proscribed.[111] The likeliest reason, however, for the actions taken against 'Alā' Ḥāmid was expressed by the Cairo publisher Amīn al-Mahdī: 'What we are seeing is part of the Salman Rushdie affair fall-out.'[112]

Quite a different case, but far more deadly in its ultimate consequences, was that of Farag Ali Fuda (variously spelled Fouda in English). This Egyptian secularist writer was assassinated at the age of forty seven in a Cairo suburb by the group called Islamic Jihād, in June 1992.[113] The latter organisation had issued a *fatwā* against him because of his 'secular extremism'.[114] Alrawi notes that 'in his ten books he sought to dissociate Islam from the actions of those who use religion for political purposes. He contended that the arguments used to justify terrorism and bigotry in the name of Islam were far from Islamic.'[115] Yet it may have been his sense of humour, more than anything else, which, as with the cartoonist Nājī al-'Alī, precipitated his final downfall. His satire in the Cairo *October* magazine mocked the sexual problems of certain Islamic groups and condemned Egyptian sectarianism in witty, yet biting, paragraphs.[116] Farag Fuda's defenders maintain the author's reverence for Islam[117] but the Azhar remained unconvinced. Its Islamic Research Council held that Dr. Fuda's attempt to establish a political party which was non-sectarian and attractive to both Christians and Muslims 'was an affront to Islam.'[118]

The final case which we will survey here is that of Dr. Nāṣir Aḥmad Abū Zayd, a fifty year old academic at the University of Cairo, holding the rank of an Assistant Professor of Arabic Language. His writings attracted the wrath of the fundamentalists; and when he came to apply for promotion in his University he was accused of 'apostasy and atheism'[119] having, among other things, defended the right of Salman Rushdie to publish his novel *The Satanic Verses*,[120] and, in his own publications, 'cast doubt on some of the most basic tenets of Islam.'[121] Abū Zayd's books, indeed, were held to *slander* Islam.[122] In a telling paragraph, the newspaper *al-Quds al-'Arabī* noted that these events were taking place sixty years after the Ṭāhā Ḥusayn affair.[123]

Dr. Abū Zayd's application to be promoted to a Chair was turned down[124] but far worse was to follow: the whole matter did not end in a single University decision to deny promotion to one of its academics. A lawsuit was filed by Abū Zayd's fundamentalist enemies, seeking the divorce of Abū Zayd from his wife (also a teacher at Cairo University) 'on the grounds that she, as a Muslim, cannot remain married to an apostate.'[125] Although the suit was initially thrown out by an Egyptian judge, the significance of what Dr. Abū Zayd and his wife have been through remains in no doubt. And in 1995 the decision was reversed.

The cases outlined above, especially those of 'Alā' Ḥāmid, Farag Fuda and Nāṣir Abū Zayd, illustrate the power of the pen and clearly demonstrate that it can, indeed, in the reactions and responses that it generates, be just as potent in the Middle East as any sword or bomb. Imprisonment, assassination and a possible forced divorce do not conspire to make the writer's milieu an easy one – as Maḥfūẓ himself has discovered.

Of course, the Middle East is not alone in the growth and rise of what we are terming here, loosely, religious fundamentalism. This is a worldwide phenomenon which has invaded not only Islam but also Christianity, Judaism, Sikhism and Hinduism – to name just a few religions – as well.[126] This rise in fundamentalism has been paralleled by a widespread willingness to censor or ban literary and other works which is by no means confined to the Middle East and its governments.[127] Our analysis of the stratum of the present is complete if we bear in mind that, concomitant with these two factors and others mentioned above, there has been a perceived decline in reverence in the *Christian West*, generally speaking, for organised religion,[128] which contrasts markedly with the constancy, respect[129] and even increase in fervour, which characterises organised religion in the *Islamic East*.

Rushdie's *Satanic Verses*: (i) The Stratum of the Past

The strange story of the Satanic Verses has received unusual prominence in our own age because Salman Rushdie decided to name his, now notorious, novel after them. The basic historical account is easily told with reference to the version by the famous historian al-Ṭabarī (*circa* 839–923). The latter relates how the Prophet Muḥammad was concerned about his people and the affair of the Satanic Verses was a product of that concern and his desire to be at one with his own tribe of Quraysh:

> Then God revealed:
> By the star when it sets, your comrade
> does not err, nor is he deceived; nor
> does he speak out of (his own) desire . . .
>
> [Q.53: 1–3]
>
> and when he came to the words:
> Have you thought upon al-Lāt and al-'Uzzā
> and Manāt, the third, the other?
>
> [Q.53: 19–20]

> Satan cast on his tongue, because of his inner debates and what he desired to bring to his people, the words:
>
> These are the high-flying cranes
> [*tilka al-gharānīq al-'ulū*];
> verily their intercession is accepted with approval.[130]

Al-Ṭabarī tells us that the tribe of Quraysh was extremely pleased at Muḥammad's words and his apparent respect for their gods: 'The Quraysh left delighted by the mention of their gods which they had heard, saying, "Muḥammad has mentioned our gods in the most favourable way possible, stating in his recitation that they are the high-flying cranes and that their intercession is received with approval."'[131]

However, the angel of the revelation, Gabriel, then came to Muḥammad and told him that he was seriously mistaken in what he had transmitted. God abrogated the words which Satan had put into the Prophet's mouth[132] and instructed Muḥammad with the following:

> Never did we send a messenger or a prophet before you but that when he recited (the Message) Satan cast words into his recitation (*umniyyah*). God abrogates what Satan casts. Then God established his verses. God is knower, wise.[133]
>
> [Q.22: 52]

These words now replaced what had previously been revealed about 'high-flying cranes':

> Are yours the males and his the females? That indeed were an unfair division! They are but names which you have named, you and your fathers . . .[134]
>
> [Q.53: 21–23]

This, in essence, is the story of the Satanic Verses. There are a number of variant traditions, as Watt reminds us,[135] but they do not alter the import of what al-Ṭabarī narrated. And some scholars have accepted his version of events. Watt, for example, notes that 'at one time Muḥammad must have publicly recited the satanic verses as part of the Qur'ān.' He finds it 'unthinkable that the story could have been invented later by Muslims or foisted upon them by non-Muslims.' Watt concludes: 'At some later time Muḥammad announced that these verses were not really part of the Qur'ān and should be replaced by others of a vastly different import. The earliest versions do not specify how long afterwards this happened; the probability is that it was weeks or even months.'[136] Elsewhere, Watt says: 'The story is so strange that it must be true in essentials.'[137]

Yet the story of the Satanic Verses has by no means been accepted uncritically down the ages, either in the past or in the present, M.M. Ahsan provides us with a list of very distinguished Muslim writers who 'have all rejected the story as preposterous and without foundation.'[138] Ahsan hits out at what he perceives to be the past distortions of Western orientalists, when dealing with such matters as Islam and the Qur'ān.[139] It is therefore interesting that one of the most notable and powerful rejections of the story of the Satanic Verses comes from the pen of the Western orientalist Professor John Burton of St. Andrews University.[140]

In what is indeed a magisterial and seminal article in the study of the Satanic Verses, Burton argued as long ago as 1970 that 'this story must be decisively rejected once and for all.'[141] Here he sided with the Italian L. Caetani whose 'impression . . . was that here we have to do with a later fabrication, partly because the *isnāds* of the various versions of the tale merit little confidence, but primarily because, had these *ḥadīths* even a degree of historical basis, Muḥammad's reported conduct on this occasion would have given the lie to the whole of his previous prophetic activity.'[142] Burton himself concluded, at the end of his carefully argued article: 'There existed . . . a compelling theoretical motive for the invention of these infamous *ḥadīths*. If it be felt that this has now been demonstrated, there should be no further difficulty in suggesting that those *ḥadīths* have no historical basis.'[143]

M.M. Ahsan believes that 'it is unfortunate that an eminent historian like al-Ṭabarī mentioned this story in his *Ta'rīkh* and did not make any comment on it . . . The fact that al-Ṭabarī, Ibn Sa'd and some other historians and scholars recorded this story in their works does not prove that the story itself is true.'[144] There are other areas of Ṭabari's *History* where this author is not wholly reliable or correct as well.[145]

This historical background of controversy and virulent dissent was the background, the stratum of the past, against which Salman Rushdie produced his novel *The Satanic Verses*. Not only did it come down on one side of the debate, i.e. that the incident actually took place, but the author chose to fictionalise and extend the incident in a way undreamed of before by those who had accepted the story as true: *The great angel of God's revelation, Gabriel himself, is portrayed as the author of the Satanic Verses*! This constitutes a literary paradigm shift in the story of earthquake proportions. Thus where, as I have noted before, the Western reader might peruse the entire novel as basically a study in cultural alienation, the educated Muslim reader can hardly avoid reading it in a completely different register and on a completely different level, at least initially. What constituted the real blasphemy for the Muslim of the present was what he perceived to be the re-articulation of an ancient lie, clothed in what was regarded as a further gratuitous falsehood and presented to a largely unschooled world as a literary entertainment.

Rushdie's *Satanic Verses*: (ii) The Stratum of the Present

Had the Iranian Revolution of 1978–1979[146] not taken place and brought the Imām Khomeini to such a position of vital prominence and charismatic authority, it is at least possible that no *fatwā* would have been issued by that Imām against Salman Rushdie. For such an edict to have been issued, for example, from his place of exile in Neauphle-le-Château, twenty five miles outside Paris,[147] by the Imām would have been a mere empty gesture by one yet to reach the plenitude of his authority. The *fatwā*'s power and, indeed, terror, derived (and still derives) from the power, authority and capacity to judge vested in the Imām Khomeini by the Revolution. So, although that Revolution took place several years before the publication of Rushdie's *Satanic Verses*, it necessarily constitutes a key aspect of the stratum of the present which is to be excavated here.

The revolutionary agenda of Iran, not unsurprisingly, opposed all that might oppose a principal engine of that Revolution, Islam itself. Khomeini, as we suggested earlier, was not only the Father of a revolution but also the product of a preceding revolutionary climate as was his *fatwā*. In this section, then, we will review briefly (a) the immediate climate that prepared Iran for its Revolution and the leadership of Khomeini, and (b) the vital role of Islam in that Revolution. These twin politico-religious foci were not unknown to the author of *The Satanic Verses*: we note Rushdie's parody of the Imām Khomeini and his exile in Chapter Four of the novel. The significance of Khomeini's *fatwā*, apart from the danger in which it put Salman Rushdie, was that it spoke not only to an *internal* Iranian constituency but it attempted, at least, to address an *external* pan-Islamic constituency. The *fatwā* aspired to a *religious* universalism and legitimacy just as Rushdie's novel aspired to a *literary* universalism and authorial right.

In the years leading up to the Iranian Revolution there were numerous discontented groups. Robert Graham identifies five main ones: '(a) the students; (b) the small underground guerilla movement; (c) the clergy; (d) the new rootless urban proletariat; (e) the bazaar merchant communities.'[148] This is not to mention such banned groups as the Iranian Communist Party (the Tudeh Party), and the Iran Liberation Movement.[149] The 'modern middle class' was unhappy with its lot as well.[150]

All these different constituencies had much to be discontented and unhappy about.

Massive corruption in high places was routinely tolerated and the regime seemed unable to do anything about it.[151] There were also massive problems of culture clash: many Iranians suffered under the 'acute psychological strain' inflicted on them by the need for their age old culture to adapt to 'the impact of new and alien influences.'[152] The economy posed a third major problem. Many foreign and Iranian scholars and observers believe that the deteriorating economy in the middle of the 1970s was one of the triggers of the Revolution.[153] Certainly, it is true to say with Misagh Parsa that 'after 1975, broad segments of the bazaar faced severe economic pressures.'[154] Finally, the power held at the centre by the authoritarian Shah and his immediate circle constituted an almost fascist absolute.[155] This power was sustained by military might and the brutalities of, and use of widespread torture by, the secret police and intelligence service, SAVAK.[156] This huge power, embodied in and represented by the monarchy, was a matter of particular distaste to Khomeini who openly attacked the institution of monarchy on the occasion of the lavish ceremonies at Persepolis in 1971 in celebration of two and a half millenia of the Persian monarchy. He reminded his audience that the Prophet Muḥammad had said God objected strongly to the title 'King of Kings' and that Islam in its essence opposed the entire conception of monarchy.[157]

This, then, in a nutshell was the climate of pre-revolutionary Iran. It was a potent and subversive cauldron whose ingredients included, *inter alia*, corruption, state terror, a deteriorating economy, culture clash and a hugely authoritarian ruler. But there was another factor in all this which helped to precipitate that 'volcanic political explosion that ended the Pahlavi dynasty in February 1979', as Amuzegar neatly puts it.[158] This was the role of the Islamic religion both before and during the Revolution.

Mansoor Moaddel believes that '*ideology is the constitutive feature of revolution*'[159] and that 'Shi'i revolutionary discourse . . . transformed the economic difficulties and social discontents of the 1970s into a revolutionary crisis.'[160] Most other commentators too are keen to stress the vital role of Islam in the Revolution. Graham notes that 'the clergy [as he wrongly calls them] had a genuine constituency – the conservative mass of the population who were puzzled, confused and bitter about the contradictory policies and broken promises of the Shah.'[161] These religious leaders themselves were deeply discontented, particularly as the Shah attempted to suppress them by arrest, imprisonment or exile.[162]

Hiro stresses that 'the mosque played a crucial part in the revolution, both as an institution and as a place of prayer and congregation.'[163] Dabashi holds that 'the Islamic Ideology' was the crucial and probably indispensable factor in the mobilization of overt public opinion, discontented with the rule of the Shah.[164]

Khomeini himself was convinced that the real motor of the Revolution was to be religion,[165] and when his hour came he cleverly used all things religious to give a dynamic momentum to the Revolution and the events which led up to it.[166] Interpretations of the religious results of what he achieved vary. One article, for example, accuses Khomeini of bequeathing to Shī'ism 'an ideology of revolutionary violence.'[167] What cannot be denied is the role of religion in the Revolution. This is not surprising. 'Religion,' Graham tells us, 'is still the biggest single binding cultural influence, and acts as the most common point of reference for all classes of Iranians.'[168]

Amuzegar provides three distinct reasons why we are entitled to describe the Iranian Revolution as religious and Islamic: it led to the emergence as leader of Khomeini; it used religion as its revolutionary network; it established an Islamic Republic in Iran.[169] Religion played a role in mobilising the discontented, supporting 'nationalist and populist banners of independence and prosperity', presenting the Revolution as a Shī'ite 'passion play', and substituting Islamic ideas for all others.[170]

The uniqueness, however, of the Revolution was its mighty elevation of the doctrine of *Wilāyat al-Faqīh* (*Vilāyat-i Faqīh* in Persian), that is, 'Government by the Jurist.'[171] In a very real sense, this formally marked the end of a transition from a period of traditional Shī'ite quietism to religious activism, an intellectual transition already begun in the 1960s and 1970s.[172] Khomeini contended that a *faqīh* should not just be one of many high-ranking civil servants or administrators but oversee the state administration as judge, guardian and ruler.[173] And that state and government must assuredly be Islamic, for that, proclaimed Khomeini, was the ultimate logic of the doctrine of *Wilāyat al-Faqīh*.[174] It seemed to some that Plato's Philosopher-King, clad in the garb of religion, was to rule with supreme arbitrary authority.[175] Indeed, Khomeini himself was not averse to enlisting the full authority of Plato.[176] And so it was with the plenitude of the doctrine of *Wilāyat al-Faqīh* behind him that the Imām Khomeini directed his devastating *fatwā*[177] at Salman Rushdie in February 1989.

Kazantzakis' and Scorsese's *Last Temptation*: (i) The Stratum of the Past

Arianism, that famous Christian heresy named after the Alexandrian priest Arius (died *circa* 336),[178] has frequently been considered to be 'the archetypal Christian deviation', as Rowan Williams reminds us.[179] It was a heresy which, contrary to Christian orthodoxy, reduced the rank of Jesus Christ to that of a demigod.[180] In a nutshell Arianism taught 'that the Son does not participate in the Divinity of the Father but is subordinate to the Father. The Son is merely the first and greatest of the creatures of the Father because "there was a time when he did not exist."'[181]

Arius' intention was clearly to stress the utter transcendence of God and His complete 'otherness.'[182] However, in doing so, he also held that the Logos was created by God in time as the latter's first creation and later in history, united with the man Jesus Christ.[183] It is thus clear that not only did the Arians hold that The Word/The Son/Jesus Christ was not God, but they believed he was 'dependent [on] and subordinate' to God[184] and cannot be considered God's equal.[185]

Williams cites a statement of faith by the Arians which neatly encapsulates their theology concerning 'the Son':

> . . . God, being the cause of all things, is without beginning and supremely unique (*monōtatos*), while the Son, timelessly (*achronōs*) begotten by the Father, created and established before all ages, did not exist prior to his begetting, but was timelessly begotten before all things; he alone was given existence [directly] by the Father. For he is not eternal or co-eternal or equally self-sufficient (*sunagennētos*) with the Father, nor does he have his being alongside the Father . . .[186]

What we have, then, in Arianism, to cite Kelly's succinct summary, is a corpus of teachings which believes that the Son of God is a creature created *ex nihilo* by the Father's will,[187] that this Son 'had a beginning',[188] that the Son has no direct contact with, and knowledge about, the Father[189] and that the Son was 'liable to change and even sin.'[190] Kelly notes that when the Arians called the Son 'God' or 'Son of God', they used these titles as 'courtesy titles' only.[191] And not only was the Son ignorant of the Father, according to the Arians: they held, too, that the Son was ignorant of his own substance (*ousía*).[192]

From the above, it will be clear why I have characterised the Jesus of

The Last Temptation as Arian: Kazantzakis tends often to 'humanise' his hero,[193] and demythologise, explain or clothe in dreams such traditional features of Jesus' life as the operation of miracles.[194] There is, at the very least, a latent neo-Arianism at work here in Kazantzakis' novel, perhaps deriving from the seminal impact of such theologians on the Twentieth Century theological milieu as Rudolf Bultmann (1884–1976) with his demythologising instincts.[195]

Related to, and certainly deriving from, the intricacies of Arianism in its downplaying of the divine Person and nature of Christ, was that theology which *did* accept Jesus Christ's intrinsic divinity but which *denied that he himself was aware of it.* This might be labelled a species of neo-Arianism. Aspects of this are to be found in the portrait of Christ in Kazantzakis' work, especially where his hero queries his own identity and mission. The *traditional* Christian theological paradigm, of course, despite much debate, was that Jesus' 'self-consciousness was always consciously of Himself as God.'[196] This has been disputed by much modern scholarship[197] and it is clear that the deliberations of the latter became known to Kazantzakis in some form or another.

Another feature of the stratum of the past, the more recent past, is the way in which old Christian heresies have reappeared in later ages, clothed sometimes in new garb but often with the same message. There are, for example, aspects of Arianism or neo-Arianism, as well as Gnosticism,[198] in the early Twentieth Century heresy or movement which became characterised as Modernism, which are of significance to our discussions here. It was early recognised that Modernism was infused by a variety of different heresies. Pope Pius X (*reg.* 1903–1914) called it *cumulatio omnium haeresium* (the synthesis of all heresies).[199] In a decree entitled *Lamentabili Sane* (3rd July 1907), Pius X condemned and proscribed among the propositions of the Modernists the following:

> [Prop.] 34. The critics can ascribe to Christ a knowledge without limits only on a hypothesis which cannot be historically conceived and which is repugnant to the moral sense. That hypothesis is that Christ as man possessed the knowledge of God and yet was unwilling to communicate the knowledge of a great many things to His disciples and posterity.
>
> [Prop.] 35. Christ did not always possess the consciousness of His Messianic dignity.[200]

A little later, in the much more famous Encyclical Letter *Pascendi Gregis* (8th September 1907), Pius X noted: 'In the Person of Christ, [the Modernists] say, science and history encounter nothing that is not human. Therefore, in virtue of the first canon deduced from agnosticism, *whatever there is in His history suggestive of the divine, must be rejected.*'[201] Pope Pius went on to accuse the Modernists of preaching a kind of 'double-truth' doctrine:[202]

> Science is entirely concerned with phenomena, into which faith does not at all enter; faith, on the contrary, concerns itself with the divine, which is entirely unknown to science. Thus it is contended that there can never be any dissension between faith and science, for if each keeps on its own ground they can never meet and therefore never can be in contradiction . . . Should it be further asked whether Christ has wrought real miracles, and made real prophecies, whether he rose truly from the dead and ascended into Heaven, the answer of agnostic science will be in the negative and the answer of faith in the affirmative – yet there will not be, on that account, any conflict between them. For it will be denied by the philosopher as a philosopher speaking to philosophers and considering Christ only in His *historical reality*; and it will be affirmed by the believer as a believer speaking to believers and considering the life of Christ as *lived again* by the faith and in the faith.[203]

Pius detected a kind of methodological schizophrenia in the Modernists: 'When they write history they make no mention of the divinity of Christ, but when they are in the pulpit they profess it clearly.'[204] The neo-Arian legacy of all this was the distinction which was made 'between the Christ of history and the Christ of faith.'[205] Pius concludes that the method of the Modernists

> is to put themselves into the position and person of Christ, and then to attribute to Him what they would have done under like circumstances. In this way, absolutely *a priori* and acting on philosophical principles which they hold but which they profess to ignore, they proclaim that Christ, according to what they call His *real* history, *was not God and never did anything divine*, and that as man He did and said only what they, judging from the time in which He lived, consider that he ought to have said or done.[206]

The theological trends to which Pius X is objecting here in *Pascendi Gregis* may easily and neatly be labelled neo-Arian because of their profound emphasis on the *humanity* of Christ at the expense of His divinity. They have been surveyed here to give some indication of the controversial and tempestuous theological climate prevailing at the beginning of the Twentieth Century in Christendom.[207] That climate constitutes a part of the stratum of the past within which, and from which, both the spirit-torn Kazantzakis and the former seminarian Scorsese took their cultural, intellectual and theological bearings.

Kazantzakis' and Scorsese's *Last Temptation*: (ii) The Stratum of the Present

This section will examine two main phenomena: (a) the extension, or re-apparition, of an entrenched religious orthodoxy's traditionalist wing with its roots in the past, with particular reference to Catholic, Protestant and Orthodox manifestations of this; and (b) the often related rise of Christian fundamentalism in its Catholic and Protestant incarnations. The two phenomena will be considered here together.

In the Roman Catholic Church prior to the Second Vatican Council (1962–1965),[208] the suppression of the Modernist heresy, from the time of Pope Pius X onwards, cast a long shadow. Until recent times all 'clergy, pastors, confessors, preachers, religious superiors, and professors in philosophical-theological seminaries' were required to swear 'The Oath against Modernism' (*Sacrorum Antistitum*) instituted by Pius on 1st September 1910.[209] This oath included a declaration of submission and adherence to the contents of the decree *Lamentabili* and the Encyclical *Pascendi Gregis*;[210] and a condemnation of any kind of 'double-truth' position by a believing historian.[211] Prudence and restraint were to be accepted as necessary in the use of textual criticism which was never to be used as the only critical norm.[212]

Furthermore, a rigorous control was exercised in the pre-Vatican II Church over the work of theologians like the Jesuit Teilhard de Chardin, as we have seen, and Henri de Lubac (1896–1991). The latter, like Teilhard, was banned from teaching and 'exiled', in his case from the Theology School in Lyons. A ban was placed on de Lubac's books and he was silently ostracised by his Church and his Order, the Jesuits.[213]

Yet the career of de Lubac also constitutes a kind of paradigm for the almost invisible theological and cultural change sweeping through the Catholic Church, even before the heady days of the Second Vatican Council. De Lubac was slowly rehabilitated: leading hierarchs encouraged him; he was elected a member of the prestigious Institut de France and finally, nominated by Pope John XXIII (*reg.* 1958–1963) to be a *consultor* for the Vatican Council's preparatory theological Commission.[214] He ended with a Cardinal's red hat.

De Lubac's 'passion and resurrection' seem strange to us from the perspective of the 1990s. Joseph Fessio, the editor of Ignatius Press, had no hesitation in describing de Lubac as 'above all else a man of the Church, *homo ecclesiasticus* . . . He has received all from the Church. He has returned all to the Church.'[215] Yet his 'passion' is certainly symptomatic of a certain kind of orthodox rigidity which prevailed in Roman Catholic circles before the Second Vatican Council.

This rigidity, if that *is* the right word, was not total, however. We have noted above that change was seeping through the Catholic Church and this was not simply the product of allegedly dissident or difficult theologians. It was happening at the highest levels. Cardinal Augustin Bea, then member of the Pontifical Biblical Commission and President of the Vatican's Secretariat for Promoting Christian Unity, stressed[216] that, without the doctrinal preparation of Pope Pius XII (*reg*. 1939–1958), the Second Vatican Council could not have taken place. He points out that three major Council documents – on the Church,[217] on Divine Revelation,[218] and on the Sacred Liturgy[219] – were foreshadowed and prepared for by Pius XII's three major Encyclicals *Mystici Corporis*[220](29th June 1943), *Divino Afflante Spiritu*[221] (30th September 1943) and *Mediator Dei*[222] (20th November 1947). Brown, Fitzmyer and Murphy draw particular attention to *Divino Afflante Spiritu* 'as a Magna Carta' which permitted Catholics to employ modes of historical and literary criticism which had long been the focus for profound suspicion.[223]

The Second Vatican Council, inaugurated by Pope John XXIII, defended many of the results of that historico-literary criticism.[224] This Council 'opened up' the Roman Catholic Church or, to use the word which became current in the 1960s, espoused a radical *aggiornamento* (updating)[225] which stressed that, while old traditional dogmas could never be changed in their essences, they *could* be interpreted or rewritten in new words. Such changes, inevitably, brought a backlash in their train,both in the form of the extension or re-apparition of an entrenched religious orthodoxy in triumphalist and traditionalist mode, which carried over from the past rituals and religious apparatus which had never really died; and the rise of Catholic fundamentalism.

There is no doubt that the Second Vatican Council constitutes a complex factor in any attempt to account for the rise of traditionalism in the USA and elsewhere.[226] Many conservative Catholics abhorred both the new *aggiornamento*[227] and the speed of change itself.[228] They yearned for a mythical Golden Age, the pontificate of Pope Pius XII[229] –

mythical since that pontificate, as we have shown, *did* witness some profound changes – rather in the same way that some Islamic fundamentalists yearn for a perceived Golden Age during the caliphates of the first four successors of the Prophet Muḥammad, the *Rāshidūn*.

The fundamentalist consequences of such a traditionalist strain may be summarised here briefly: they included, *inter alia*, the Lefebrist schism led by the rebel French Archbishop Marcel Lefebvre[230] (1905–1991); the rise of 'an antimodernist world view' among traditionalists 'rooted in adherence to religious and epistemological categories that have lost much of their plausibility and privileged status in the wake of institutional and intellectual change and adaptation';[231] a rise in conservative Catholic activism;[232] a deep crisis of authority;[233] and the spread of conservative groups like Opus Dei,[234] and conservative Catholic newspapers like *The Wanderer*.[235] The institutional ecclesiastical consequences of that traditionalism always latent in the Roman Catholic Church included the promulgation of the Encyclical in 1968 by Pope Paul VI (*reg*. 1963–1978) entitled *Humanae Vitae*[236] which reaffirmed the age-old traditional ban on the use of artificial means of birth control; the promulgation of the Encyclical on morals in 1993 by Pope John Paul II entitled *Veritatis Splendor*;[237] and the issue of a Universal Catechism, first in French[238] and later in English,[239] in 1992 and 1994 respectively.

Thus, while the orthodox hierarchy in Rome was concerned to uphold traditional dogmas which it believed were under attack from all sides, the right-wing traditionalist Catholic laity worldwide were concerned to uphold traditional rituals such as the Tridentine Mass. And it was the antique fabric of orthodoxy and tradition which constituted the hidden backdrop against which Scorsese produced his film based on Kazantzakis' novel.

Of course, as we have seen, it was not only Catholics who objected to the book and later the film. There were vociferous protests from Protestantism and Greek Orthodoxy as well. Thus it is useful to trace here, briefly, the dogmatic and fundamentalist strains which have, at times, imbued both and still do.

Some writers have highlighted the increasing secularisation in Twentieth Century North American life.[240] In the 1920s and 1930s there was a decline in the vigour of Protestant morale, but this was matched by the post-Second World War revival, particularly in evangelical Protestantism, under the impetus of such popular evangelists as Billy Graham.[241] Nancy Ammerman detects a period of 'apparent hibernation' which preceded the re-emergence of North American fundamentalism in the later part of the Twentieth Century.[242] A name much associated with that kind of fundamentalism was that of the independent Baptist minister Jerry Falwell.

In some senses, the development of Protestant fundamentalism parallels that of Catholic fundamentalism. Like the latter it emerged as a reaction to attempts at 'modernisation.'[243] Many, however, viewed such attempts as heresy and, for example, in the 1920s fought losing battles against such 'modernism' over issues like the teaching of evolution in the schools.[244] North American Protestant fundamentalists, like their counterparts elsewhere, laid much stress on the idea that they were saved, on an inerrant Bible, an over-riding preoccupation with the End Times (with 'the Rapture' as a key event of those Times), and a separatist dislike of those who did not hold the same beliefs.[245] Few, if any, of the partisans of the ecumenical movement are to be found in their ranks. Significantly for our book, Ammerman notes: 'If pickets at the doors of a movie such as "The Last Temptation of Christ" will keep even a single soul from the fires of hell, then the effort is worth it. But if confrontation is likely only to drag the believer down to the level of the sinner, better to avoid the situation.'[246] She insists, too, that modern American Protestant fundamentalism retrieves a past in which it was born in largely urban areas of the North East USA and Canada, after 1850.[247] Of fundamentalism itself she noted: '*Fundamentalism, then, differs from traditionalism or orthodoxy or even a mere revivalist movement. It differs in that it is a movement in conscious, organized opposition to the disruption of those traditions and orthodoxies.*'[248]

The events of the 1960s in the USA, an era of rapid change in society, galvanized fundamentalism into assuming a social agenda again.[249] The anxieties generated by social change led many to search for a more stable truth if one were to be found.[250] The culmination was the establishment in 1979 of an organization called Moral Majority led by Jerry Falwell (Independent Baptist), James Kennedy (Presbyterian), Greg Dixon (Independent Baptist), Tim LaHaye ('conservative ideologue') and Charles Stanley (Southern Baptist).[251] As we have noted earlier, American Protestant fundamentalists mounted a campaign to have Kazantzakis' work removed from library shelves and were later prominent in the protests and demonstrations which greeted Scorsese's film version of Kazantzakis' novel.[252]

We turn finally to the theological and other developments which took place in the Orthodox Churches. Of particular interest is the Greek Orthodox Church. The latter, as we saw, condemned Kazantzakis' novel and later, when Scorsese's film was shown in Greece, the Church was instrumental in having the film banned.[253]

The Orthodox Churches did not undergo the equivalent of what some Catholic traditionalists regarded as the 'trauma' of the Second Vatican Council and the consequent vehement reaction of a group of traditionalists. These Churches simply retained their age-old traditionalism. Lawrence Cross believes that 'on the level of theological life the orthodox world faces a number of urgent but related tasks. There is a deep need for an authentic return to the 'mind' of the fathers of the church. The church must relearn to reflect and act with the mind of patristic tradition.'[254] In Russia, the Russian Orthodox Church for much of this century has been a persecuted Church forever turning inward upon itself, and thus there has been scant room for innovation or radical renewal.[255] An ingrained conservatism and unwillingness to change in almost every area of ecclesiastical life has remained a characteristic feature of Russian Orthodox life.[256] Ellis believes that its traditionalism has enabled the Church to survive the years of persecution,[257] but she also points out that persecution does not predispose one to reform.[258] Whether such deep-rooted traditionalism can be reformed, even after the fall of communism, is debatable. What is not in doubt is that *glasnost* is by no means the same as *aggiornamento*.

If we now turn to the theology and practices of another branch of the Orthodox Church, the Greek Orthodox Church (that of Kazantzakis' own homeland and the immediate religious backdrop, as it were, against which he wrote), we find ourselves considering, by contrast with the Russian experience, a *major* Orthodox Church which is uniquely recognised also as a National Church.[259] It has continued up to the present to play a central and traditional role in Greek life and society.[260] It is no exaggeration to say that the very fabric of society is soaked in the Greek Orthodox Church.[261] Campbell has movingly described the Greek village itself as 'a communion under the necessary protection of God . . .' whose 'moral centre' is the Church.[262] The Greek family is similarly characterised in religious terms as 'a religious community with icons and other sacred objects, a channel of grace for fertility and protection.'[263]

It is worth reiterating here Malik's statement about Orthodoxy in general: 'The very soul of Orthodoxy breathes mystery, otherness, transcendence. Morals are considered important, but Orthodoxy is not moralistic: its intention is to bring out the mystery and freedom of Being.'[264] No one will dispute that the Greek branch of the Orthodox Church shares in these charismata of mystery, otherness and transcendence and it is clear that the moral conscience of that Church was outraged both by the book and the film of *The Last Temptation*; it acted accordingly.

Orthodoxy believes that it is a universal Church, Christ's own Church on earth;[265] as such, it would not be an exaggeration to say that it cherishes its own traditions to the point of being in love with tradition and traditionalism, especially where that is based upon the Bible, the teaching of the Fathers, the Ecumenical Councils,[266] later Councils and major doctrinal statements.[267] 'All Orthodox formularies and pronouncements claim clearly and distinctly *that the Orthodox Church has kept the faith immaculate and intact*, without addition or subtraction, without alteration or omission, as taught by Holy Scripture *and Sacred Tradition.*'[268] Heresy deprived one of union with the Church.[269]

Ware reminds us that 'Orthodoxy' is a word which means both 'right belief' and 'right glory'[270] and that this Church suffered no doctrinal or political Reformation or Counter-Reformation in the Western sense of those terms. History itself is perceived differently.[271] Writing in 1976, well before the collapse of communism, George Maloney observed: 'Many Greek theologians seem to feel that, as representatives of the only free Orthodox nation, they have a mission to return to patristic sources and to defend the early traditions. As a result, modern Greek theology has been more conservative than original, more traditional than creative.'[272]

Yet although such traditionalism and such attitudes have undoubtedly brought some stagnation and torpor to the Church,[273] there *has* been theological development as well. The application by Greek theologians in the Twentieth Century of German scholarship in theology has produced a plethora of theological writings though not without a concomitant reaction.[274] In Greek Orthodoxy in recent times, it must also be noted that it has often been the *lay* theologians, rather than the clerical, who have been at the forefront of whatever developments in theology there have been.[275] There has, nonetheless, been a considerable improvement in the theological education of the clergy as well. Furthermore, while it is true that the earlier Greek theologians of this century, like Christos Androutsos (1869–1935), Panagiotis Trembelas (1886–1977) and Ioannis Karmiris (1904–1991), were more scholastic than mystical on the Russian model, and much influenced by Western methodologies, there has been a sea change in orientation. A later and younger group of Greek theologians has become less Western and more mystical in their approach using, for example, not only Heidegger but the ascetical works of the great Fathers of the Church.[276]

Theologically, then, one may agree with Timothy Ware that, despite difficulties, Greek Orthodoxy is still imbued with 'vigour and new life.'[277] Sociologically, the Church's links with the State have been weakened, though by no means severed;[278] it remains a conservative body. For example, it strongly but unsuccessfully opposed the introduction by the government of legalized abortion in the 1980s.[279] And we have already noted the profound opposition by the Greek Orthodox Church both to Kazantzakis' novel[280] and Scorsese's film.

In sum, then, *The Last Temptation* in both its fictional and celluloid incarnations may be said to have collided with two powerful enemies, an Eastern and a Western Christian fundamentalism. The first was born of persecution in Russia and a general attempt elsewhere to preserve an unchanging theological *status quo* which prized the sacred tradition as a God-given cultural and religious heritage; the second was born of both Catholic and Protestant attempts to preserve traditional rituals and, admittedly disparate, theological norms which seemed threatened by the advance of 'modernism' and modernisation, incarnated in a Scorsese or a Kazantzakis. The modern 'Reformation' in the Catholic Church, the Second Vatican Council, far from sweeping away old pieties and fundamentalisms, enhanced and drew attention to what had always been present but had rarely been articulated in so passionate and vocal a fashion as it was by the small post-Vatican II traditionalist constituency which felt betrayed and abandoned by that Council.

An atmosphere was thus created, from all the factors delineated above, which was both religiously defensive *and* offensive: it sought to defend the purity of religion from attack, and, as we have seen, had little difficulty in generating attacks, by means of riot, demonstration and other methods, on those who threatened established religion by word or work. In the final analysis anti-clericalism might be tolerated; but what was perceived to be a directly blasphemous assault, for example, the film *Je Vous Salue, Marie*, evoked a more vehement response.[281] Scorsese's *Last Temptation of Christ* was made, and opened, against the simmering background of religious controversy already generated by Godard's *Je Vous Salue, Marie* in France and elsewhere.[282]

Thus Kazantzakis was nearly excommunicated by the Greek Orthodox Church.[283] The German text of *The Last Temptation* was place on the *Index of Forbidden Books* by the Roman Catholic Church.[284] Jean-Luc Godard was condemned by Pope John Paul II for having 'distorted and reviled' the Gospel message.[285] Scorsese was excoriated by, among others, Catholics, Baptists, the Eastern Orthodox Church of America, Archbishops, members of the US House of Representatives, Jews and Mother Teresa of Calcutta.[286] It becomes a truism, then, to observe that the environment within which Kazantzakis wrote and Scorsese directed was, at least from a religious perspective, inimical both to the content and the style of their book and film. Maḥfūẓ and Rushdie encountered the same problem.

NOTES

1 See Q.33:40; 'Khatam al-Nabiyyīn' in Netton, *Popular Dictionary of Islam*, pp. 24–25, 146.
2 Yaḥyā & Shukrī, *al-Ṭarīq*, p. 5 (my italics).
3 Q.6:91, trans. by Arberry, *Koran Interpreted*, vol. 1, p. 160.
4 Yaḥyā & Shukrī, *al-Ṭarīq*, p. 148.
5 *The Guardian*, 3rd March 1989, cited in Appignanesi & Maitland (eds.), *The Rushdie File*, pp. 189–190 (my italics).
6 See Yaḥyā & Shukrī, *al-Ṭarīq*, p. 99.
7 See ibid., pp. 6, 147.
8 Ibid., p. 99. For Maḥfūẓ's real intentions in writing *AH*, see El-Enany, *Naguib Mahfouz: The Pursuit of Meaning*, p. 100. See also the interview with Maḥfūẓ in the Egyptian weekly magazine *Ākhir Sā'a* (10th May 1989) whose headline proclaims: '*Awlād Ḥāratinā* does not violate the faith.'
9 Q.2:23–24, trans. by Yusuf Ali, *Qur'an*, pp. 21–22; see also Q.10:38, Q.11:13.
10 G.E. Von Grunebaum, art. 'I'djāz', *EI*[2] vol. 3, pp. 1018–1020.
11 Ibid., p. 1018.
12 Ibid., p. 1020.
13 El-Enany, *Naguib Mahfouz: The Pursuit of Meaning*, p. 143.
14 Ibid.
15 Ibid.
16 See H.A.R. Gibb, *Mohammedanism: An Historical Survey*, 2nd edn., Home University Library of Modern Knowledge, no. 197, (London: Oxford University Press, 1964), pp. 58–59.
17 See ibid. and n.1 above.
18 See Wilfred Cantwell Smith, art. 'Aḥmadiyya', *EI*[2] vol. 1, pp. 301–303.
19 L. Gardet, art. 'Al-Asmā' al-Ḥusnā', *EI*[2] vol. 1, p. 717; see Q.55:27.
20 Gardet, art. 'Al-Asmā' al-Ḥusnā', p. 716.
21 See Wehr, *Dictionary of Modern Written Arabic*, p. 800 s.v. *al-qayyūm*; see the trans. by Yusuf Ali (*Qur'an* p. 102) of the famous 'Throne Verse', Q.2:255, and the same translator's rendition of Q.20:111 (Yusuf Ali, *Qur'an*, p. 813); see also 'al-Qayyūm' in Netton, *Popular Dictionary of Islam*, pp. 205, 45, and Netton, *Allāh Transcendent: Studies in the Structure and Semiotics of Islamic Philosophy, Theology and Cosmology*, (London & New York: Routledge, 1989), p. 151.
22 See. Q.28:88, Q.55:26–27.
23 Wehr, *Dictionary of Modern Written Arabic*, pp. 748–749 s.v. *qidam*.
24 L. Gardet, art. 'Allāh', *EI*[2] vol. 1, p. 411.
25 Ibid.
26 Ibid.
27 Yaḥyā & Shukrī, *al-Ṭarīq*, e.g. pp. 6, 147.
28 Significantly, Maḥfūẓ's translator of *AH*, Philip Stewart, notes in his

'Translator's Introduction': 'Gebelawi represents God, or rather "not God, but a certain idea of God that men have made", as Mahfouz put it in the course of discussion with me.' (Stewart, *CG*, p. VII).

29 See Thomas J.J. Altizer (ed.), *Towards a New Christianity: Readings in the Death of God Theology*, (New York: Harcourt, Brace & World Inc., 1967), esp. pp. 1–14 ('Introduction to the Readings'), and pp. 303–320 (Altizer, 'A Wager' from his *The Gospel of Christian Atheism* (Philadelphia: Westminster Press, 1966)). A superb selected bibliography for the whole subject of 'Death of God' Theology will be found on pp. 365–374.

30 Carl A. Raschke, 'The Deconstruction of God' in Thomas J.J. Altizer *et al.*, *Deconstruction and Theology*, (New York: Crossroad, 1982), p. 3. See also Netton, *Allāh Transcendent*, pp. 30, 44 n.212, 325.

31 Jan Milic Lochman, art. 'Atheism' in Nicholas Lossky *et al.*, (eds.), *Dictionary of the Ecumenical Movement*, (Geneva: WCC Publications, 1991), p. 62.

32 Friedrich Nietzsche, *Thus Spoke Zarathustra*, Penguin Classics, (Harmondsworth: Penguin Books, 1969), p. 41. See also idem., 'Passages on the Death of God, from *The Gay Science* and *Thus Spoke Zarathustra*' in Altizer (ed.), *Towards a New Christianity*, pp. 83–90.

33 John Llewelyn, 'Value, Authenticity and the Death of God' in G.H.R. Parkinson (ed.), *An Encyclopaedia of Philosophy*, (London: Routledge, 1988), p. 641.

34 Ibid., p. 645.

35 Roger Scruton, *A Short History of Modern Philosophy from Descartes to Wittgenstein*, (London: Ark Paperbacks, Routledge & Kegan Paul, 1984), pp. 190–191.

36 J.P. Stern, *Nietzsche*, Fontana Modern Masters, (London: Fontana Press, Harper Collins, 1985), Ch. 5, Sect. 3 'The God-less Theology', p. 90.

37 Paul Ramsey, 'Preface' to Gabriel Vahanian, *The Death of God: The Culture of Our Post-Christian Era*, (New York: George Braziller, 1961), p. XIII.

38 Vahanian, *The Death of God*, pp. 228–229.

39 Ibid., pp. 106–107.

40 See above n.30.

41 Raschke, 'The Deconstruction of God', p. 3.

42 Alan Bullock, Oliver Stallybrass, & Stephen Trombley (eds.), *The Fontana Dictionary of Modern Thought*, 2nd rev. edn., (London: Fontana Press, Harper Collins, 1988), s.v. 'death of God theology', p. 203.

43 Don Cupitt, *The Long-Legged Fly: A Theology of Language and Desire*, (London: SCM Press, 1987), pp. 157–158.

44 Ibid., p. 158. For Cupitt, 'the most powerful religious images are now non-realist.' He castigates the Church for clinging to 'Michaelangelo's sort of God, an objective personal being' and asks why ('God in whose image?', [Letter to] *The Independent*, 22nd September 1993.)

45 (London: SCM Press, 1993).

46 Ibid., p. 11.

47 Walter Schwarz, 'Wide eyed and Godless', *The Guardian: Outlook*, 4th–5th September 1993, p. 19; see also 'Anglican Priest Sacked for Unorthodoxy', *The Tablet*, 28th August 1993, p. 1111.

48 Charles I. Glicksberg, *Modern Literature and the Death of God*, (The Hague: Martinus Nijhoff, 1966), p. 117.

49 El-Enany, *Naguib Mahfouz: The Pursuit of Meaning*, pp. 13–16.

50 See also ibid., pp. 48, 153.

51 See Schwarz, 'Wide eyed and Godless', p. 19; see also the following articles in *The Times*, 15th December 1993: Ruth Gledhill, 'Bishop [Jenkins] feels the heat over views on hell' (p. 6); Martin Ivens, 'A brief history of hell' (p. 15); and the editorial for that day: 'To Hell from Durham: More Thoughtful Provocation from the Bishop' (p. 17).

52 Schwarz,' Wide eyed and Godless', p. 19.

53 A.N. Wilson, *Jesus*, (London: Sinclair-Stevenson, 1992).

54 Barbara Thiering, *Jesus the Man: A New Interpretation from the Dead Sea Scrolls*, (London: Doubleday, 1992).

55 See A.N. Wilson, 'Faith to Face', *The Times Saturday Review*, 19th September 1992, pp. 10–11; see also Cristina Odone, 'The Impertinent Conception', *The Guardian*, 19th September 1992. Henry Chadwick believes that 'the book is bound to be read as the author's apologia for his own very public apostasy, and a sequence of passages, mainly non-historical, will go far to justify that autobiographical reading.' (*The Tablet*, 26th September 1992, p. 1198).

56 Humphrey Carpenter, 'Unwrapping the Presence', *The Sunday Times Books*, 20th September 1992, p. 4.

57 E.g. see Frank Longford, 'Was Jesus just a Good Jew?', *The Times*, 19th September 1992; Jan Morris, 'Believe it or Not', *The Independent*, 19th September 1992.

58 E.g., Elspeth Barker, 'True Stories of Good and Evil', *The Independent on Sunday: The Sunday Review*, 20th September 1992, p. 26; Gerald O'Collins, 'Selling Jesus', *The Tablet*, 26th September 1992, pp. 1184–1186.

59 (London: SCM Press, 1977; 2nd edn. with new Preface 1993); for Hick and Cupitt, see Daniel W. Hardy, 'Theology Through Philosophy' in David F. Ford (ed.), *The Modern Theologians: An Introduction to Christian Theology in the Twentieth Century*, (Oxford: Basil Blackwell, 1989), vol. 2, esp. pp. 54–59, 59–65.

60 Its full title was *The Sacred Mushroom and the Cross: A Study of the Nature and Origins of Christianity within the Fertility Cults of the Ancient Near East*, (London: Hodder & Stoughton, 1970). Allegro held that the aberrations of some of the proper names in the New Testament were extremely important: 'They provide us with a clue to the nature of original Christianity. Concealed within are secret names for the sacred fungus, the sect's "Christ"' ('Introduction', ibid., p. XX). The reviewers were not impressed: see, for example, Eric Marsden, 'Jews Stand up for Jesus', *Sunday Times*, 20th December 1970. Allegro's obituarists were not impressed either: see Hugh Montefiore below, n.62. See also Hyam Maccoby 'Obituary: Dr. John Allegro', *The Independent*, 24th February 1988 which notes that '*The Sacred Mushroom and the Cross* (1970) . . . made [Allegro] a celebrity, but destroyed his standing as a serious scholar'; and 'Obituary: Dr. John Allegro', *The Times*, 22nd February 1988, which lamented: 'It is, perhaps, a tragedy that the controversy which surrounded Allegro (albeit of his own making) overshadowed his long devotion to interpreting the Dead Sea Scrolls.'

61 E.g., see his *The Dead Sea Scrolls; A Reappraisal*, (Harmondsworth: Penguin, 1956; 2nd edn. repr. 1972).

62 Hugh Montefiore, 'Obituary: John Allegro', *The Guardian*, 20th February 1988.

63 See Pierre Teilhard de Chardin, *The Phenomenon of Man*, (London: Fontana Books, Collins, 1969); Maurice Keating with H.R.F. Keating, *Understanding Pierre Teilhard de Chardin: A Guide to The Phenomenon of Man*, (London: Lutterworth Press, 1969). 'In 1944 [Teilhard] was refused ecclesiastical permission to publish *The Phenomenon of Man* which he had submitted to Rome' (Keating & Keating, *Understanding Pierre Teilhard de Chardin*, p. X).

64 See Vernon Sproxton, *Teilhard de Chardin*, (London: SCM Press, 1971), esp. pp. 60, 61, 98–99. For an introduction to his thought, see N.M. Wildiers, *An Introduction to Teilhard de Chardin*, The Fontana Library of Theology and Philosophy, (London: Fontana Books, 1971). See also Michael Le Morvan, *Pierre Teilhard de Chardin: Priest and Evolutionist*, (London: Catholic Truth Society, 1969), pp. 6–7.

65 (London: Collins, 1971).

66 See Werner G. Jeanrond, 'Hans Küng' in David F. Ford (ed.), *The Modern Theologians: An Introduction to Christian Theology in the Twentieth Century*, (Oxford: Basil Blackwell, 1989), vol. 1, p. 165.

67 Edward Schillebeeckx, *Jesus: An Experiment in Christology*, trans. by Hubert Hoskins, (London: Collins, 1979) [first published in Dutch in 1974].

68 John Bowden, *Edward Schillebeeckx: Portrait of a Theologian*, (London: SCM Press, 1983), p. 35.

69 Ibid.

70 Matthew Fox, *Original Blessing: A Primer in Creation Spirituality*, (Santa Fe: Bear & Company, 1983, 1990). Matthew Fox directs the Institute in Culture and Creation Spirituality (ICCS) at Holy Names College in Oakland, California. He has produced twelve books on spirituality and culture of which the most famous or notorious is *Original Blessing*. In his Introduction to this book Fox poses two questions: '(1) In our quest for wisdom and survival, does the human race require a new religious paradigm? (2) Does the creation-centred spiritual tradition offer such a paradigm?' (*Original Blessing*, p. 9). Since Fox gives a resounding *yes* to both these questions, it is perhaps hardly surprising that he found himself in trouble with his Church (Roman Catholic) which had little sympathy with what he was trying to do.

71 See Malachi Martin, *The Jesuits*, (New York: Simon & Schuster, 1988), p. 99.

72 See ibid., p. 44.

73 See ibid., pp. 31–32.

74 See ibid., p. 44.

75 See 'al-Ḥallāj, al-Ḥusayn b. Manṣūr' in Netton, *Popular Dictionary of Islam* p. 94; see also idem., *Allāh Transcendent*, p. 49; L. Massignon & L. Gardet, art. 'Al-Ḥallādj', *EI*[2] vol. 3, pp. 99–104; al-Ḥallāj, *Kitāb Akhbār al-Ḥallāj*, ed. Louis Massignon & Paul Kraus, (Paris: Éditions Larose, Imprimerie 'au Calame', 1936); Louis Massignon (trans.), *The Passion of al-Ḥallāj*, trans. with a biographical foreword by Herbert Mason, Bollingen Series, no. 98, (4 vols, Princeton: Princeton University Press, 1982).

76 See 'al-Ma'arrī, Abū 'l-'Alā'' in Netton, *Popular Dictionary of Islam*, p. 155; al-Ma'arrī, *Risālat al-Ghufrān*, Dhakhā'ir al-'Arab, no. 4, 3rd edn., ed. by 'Ā'isha 'Abd al-Raḥmān Bint al-Shāṭi', (Cairo: Dār al-Ma'ārif, 1963). See also A.M. Zubaidi, 'The Impact of the Qur'ān and *Ḥadīth* on Medieval Arabic Literature' in A.F.L. Beeston *et al.* (eds.), *Arabic Literature to the End of the Umayyad Period*, Volume 1: The Cambridge History of Arabic Literature, (Cambridge: Cambridge University Press, 1983), p. 337; and 'Ā'isha 'Abd al-Raḥmān ("Bint al-Shāṭi'"), 'Abū 'l-'Alā' al-Ma'arrī' in Julia Ashtiany *et al.* (eds.), *'Abbasid Belles Lettres*, Volume 2: The Cambridge History of Arabic Literature, (Cambridge: Cambridge University Press, 1990), pp. 328–338.

77 R.A. Nicholson, *Studies in Islamic Poetry*, (Cambridge: Cambridge University Press, 1921, repr. 1969), p. 166. See also idem., *A Literary History of the Arabs*, (Richmond: Curzon Press, 1993, repr. of 1930 CUP edn.), pp. 318–319.

78 See 'Ā'isha 'Abd al-Raḥmān, 'Abū 'l-'Alā' al-Ma'arrī', p. 333.

79 Ibid., p. 338.

80 For an erudite survey of that controversial dictum, see Francis A. Sullivan, *Salvation outside the Church?*, (London: Cassell, Geoffrey Chapman, 1992).

81 See Nicholson, *Literary History of the Arabs*, p. 318.

82 See Cachia, *Ṭāhā Ḥusayn*, esp. pp. 167–179.

83 Ṭāhā Ḥusayn, *Fī 'l-Shi'r al-Jāhilī*, (Cairo: Maṭba'a Dār al-Kutub al-Miṣriyya, 1926).

84 'Ḥusayn, Ṭāhā' in Netton, *Popular Dictionary of Islam*, pp. 107–108.

85 Cachia, *Ṭāhā Ḥusayn*, p. 60.

86 Ibid.

87 Ibid.

88 Ibid., p. 61.

89 *Ākhir Sā'a*, 10th May 1989.

90 See El-Enany, *Naguib Mahfouz: The Pursuit of Meaning*, p. 14. Maḥfūẓ concluded his acceptance speech to the Swedish Academy and its Nobel Committee, when he received the Nobel Prize, with a quotation from al-Ma'arrī (see 'Nobel Lecture by Naguib Mahfouz' in El-Batrik (ed.), *The World of Naguib Mahfouz*, p. 87).

91 Ruthven, *A Satanic Affair*, p. 116. Such *fatwā*s seem to be becoming more common: in October 1993, for example, a group of Bangladeshi *'ulamā'* issued a *fatwā* against a thirty one year old Bangladeshi poet and feminist, Taslima Nasreen, for alleged blasphemy. She had published, in January 1993, a novel entitled *Lajja* (*Shame*) which sold 60,000 copies before the Bangladeshi government banned it in July on the grounds that it was inflammatory. Not surprisingly, Taslima Nasreen has been described as the Salman Rushdie of Bangladesh. (See Tim McGirk, 'Fatwa is a feminist issue in Dhaka', *Independent on Sunday*, 5th December 1993, p. 16.) Worthy of comparison with Nasreen's case is that of the twelve year old Pakistani Christian, Salamat Masih, charged with 'defaming the Prophet.' The boy suffered a six month long imprisonment before being released on bail. Fundamentalist Muslims in Pakistan have called for the boy's execution. (See Jennifer Griffin, 'Boy faces death for "blasphemy"', *The Observer*, 28th November 1993.)

92 For an excellent analysis of this complicated subject, see Youssef M. Choueiri, *Islamic Fundamentalism*, Twayne's Themes in Right-Wing Politics and Ideology Series, (Boston: Twayne Publishers, 1990). There have been many reservations about the use of this term 'Islamic Fundamentalism'. See, therefore *British Association for the Study of Religions Bulletin*, no. 70 (November 1993), pp. 47–48 where Paul Gifford reviews Martin E. Marty & R. Scott Appleby (eds.), *Fundamentalisms Observed*, (Chicago & London: University of Chicago Press, 1991), and draws attention to the reservations expressed by the editors and many of the contributors 'about the use of the term "fundamentalism".' Gifford notes that 'Martin Marty has elsewhere remarked that those who say that the group in question might more adequately be labelled 'belligerent neo-radical protorevolutionary extremist conservative' cannot hope to command wide acceptance of their term [!], and anyway when they unpack what they mean by that mouthful they almost invariably come near to what others commonly mean by the word 'fundamentalist'.' See also J.W. Bowker's review of ibid., (*BSOAS*, vol. LVI: 3 (1993), p. 589) where he notes: 'Like "time" for Augustine, we all know perfectly well what [Islamic Fundamentalism] is until we are asked to define it.'

93 See, for example, the attempted assassination of Atef Sedki, the Egyptian Prime Minister, on 25th November 1993. Mr. Sedki escaped but a fifteen year old schoolgirl was killed and nine other people were wounded (*The Times*, 26th November 1993).

94 *Menas Associates' Egypt Focus*, vol. 2, no. 3 (March 1992), p. 5.

95 *Index on Censorship*, no. 7 (1992), p. 39.

96 *Cities of Salt*, trans. by Peter Theroux, (London: Cape, 1988); for the original Arabic see *Mudun al-Milḥ*, (Beirut: Arab Institute for Research and Publishing, 1984).

97 Rasheed El-Enany, 'An Introduction [to Munif]' in *Review Guardian*, 14th May 1992, p. 21. Dr. El-Enany's 'Introduction' accompanies a longer article written by Munīf himself entitled 'Moving beyond Lines in Sand' (ibid., pp. 21–22).

98 'Alā' Ḥāmid, *Masāfa fī 'Aql Rajul*, (Cairo: n.p., 1988). The growing saga of this book may be traced in a variety of organs of the Arab press including: *al-Ahrām*, 28th March 1990; *al-Quds al-'Arabī*, 14th–15th April 1990; *al-Ḥayāt*, 2nd July 1990; *al-Quds al-'Arabī*, 30th December 1991; *al-Quds al-'Arabī*, 6th January 1992; *al-Quds al-'Arabī*, 8th January 1992; *al-Quds al-'Arabī*, 20th January 1992; *al-Quds al-'Arabī*, 25th–26th January 1992; *al-Quds al-'Arabī*, 28th January 1992. The case was also reported in the British press (e.g., *The Independent*, 16th January 1992) and was the subject of a BBC2 Television programme at 11:15pm on Monday 9th March 1992 entitled *The Late Show*.

99 E.g., see the headline in *al-Quds al-'Arabī*, 14th–15th April 1990: *Tajdīd ḥabs "Salmān Rushdī" al-Miṣrī*; see also *The Independent*, 9th March 1992, p. 24 (Television and Radio) which advertised the BBC2 *Late Show* mentioned above in the following terms: 'Writer Alaa Hamíd, *dubbed Egypt's Salman Rushdie* after writing an allegedly blasphemous novel called *A Distance in a Man's Mind* (my italics).'

100 For example, see *The Catholic World Report*, (March 1992), p. 10 s.v. 'Egypt'.

101 See Adel Darwish, 'The Hydra grows another head', *Index on Censorship*, vol. 21, no. 6 (June 1992), p. 27; see also *The Late Show*, BBC2, 9th March 1992.
102 See Darwish, 'The Hydra grows another head', p. 33; *The Late Show*, 9th March 1992; *The Independent*, 16th January 1992; *al-Quds al-'Arabī*, 6th January 1992.
103 See above n. 98.
104 See *The Late Show*, 9th March 1992.
105 'The Hydra grows another head', p. 27.
106 Ibid.
107 Ibid.; *The Late Show*, 9th March 1992.
108 *The Late Show*, 9th March 1992.
109 For example, see *al-Quds al-'Arabī*, 6th January 1992; *al-Quds al-'Arabī*, 8th January 1992.
110 *The Late Show*, 9th March 1992.
111 Ibid.
112 Cited in Darwish, 'The Hydra grows another head', p. 33.
113 Karim Alrawi, 'Farag Fouda Murdered', *Index on Censorship*, no. 7 (1992), p. 90; Bassam S.A. Haddad, 'The Assassination of Fuda', *The Arab Studies Journal*, vol. 1, no. 1 (Spring 1993), pp. 16–19.
114 Haddad, 'Assassination of Fuda', p. 16.
115 Alrawi, 'Farag Fouda Murdered', p. 90.
116 Ibid.
117 Haddadh, 'Assassination of Fuda', p. 16.
118 Alrawi, 'Farag Fouda Murdered', p. 90.
119 Adel Darwish, 'Egypt Islamists try to force foe to divorce', *The Independent*, 10th July 1993.
120 Ibid.
121 Helen Miles, 'Zealots set time bomb under Egypt's law', *The Sunday Times*, 27th June 1993, p. 16 (World News).
122 *al-Quds al-'Arabī*, 2nd April 1993.
123 Ibid.
124 Ibid.; see also Miles, 'Zealots set time bomb', p. 16.
125 Darwish, 'Egypt Islamists'; Miles, 'Zealots set time bomb', p. 16; see also Shyam Bhatia, 'Unadulterated Islam says couple must face divorce', *The Observer*, 12th December 1993, p. 18.
126 For *Islamic Fundamentalism* see Choueiri, *Islamic Fundamentalism*, passim; Dilip Hiro, *Islamic Fundamentalism*, Paladin Movements and Ideas, (London: Collins, Paladin Grafton Books, 1989); R.M. Burrell (ed.), *Islamic Fundamentalism*, Royal Asiatic Society Seminar Papers no. 1, (London: Royal Asiatic Society, 1989); See also Sami Zubaida, 'The Quest for the Islamic State: Islamic Fundamentalism in Egypt and Iran' in Lionel Caplan (ed.), *Studies in Religious Fundamentalism*, (London & Houndmills: Macmillan, 1987), pp. 25–50; and John O. Voll, 'Fundamentalism in the Sunni World: Egypt and the Sudan' in Martin E. Marty & R. Scott Appleby (eds.), *Fundamentalisms Observed*, The Fundamentalist Project, vol. 1, (Chicago & London: University of Chicago Press, 1991), pp. 345–402. For *Christian Fundamentalism* see the discussions in James Barr, *Fundamentalism*, 2nd edn. (London: SCM Press, 1981) and idem.,

Escaping from Fundamentalism, (London: SCM Press, 1984). See also Nancy T. Ammerman, 'North American Protestant Fundamentalism' in Marty & Appleby (eds.), *Fundamentalisms Observed*, pp. 1–65. For *Jewish Fundamentalism* see Ian Lustick, *For the Land and the Lord. Jewish Fundamentalism in Israel*, (New York, N.Y.: Council on Foreign Relations, 1988); see also Jonathan Webber, 'Rethinking Fundamentalism: The Readjustment of Jewish Society in the Modern World' in Caplan (ed.), *Studies in Religious Fundamentalism*, pp. 95–121; and Gideon Aran, 'Jewish Zionist Fundamentalism: The Bloc of the Faithful in Israel (Gush Emunim)' in Marty & Appleby (eds.), *Fundamentalisms Observed*, pp. 265–344. For *Sikh Fundamentalism* see Angela Dietrich, 'The *Khalsa* Resurrected: Sikh Fundamentalism in the Punjab' in Caplan (ed.), *Studies in Religious Fundamentalism*, pp. 122–137. See also T.N. Madan, 'The Double-Edged Sword: Fundamentalism and the Sikh Religious Tradition' in Marty & Appleby (eds.), *Fundamentalisms Observed*, pp. 594–627. For an example of *Hindu Fundamentalism* see Donald Taylor, 'Incipient Fundamentalism: Religion and Politics among Sri Lankan Hindus in Britain' in Caplan (ed.), *Studies in Religious Fundamentalism*, pp. 138–155. See also Daniel Gold, 'Organized Hinduisms: From Vedic Truth to Hindu Nation' in Marty & Appleby (eds.), *Fundamentalisms Observed*, pp. 531–593.

127 One has only to think of the *Spycatcher* Affair (1985–88) in the UK: '*Spycatcher*, the memoirs of retired agent Peter Wright, were finally published in the U.K. in 1988, after prolonged legal action by the British Government had failed to stop publication and sale abroad.' (Clive Ponting, *Secrecy in Britain*, Historical Association Studies, (Oxford: Basil Blackwell, 1990), pp. 24, see also pp. 40–41, 65–66, 74). See also Ṣādiq Jalāl al-'Aẓm, *Dhihniyyat al-Taḥrīm*, (London & Cyprus: Riad El-Rayyes Books, 1992); idem., *Naqd al-Fikr al-Dīnī*, 6th impression, (Beirut; Dār al-Ṭalī'a, 1988); Rasheed El-Enany, 'al-Shayṭān al-Sākit: al-Kashf 'an al-Mafqūd bayn al-Nāqid wa 'l-Manqūd', *al-Nāqid*, vol. 6, no. 63 (September 1993), pp. 36–40.

128 See Medved, *Hollywood Vs. America*, esp. pp. 50, 37–49. See also 'Nude Christ film hits screen', *The Guardian*, 12th March 1992 (which describes a Danish film *The Return* in which Jesus Christ is shown naked 'and in love with a woman terrorist') and 'Portugal's Book of the Profits', *The European*, 21st–24th May 1992 (which reviews a 1991 novel by the Portuguese novelist José Saramago entitled *The Gospel According to Jesus Christ* in which Jesus is 'fully human' and 'cohabits with Mary Magdalene, who supports him from her earnings as a prostitute.') It is, perhaps, a dubious criterion but the last person imprisoned in England for atheism, in 1841, was G.J. Holyoake (1817–1906) (*The Guardian*: 2, 8th December 1993, p. 3).

129 A very simple but relevant example is the enormous respect accorded throughout history to the figure and person of the Prophet Muḥammad: because Islamic tradition holds that he received the revelation of the Qur'ān veiled, Islamic illustrations of his *Mi'rāj* (Ascension) may show his face 'partially obliterated' or veiled. See B.W. Robinson, art., '(5) The *Mi'rādj* in Islamic Art' in art., 'Mi'rādj', *EI*[2], vol. 7, pp. 104–105; Marie-Rose

Séguy (ed.), *The Miraculous Journey of Mahomet: Mirâj Nâmeh*, Bibliothèque Nationale, Paris, (Manuscrit Supplément Turc 190), (London: The Scolar Press, 1977), p. 21; and S.M. al-Ani, *The Early Representations of the Prophet Muḥammad with Special Reference to the Mi'rāj Scenes*, 2 vols., PhD Thesis, University of Edinburgh, 1979, esp. vol. 1, pp. 131, 137, 159, 343, 344, 348, 352, 356, 358, 361, 362, 363, 365, 366, 368, 369, 370, 371. See also Sir Thomas Arnold, *Painting in Islam*, (New York: Dover, 1965, repr. of O.U.P. edn. of 1928), pp. 98, 99, 122. This kind of respect has been paralleled in our own age with the 1977 film *The Message* (called, in the Arabic version *al-Risāla*) which, although a lengthy screen account of the life of Muḥammad, never actually shows the Prophet. See Leonard Maltin's *Movie and Video Guide, 1993 Edn.*, p. 815 s.v. *Mohammad, Messenger of God*; Milne (ed.), *Time Out Film Guide*, p. 16 s.v. *Al-Risalah (The Message/Mohammad, Messenger of God)*.

130 Trans. by W. Montgomery Watt & M.V. McDonald, *The History of al-Ṭabarī (Ta'rīkh al-rusul wa 'l-mulūk): Volume VI: Muḥammad at Mecca*, SUNY Series in Near Eastern Studies (Bibliotheca Persica), (Albany, N.Y.: State University of New York Press, 1988), p. 108; for the original Arabic see al-Ṭabarī, *Ta'rīkh al-Rusul wa 'l-Mulūk*, ed. Muḥammad Abū 'l-Faḍl Ibrāhīm, Dhakhā'ir al-'Arab, no. 30, (Cairo: Dār al-Ma'ārif, 1961), vol. 2, pp. 337–338; see also al-Ṭabarī, *Jāmi' al-Bayān fī Tafsīr al-Qur'ān*, (Beirut: Dār al-Ma'rifa, 1972 [repr. of AH 1328 edn. published by Būlāq: al-Maṭba'a al-Kubrā al-Amīriyya]), vol. 17, p. 132; al-Ṭabarsī, *Majma' al-Bayān fī Tafsīr al-Qur'ān*, (Beirut: Dār Iḥyā' al-Turāth al-'Arabī, AH 1379), vol. 7, pp. 90–91; W. Montgomery Watt, *Muhammad at Mecca*, (Oxford: Clarendon Press, 1972), pp. 101–109; idem., *Muhammad, Prophet and Statesman*, (London: Oxford University Press, 1967), pp. 60–65; 'Satanic Verses, The' in Netton, *Popular Dictionary of Islam*, p. 226; Ṣādiq Jalāl al-'Aẓm, '"Āyāt Shayṭāniyya" Karnifāl Sākhir', *Al-Nāqid*, no. 54 (December 1992), pp. 6–39, esp. 23–24; idem., *Dhihniyyat al-Taḥrīm*, esp. pp. 276–280.

131 Watt & McDonald (trans.), *The History of al-Ṭabarī: Vol. VI: Muhammad at Mecca*, p. 109; al-Ṭabarī, *Ta'rīkh*, vol. 2, p. 338.

132 Watt & McDonald (trans.), *The History of al-Ṭabarī: Vol. VI: Muhammad at Mecca*, p. 109; al-Ṭabarī, *Ta'rīkh*, vol. 2, pp. 338–339.

133 Ibid.

134 Trans. by Watt & McDonald, *The History of al-Ṭabarī: Vol. VI: Muhammad at Mecca*, p. 110; al-Ṭabarī, *Ta'rīkh*, vol. 2, p. 339.

135 Watt, *Muhammad at Mecca*, p. 102.

136 Ibid., p. 103.

137 Idem., *Muhammad, Prophet and Statesman*, p. 61.

138 M.M. Ahsan, 'The Muslim Argument: The 'Satanic' Verses and the Orientalists' in Ahsan & Kidwai (eds.), *Sacrilege Versus Civility*, p. 132.

139 Ibid., pp. 131–132.

140 J. Burton, 'Those are the High-Flying Cranes', *Journal of Semitic Studies*, vol. 15, no. 2 (1970), p. 246–265.

141 Ibid., p. 248.

142 Ibid.

143 Ibid., p. 265.

144 Ahsan, 'The Muslim Argument', pp. 138–139.
145 Ibid., p. 139.
146 The Iranian Revolution seems to have spawned almost as many books and articles on the subject as there were revolutionaries! For an extended, but very clear and very readable introduction to the subject, see Dilip Hiro, *Iran Under the Ayatollahs*, (London: Routledge & Kegan Paul, 1985), esp. pp. 66–100, 103–135. For a magisterial survey of the Islamic ideology, and the ideologues, see Hamid Dabashi, *Theology of Discontent: The Ideological Foundations of the Islamic Revolution in Iran*, (New York & London: New York University Press, 1993); for a succinct, mainly political, analysis, see Fred Halliday, 'The Genesis of the Iranian Revolution', *Third World Quarterly*, vol. 1:4 (October 1979), pp. 1–16.
147 Mohamed Heikal, *The Return of the Ayatollah: The Iranian Revolution from Mossadeq to Khomeini*, (London: André Deutsch, 1981), pp. 135, 142–143.
148 Robert Graham, *Iran: The Illusion of Power*, rev. edn., (London: Croom Helm, 1979), p. 213.
149 Ibid.
150 Hiro, *Iran Under the Ayatollahs*, p. 63.
151 Graham, *Iran*, p. 210; Hiro, *Iran Under the Ayatollahs*, p. 95.
152 Graham, *Iran*, p. 192, see also p. 201.
153 Jahangir Amuzegar, *The Dynamics of the Iranian Revolution: The Pahlavis' Triumph and Tragedy*, (Albany, N.Y.: State University of New York Press, 1991), pp. 53 ff, 192.
154 Misagh Parsa, *Social Origins of the Iranian Revolution*, (New Brunswick & London: Rutgers University Press, 1989), p. 102; see also Hiro, *Iran Under the Ayatollahs*, p. 62.
155 See Graham, *Iran*, pp. 131ff; Amuzegar, *Dynamics of the Iranian Revolution*, pp. 67ff.
156 See Graham, *Iran*, pp. 170, 144–151; Heikal, *The Return of the Ayatollah*, esp. pp. 121–122; Amuzegar, *Dynamics of the Iranian Revolution*, pp. 157 ff; Hiro, *Iran Under the Ayatollahs*, pp. 52, 54.
157 Hiro, *Islamic Fundamentalism*, p. 161. See Amuzegar, *Dynamics of the Iranian Revolution*, pp. 117 ff. See also Dabashi, *Theology of Discontent*, p. 481.
158 *Dynamics of the Iranian Revolution*, p. 9.
159 Mansoor Moaddel, *Class, Politics and Ideology in the Iranian Revolution*, (New York: Columbia University Press, 1993), p. 2.
160 Ibid., p. 24, see also pp. 258–259.
161 Graham, *Iran*, p. 223.
162 Ibid., pp. 220–221.
163 Hiro, *Iran Under the Ayatollahs*, p. 100; see idem., *Islamic Fundamentalism*, p. 168.
164 Dabashi, *Theology of Discontent*, p. 4, see also pp. 2, 7.
165 Heikal, *Return of the Ayatollah*, p. 143.
166 See Hiro, *Islamic Fundamentalism*, p. 165.
167 Martin Zonis & David Brumberg, 'Shi'ism as Interpreted by Khomeini: An Ideology of Revolutionary Violence' in Martin Kramer (ed.), *Shi'ism, Resistance and Revolution*, Collected Papers Series of the Dayan Center

for Middle Eastern and African Studies, The Shiloah Institute, (Boulder, Colorado: Westview Press/London: Mansell, 1987), pp. 47–66.

168 Graham, *Iran*, p. 200.

169 Amuzegar, *Dynamics of the Iranian Revolution*, p. 24; see also Moaddel, *Class, Politics and Ideology*, pp. 130–163.

170 Amuzegar, *Dynamics of the Iranian Revolution*, p. 31.

171 'Khumaynī, Āyatullāh Rūḥullāh' in Netton, *Popular Dictionary of Islam*, p. 148. See Hamid Enayat, 'Ayatollah Sayyid Ruhullah Musawi Khumayni and *Wilayat-i Faqih*' in Seyyed Hossein Nasr, Hamid Dabashi & Seyyed Vali Reza Nasr (eds.), *Expectation of the Millenium: Shi'ism in History*, (Albany, N.Y.: State University of New York Press, 1989), esp. pp. 334–335. See also Dabashi, *Theology of Discontent*, pp. 11–12, 437, 491–493; Gregory Rose, '*Velayat-e Faqih* and the Recovery of Islamic Identity in the Thought of Ayatollah Khomeini' in Nikki R. Keddie (ed.), *Religion and Politics in Iran: Shi'ism from Quietism to Revolution*, (New Haven & London: Yale University Press, 1983), pp. 166–188. For Khomeini's thought, see the extensive Chapter 8 ('Ayatollah Khomeini: The Theologian of Discontent') in Dabashi, *Theology of Discontent*, pp. 409–484. See, finally, Said Saffari, 'The Legitimation of the Clergy's Right to Rule in the Iranian Constitution of 1979', *British Journal of Middle Eastern Studies*, vol. 20:1 (1993), pp. 64–82.

172 Mangol Bayat, 'Ayatollah Sayyid Ruhullah Musawi Khumayni and *Wilayat-i Faqih*' in Nasr, Dabashi & Nasr (eds.), *Expectation of the Millenium*, p. 349; see also Amuzegar, *Dynamics of the Iranian Revolution*, pp. 26–27.

173 Enayat, 'Ayatollah Sayyid Ruhullah Musawi Khumayni', pp. 334–335.

174 Dabashi, *Theology of Discontent*, p. 440.

175 See Amuzegar, *Dynamics of the Iranian Revolution*, p. 27; Dabashi, *Theology of Discontent*, p. 413.

176 'The Ayatollah also enlists the support of Plato, arguing that the Greek philosopher anticipated the rule of the clergy in his call for government by "the pious and the wise, in *The Republic*"' (Amir Taheri, *The Spirit of Allah: Khomeini and the Islamic Revolution*, (London: Hutchinson, 1985), pp. 163, 316 n. 11).

177 The *fatwā* 'was the language with which Khomeini was most comfortable' (Dabashi, *Theology of Discontent*, p. 481).

178 For an excellent appraisal of the life, theology and philosophy of Arius, see Rowan Williams, *Arius: Heresy and Tradition*, (London: Darton, Longman & Todd, 1987).

179 Ibid., p. 1.

180 See J.N.D. Kelly, *Early Christian Doctrines*, 5th rev. edn., (London: Adam & Charles Black, 1977), p. 230.

181 Pier Franco Beatrice, *Introduction to the Fathers of the Church*, (Vicenza: Edizioni Istituto San Gaetano, 1987), p. 195.

182 See Kelly, *Early Christian Doctrines*, p. 227.

183 See Hermann Bauke, 'The History of Christological Doctrine' in Jaroslav Pelikan (ed.), *Twentieth Century Theology in the Making: Vol. 11: The Theological Dialogue: Issues and Resources*, The Fontana Library: Theology and Philosophy, (London: Collins/New York: Harper & Row, 1970), p. 108.

184 Williams, *Arius*, p. 177.
185 Ibid., p. 248
186 Ibid.
187 Kelly, *Early Christian Doctrines*, pp. 227–228.
188 Ibid., p. 228; see also Bauke, 'The History of Christological Doctrine', p. 108.
189 Kelly, *Early Christian Doctrines*, p. 228.
190 Ibid., p. 229.
191 Ibid.
192 Williams, *Arius*, pp. 103, 105–106.
193 See Levitt, *The Cretan Glance*, pp. 75–76.
194 Ibid., p. 66.
195 See Robert Morgan, 'Rudolf Bultmann' in Ford (ed.), *The Modern Theologians*, vol. 1, pp. 108–133.
196 Francis McAndrew, 'Christ's Self-Knowledge', *Christian Order*, vol. 34, no. 6/7 (June/July 1993), p. 355; see also Ludwig Ott, *Fundamentals of Catholic Dogma*, (Rockford, Illinois: Tan Books, 1974 [repr. of Cork: Mercier Press, 1960, 4th English edn.]), pp. 129–134, 162–168.
197 See John Hick, *The Metaphor of God Incarnate*, (London: SCM Press, 1993), esp. pp. 27–39. See also E.P. Sanders, *The Historical Figure of Jesus*, (London: Allen Lane, The Penguin Press, 1993), esp. pp. 238–248.
198 See Paul H. Hallett, 'Introduction' to Michael Davies, *Partisans of Error: St. Pius X Against the Modernists*, (Long Prairie: The Neumann Press, 1983), p. XIII.
199 Ibid.; see Pius X, *Encyclical Letter "Pascendi Gregis" . . . On the Doctrines of the Modernists* [Hereafter referred to as *Pascendi Gregis*], (London: Burns & Oates, 1907, repr. Long Prairie: The Neumann Press, 1983), p. 48.
200 Appendix 2: *Lamentabili Sane* in Davies, *Partisans of Error*, p. 98.
201 *Pascendi Gregis*, p. 11 (my italics).
202 See, and compare, Netton, *Allāh Transcendent*, pp. 326–327.
203 Pius X, *Pascendi Gregis*, pp. 18–19.
204 Ibid., p. 21.
205 Ibid., pp. 36, 38.
206 Ibid., p. 37 (my italics).
207 For the Catholic side, see Davies, *Partisans of Error*, *passim*. The works of Rudolf Bultmann, for the Protestant side, provide an excellent example of what would rouse the ire of traditionalists like Pope Pius X and his successors.
208 For the documents of this major Council, see Austin Flannery (ed.), *Vatican Council II: The Conciliar and Post-Conciliar Documents*, rev. edn., Vatican Collection, (Dublin: Dominican Publications/Leominster: Fowler Wright Books/New Town, NSW: Dwyer, 1988), vol. 1.
209 See Davies, *Partisans of Error*, Appendix 2, pp. 104–107.
210 Ibid., p. 106.
211 Ibid.
212 Ibid.
213 See Hans Urs Von Balthasar, *The Theology of Henri de Lubac: An Overview*, (San Francisco: Ignatius Press, Communio Books, 1991), pp. 17–18.

214 See ibid., pp. 18–19.
215 Joseph Fessio, 'Dedication' to a re-edition of one of Henri de Lubac's most famous works, *The Splendour of the Church*, trans. by Michael Mason, (San Francisco: Ignatius Press, 1986).
216 Augustin Bea, 'Foreword to *The Jerome Biblical Commentary* (1968),' repr. in Brown, Fitzmyer & Murphy (eds.), *The New Jerome Biblical Commentary*, (1989), p. XVII.
217 See *Lumen Gentium* (The Dogmatic Constitution on the Church: 21st November 1964) in Flannery (ed.), *Vatican Council II*, vol. 1, pp. 350–426.
218 See *Dei Verbum* (The Dogmatic Constitution on Divine Revelation: 18th November, 1965) in Flannery (ed.), *Vatican Council II*, vol. 1, pp. 750–765.
219 See *Sacrosanctum Concilium* (The Constitution on the Sacred liturgy: 4th December 1963) in Flannery (ed.), *Vatican Council II*, vol. 1, pp. 1–37.
220 Pius XII, *Mystici Corporis* in *Acta Apostolicae Sedis* (Rome), vol. 35 (1943), pp. 193–248. For an English translation see *Mystici Corporis Christi: Encyclical Letter on the Mystical Body of Christ*, with discussion club outline by Gerald C. Treacy, (New York: Paulist Press, 1943).
221 Pius XII, *Divino Afflante Spiritu* in *Acta Apostolicae Sedis* (Rome), vol. 35 (1943), pp. 297–326. For an English translation see *Encyclical Letter of . . . Pope Pius XII . . . on the Most Opportune Way to Promote Biblical Studies*, (Vatican: Tipografia Poliglotta Vaticana, 1943). See also Augustin Bea, '"Divino Afflante Spiritu": De Recentissimis Pii PP.XII Litteris Encyclicis', *Biblica*, vol. 24 (1943), pp. 313–322.
222 Pius XII, *Mediator Dei* in *Acta Apostolicae Sedis* (Rome), vol. 39 (1947), pp. 521–595. For an English translation see *On the Sacred Liturgy: Encyclical Letter "Mediator Dei" of Pope Pius XII*, with Introd. and Notes by Gerald Ellard, (New York: America Press, 1948).
223 'Preface' to Brown, Fitzmyer & Murphy (eds.), *The New Jerome Biblical Commentary*, p. XIX. They dedicated their book to the memory of Pius XII (whom they described as 'The Great Promoter of Catholic Biblical Studies in the Twentieth Century') and Pope Paul VI ('who defended and solidified progress in these studies during and after the Second Vatican Council.')
224 Ibid.
225 See William D. Dinges, '(1) Roman Catholic Traditionalism' (in article by William D. Dinges & James Hitchcock, 'Roman Catholic Traditionalism and Activist Conservatism in the United States') in Marty & Appleby (eds.), *Fundamentalisms Observed*, p. 67.
226 Dinges, 'Roman Catholic Traditionalism', p. 80.
227 See ibid., pp. 67, 80.
228 See ibid., p. 80.
229 Ibid.
230 Ibid., esp. pp. 66–67, 74–78.
231 Ibid., p. 98.
232 See James Hitchcock, '(2) Catholic Activist Conservatism in the United States' (in article by William D. Dinges & James Hitchcock, 'Roman Catholic Traditionalism and Activist Conservatism in the United States') in Marty & Appleby (eds.), *Fundamentalisms Observed*, pp. 101–141.
233 See ibid., pp. 114–116.

234 See ibid., pp. 118–120.
235 See ibid., pp. 122–123.
236 For the full text see *Humanae Vitae* (Encyclical Letter on the Regulation of Births: 25th July 1968), in Austin Flannery (ed.), *Vatican Council II: More Postconciliar Documents*, Vatican Collection vol. 2, (Northport, New York: Costello Publishing Company, 1982), pp. 397–416.
237 *Veritatis Splendor: Encyclical Letter . . . Regarding Certain Fundamental Questions of the Church's Moral Teaching*, (London: Catholic Truth Society/Dublin: Veritas, 1993).
238 See Bibliography s.v. Catechism.
239 See Bibliography. Publication of the English language edn. was severely delayed because of a dispute with the Vatican over the use of inclusive language, especially that which had theological implications, e.g., the substitution of the word 'human' for 'man'. See 'Start the Presses!', *The Catholic World Report*, (February 1994), pp. 20–23, esp. p. 22.
240 For example, see Richard Cawardine, 'Christianity in North America from the Sixteenth Century' in Stewart Sutherland *et al.*, (eds.), *The World's Religions*, (London: Routledge, 1988), p. 263.
241 Ibid.
242 Nancy T. Ammerman, 'North American Protestant Fundamentalism' in Marty & Appleby (eds.), *Fundamentalisms Observed*, p. 1.
243 See ibid., p. 2.
244 Ibid.
245 Ibid., pp. 4–8.
246 Ibid., p. 8.
247 Ibid., pp. 8 ff.
248 Ibid., p. 14.
249 Ibid., p. 38.
250 See ibid., p. 39.
251 Ibid., p. 43.
252 See, for example, Medved, *Hollywood Vs. America*, esp. pp. 37–40; Kelly, *Martin Scorsese*, pp. 235–241.
253 See Kelly, *Martin Scorsese*, p. 239.
254 Lawrence Cross, *Eastern Christianity: The Byzantine Tradition*, (Philadelphia/Newtown, NSW: E.J. Dwyer, 1988), p. 97.
255 See Sheridan Gilley, 'Christianity in Europe: Reformation to Today' in Sutherland *et al.* (eds.), *The World's Religions*, p. 237. See also Jane Ellis, *The Russian Orthodox Church: A Contemporary History*, (London & New York: Routledge, 1988); Michael Bourdeaux, *Gorbachev, Glasnost and the Gospel*, (London: Hodder & Stoughton, 1990).
256 Ellis, *Russian Orthodox Church*, p. 277.
257 Ibid.
258 Ibid.
259 Hugh Wybrew, 'Eastern Christianity since 451' in Sutherland *et al.* (eds.), *The World's Religions*, p. 181.
260 Timothy Ware [Bishop Kallistos of Diokleia], *The Orthodox Church*, (London: Penguin Books, rev. repr. 1993), p. 136.
261 See J.K. Campbell, 'Traditional Values and Continuities in Greek Society' in Richard Clogg (ed.), *Greece in the 1980s*, (London: Macmillan in

association with the Centre of Contemporary Greek Studies, King's College, University of London, 1983), esp. p. 189.

262 Ibid., p. 191.

263 Ibid., pp. 184–185.

264 C.H. Malik, 'The Orthodox Church' in A.J. Arberry (ed.), *Religion in the Middle East: Three Religions in Concord and Conflict*, (Cambridge: Cambridge University Press, 1969), vol. 1, p. 310.

265 Ware, *The Orthodox Church*, p. 8; see also Nicholas Lossky, art. 'Orthodoxy' in Nicholas Lossky *et al.* (eds.), *Dictionary of the Ecumenical Movement*, (Geneva: WCC Publications/London: Council of Churches for Britain and Ireland, 1991), p. 768.

266 Frank Gavin, *Some Aspects of Contemporary Greek Orthodox Thought*, (New York: AMS Press, 1970, repr. from 1923 Milwaukee edn.), pp. 207–208.

267 See Ware, *The Orthodox Church*, pp. 202–203.

268 Gavin, *Some Aspects of Contemporary Greek Orthodox Thought*, p. 250 (my italics).

269 Ibid., pp. 250–251.

270 Ware, *The Orthodox Church*, p. 8.

271 Ibid., p. 1.

272 George A. Maloney, *A History of Orthodox Theology Since 1453*, (Belmont, Mass.: Nordland Pub. Co., 1976), p. 206.

273 See Gavin, *Some Aspects of Contemporary Greek Orthodox Thought*, p. XXV.

274 See Maloney, *History of Orthodox Theology*, p. 318.

275 See Mario Rinvolucri, *Anatomy of a Church: Greek Orthodoxy Today*, (London: Burns & Oates, 1966), pp. 120, 122, 124.

276 Ware, *The Orthodox Church*, pp. 140–141.

277 Ibid., p. 144.

278 See Kallistos Ware, 'The Church: A Time of Transition' in Richard Clogg (ed.), *Greece in the 1980s*, p. 208.

279 Ware, *The Orthodox Church*, p. 137.

280 See also idem., 'The Church: A Time of Transition', p. 221: 'It is even more difficult to discover a church journal that discusses literary themes in an open and sophisticated manner: for example, that analyses, not hysterically but with objectivity, the attitude of Kazantzakis towards the Church . . .'

281 See Robin Buss, *The French Through Their Films*, (London: Batsford, 1988), pp. 68, 118.

282 Thompson & Christie, *Scorsese on Scorsese*, p. 122; see also Paul Pawlikowski, 'The Greatest Story Never Made?', *Stills*, no. 18 (April 1985), p. 13.

283 Kelly, *Martin Scorsese*, p. 165.

284 Levitt, *The Cretan Glance*, p. 61.

285 Buss, *The French Through Their Films*, p. 118.

286 Medved, *Hollywood Vs. America*, pp. 38–39.

4

INTERTEXT

The science of excavation is dependent on the interpretation of the stratification of a site.

Kenyon, *Beginning in Archaeology*, p. 69.

Julia Kristeva (born 1941) is the Twentieth Century's High Priestess of intertextuality, or 'transposition' to use *her* preferred term.[1] This distinguished Bulgarian scholar, whose work and interests have spanned fields as diverse as semiotics, feminism and psychoanalysis, has lived, in exile, in Paris since the middle of the 1960s.[2] Having defended her thesis for the *doctorat d'état* in that City in 1973 in front of Roland Barthes, she was appointed to a linguistics Chair at the University of Paris VII and she still held that appointment in 1993.[3]

Building on Bakhtin, Kristeva observes that 'Tout texte se construit comme mosaïque de citations, tout texte est absorption et transformation d'un autre texte. A la place de la notion d'intersubjectivité s'installe celle d'*intertextualité* . . .'[4]

Elsewhere, intertextuality, which Payne, following Kristeva, succinctly characterises as 'semiotic polyvalence',[5] is defined by Kristeva as a 'transposition of one (or several) sign system(s) into another'; and, fearing a banal interpretation of the term 'intertextuality', she has a preference for the term 'transposition'. Kristeva concludes that 'polysemy can also be seen as the result of a semiotic polyvalence – an adherence to different sign systems.'[6] Transposition, or intertextuality, then, is 'the signifying process' ability to pass from one sign system to another, to exchange and permutate them.'[7] And the whole idea of intertextuality 'points to the history of the text.'[8]

Four principles will guide us as we proceed: (1) In our analysis of the three texts which are the basic subject matter of this book, we will concentrate here on establishing whether or not an intertextual relationship exists between them. This will be done by focussing on, or using, Kristeva's definition of intertextuality in her *Revolution in Poetic Language* (the 'transposition of one (or several) sign system(s) into another'[9]) rather than that in her *Sēmeiōtikē* ('mosaique de citations'[10]). (2) We will remain aware that no text is, or can be, an island remote from other texts, either in the mind of the reader or that of the author.[11] As Still and Worton explain, 'the writer is a reader of texts' before the creation of his or her own text and cannot but absorb and regurgitate in some form or another what has been read.[12] (3) We will also be aware of the poetic definition of 'intertext' by Roland Barthes: 'The intertext is not necessarily a field of influences: rather it is a music of figures, metaphors, thought-words; it is the signifier as *siren*.'[13] (4) Above all, we will be aware of Michael Riffaterre's insistence that 'an intertext is one or more texts which the reader must know in order to understand a work of literature *in terms of its overall significance* (as opposed to the discrete meanings of its successive words, phrases and sentences)'.[14]

Bearing these four points in mind, this Chapter will now try to assess whether an intertextual relationship – an intertext – can be said to exist between Maḥfūẓ's *Awlād Ḥāratinā*, Rushdie's *Satanic Verses* and Kazantzakis' *Last Temptation*. The texts will be approached under the four headings of *Structure*, *Semiotics and Symbols*, *Myth* and *The Heart of the Intertext*.

Structure

As we have seen, Maḥfūẓ's novel, after a *Prologue*, is divided into five main sections, each of which bears the name of the hero who stars in that section. More significantly from the Islamic perspective, as we have also noted above, the work has 114 chapters directly and dramatically paralleling the structure of Islam's holiest text, the Qur'ān. This structure provided by Maḥfūẓ is a key semiotic indicator and its exegesis can be varied. The five main sections follow loosely one after the other in a stream of interwoven or interconnected narratives which can easily be seen to establish their own internal intertext. El-Enany has characterised the structure of *Awlād Ḥāratinā* as 'episodic'[15] but he believes that this quality of the novel was 'accidental rather than intentional' and derived from the fact that the novel was 'a religio-historical allegory meant to parallel certain 'episodes' in human history.'[16] It may be noted that the dream, *as a vital textual motor*[17] or frame, does not play a role. What *is* omnipresent is the sense of longing or yearning for peace, for a better life, for the Big House, for the return of Ḥanash, but that longing often remains unfulfilled and frustrated.

By contrast, Rushdie's text establishes no numerological parallelism with a sacred text but it does use the dream both as a motor for the narrative and a frame for much of the Islamic background. Of its nine principal sections, three are intercalated dream sequences (Chapters Two, Six and Eight) which interrupt the main narrative in one sense, yet continue it on another plane, in another. What seems episodic, and sometimes disconnected and even uncontrolled, is, in fact, tightly knit by the author. Thus, Chapter Five resumes where Chapter Three finished; Chapter Seven resumes where Chapter Five left off; and Chapter Nine takes up where Chapter Seven stopped. Although Rushdie seems to be intent on merging dimensions and planes, with regard to time and space, as much as possible, we can very loosely say that the structure of *The Satanic Verses* comprises six chapters of 'reality' and three of extended dream sequences (*or* cinema!). The latter three constitute roughly 110 pages out of a total of 547. Certainly, the way in which the author interweaves different narratives and juggles the contents of his chapters can seem structurally disconcerting at first, until one realises the games that the author is playing with space and time. In sum, where Maḥfūẓ's book is structured as an episodic allegory, Rushdie's is a picaresque, colossal and exotic panorama of reality and dream, secular and sacred, material and spiritual. And where Maḥfūẓ assumes the mantle of a Bunyan, Rushdie is closer to Cervantes.

Kazantzakis' text *does* adhere to the scriptural structuralist model discovered in that of Maḥfūẓ. As we have noted, it comprises thirty three distinct chapters. The author, in Chapter Thirty, shows, by the words he puts into Christ's mouth, that he was not unaware of the lifespan of Christ as it was traditionally perceived: '"Thirty-three", he murmured. "As many as my own years . . ."'[18] We noted, too, that Scorsese's film adheres to Kazantzakis' novel quite closely. Indeed, from the narrative point of view, one critic has noted that the film director follows the novelist's 'narrative path with utter fidelity.'[19] In our brief analysis, therefore, of the structure of *The Last Temptation* we will confine our remarks here to the Greek author's novel.

As with Rushdie's text, but unlike Maḥfūẓ's, the dream has a paramount role in the structure of Kazantzakis' work. The action of the novel takes place within a framework of dreams: there is Jesus' dream right at the beginning and there is the famous dream sequence of Chapters Thirty–Thirty Three. Peter Bien characterises this as 'the novel's ring structure.'[20] It is a device which the author uses in several of his novels to confine (control?) such elements as 'fantasy, prophecy, myth, epic exaggeration' which are often 'concentrated at the beginning and end as a kind of frame enclosing the middle.'[21] As we have seen above, in the final dream sequence there are even dreams within dreams.[22] So the motif of the dream in Kazantzakis' novel may be said to have a highly significant role, both as motor and frame. It is a frame in the manner described above and it is a motor because the dreams physically contribute to the advancement of the author's narrative. Indeed, in *The Last Temptation* it is no exaggeration to say that the dream sequence of the final chapters is a *sine qua non* of the entire work. In all this, the novel hovers between 'stylization and realism, the universal and the particular,'[23] and, with a subtle attention to detail, recreates, and infuses radically new meanings into, what is mainly a very familiar story.[24]

Kazantzakis' use of time is significant too. He creates in *The Last Temptation* 'a feeling of haste, of the need for speedy salvation' and 'time passes swiftly not only in dreams.'[25] It is a feeling which is quite absent from Scorsese's film – a radical difference, perhaps, between film and book – but which is emanated in a powerful fashion by the dynamic, whirlwind Christ of Pier Paolo Pasolini's *Il Vangelo Secondo Matteo* (*The Gospel According to St. Matthew*) (1964/1966).[26] Here Pasolini's Christ is truly 'a determinedly political animal fuelled by anger at social injustice.'[27]

Earlier, for the sake of clarity, we divided Kazantzakis' novel into five artificial sections. However, from the structural point of view, Bien points out that Kazantzakis planned a *four-stage* spiritual evolution for his Jesus in *The Last Temptation*, four phases respectively characterised as 'Son of the Carpenter', 'Son of Man', 'Son of David', and 'Son of God'.[28] These phases mirror, in a rather Arian way, the growing knowledge possessed by the hero of his own mission in the novel. As we have seen there is no omnipresent apprehension or knowledge in Kazantzakis' novel that He is the Son of God.[29] But the author, however, knows, and controls, his hero's mission in a way that that hero in the text cannot and does not.[30]

Of the four canonical Gospels, it appears to be that according to Matthew which has most influenced Kazantzakis,[31] despite his novel's almost desperate portrait of Matthew. This is certainly true in terms of the structural and spiritual articulation of the figure of Jesus Himself. It can be seen more clearly if we take Kazantzakis' fourfold spiritual progression in his portrait of Christ, outlined above – Son of the Carpenter, Son of Man, Son of David, Son of God – and relate these phrases to Matthew's Gospel.

Of course, it must be stressed that a direct and consistent structural parallelism, chapter by chapter, between Kazantzakis' novel and the

Gospel according to Matthew is not present, and was not intended or attempted by the Greek author. Matthew's Gospel has been described as 'a *dramatic account in seven acts of the coming of the Kingdom of Heaven.*'[32] In other words, there are five 'books' framed by an infancy narrative at the beginning of the Gospel and a passion narrative at the end. Each of the five 'books' comprises both narrative and discourse.[33] However, if we ignore for a moment all theological considerations arising out of Christ's own knowledge of His mission, we *can* make some analogies between novel and Gospel: we can see that Kazantzakis' 'Son of the Carpenter' phrase (a title derived from Matthew 13:55) could be a neat overall title for *Matthew* Chapters 1–8 in which the Child-Messiah is born to Joseph and Mary and proclaims the Kingdom to the world in the Sermon on the Mount;[34] his 'Son of Man' phrase (a title which embodies both the Messianic and the personal[35]) could usefully embrace *Matthew* Chapters 8–13:52 where Jesus, in His Messianic role, performs signs or miracles to prove His credentials;[36] his 'Son of David' phrase, reflecting a considerable usage of this Messianic title in *Matthew*,[37] could neatly apply to *Matthew* 13:53–18:35 where the Messiah, descended from David, establishes both His successor and His Kingdom (cf. 16:18–19);[38] while Kazantzakis' final 'Son of God' phrase, a term employed by Matthew ten times in his Gospel[39] (notably by the centurion at the crucifixion: *Matthew* 27:54) could easily be applied as an overall heading which embraces the content of *Matthew* 19–28 in which the Son prepares the final way for His Father's Kingdom and makes the final sacrifice of Himself to His Father.[40]

Kazantzakis' fourfold division of the spiritual evolution of Jesus[41] can, then, be loosely superimposed upon, or at least shown to have some affinities with, the classical sevenfold division of Matthew's Gospel by New Testament scholars. We can thus detect and establish an *intertext* where only Kazantzakis' two framing dreams, within the boundaries of which Jesus' fourfold 'spiritual evolution' is articulated,[42] have no real points of contact with Matthew's Gospel.

All that said however, it should not be assumed that the way in which Kazantzakis' four titles for Jesus have been applied to Matthew's Gospel here is intended to be rigid, unchangeable and immovable. A case could also be made for applying the term 'Son of God' as a title to cover 'the beginning of the Gospel, where Jesus is set forth as royal Son of God and Immanuel, God with us,' and the term 'Son of Man' to the conclusion 'where Jesus is given all (divine) authority as Son of Man over the kingdom of God, in heaven and on earth'[43] (see *Matthew* 28:18–20).[44] Our intertext here, then, is a fluid rather than a static or rigid arena.

Intertext

Having looked at the various structures of our three novels, it is now time to summarise and move briefly to a broader intertextual arena than that filled by Kazantzakis' novel and the Gospel of Matthew. Do the *structures* alone of our three novels allow us to establish an intertext? The brief answer must be that only a partial intertext exists from this perspective: two of the novels (*The Last Temptation* and *The Satanic Verses*) place massive emphasis in their structures on dreams; two of the novels (*The Last Temptation* and *Awlād Ḥāratinā*) employ a number with a 'sacred' significance as their total number of chapters. But there is no outstanding *structural* feature which unites all *three* texts *as an intertext*. For that we need to move to our next major sphere of analysis, that of semiotics and symbols.

Semiotics and Symbols

This section presents the signs of symbols of the fusion of two worlds. In Maḥfūẓ's *Awlād Ḥāratinā* there is a 'sacred link' between the celestial and terrestrial, the divine and the human, in the form of the 'prophet-figures' of Adham, Jabal, Rifā'a, Qāsim and 'Arafa. They are signs or symbols to suffering humanity of a world beyond the present, incarnations in a very real sense of hope itself. They exhibit a kind of ease with the two dimensions of the natural and supernatural which others do not. And it is the presence of this 'sacred link' which helps in the identification of an intertext which includes as well the novels of Rushdie and Kazantzakis surveyed above. As we shall presently see, the latters' novels also have their 'sacred link' in the form of good and bad angels.

In the Qur'ān God's messengers and prophets frequently bring warnings. The Prophet Muḥammad himself is sent as a warner, reminder, or admonisher (see Q.88:21)[45] and God, throughout history, has sent many of 'His servants' to warn mankind of the Day of Judgement and Resurrection (see Q.40:15). Prophets, then, in the Qur'ān are signs of impending punishment *and* reward for sinful humanity.

The 'prophet-figures', or 'political rebels' as El-Enany alternatively characterises them,[46] of Maḥfūẓ's novel adhere in several respects to this paradigm. As with the Qur'ānic Adam, and Maḥfūẓ's portrait of Adham, they may also receive punishment as well as signal it. Jabal joins, and speaks up for, the oppressed people of the Quarter and achieves a position of political power over them. His life is an incarnation of goodness and a warning, both to the wicked Trustee and his own people. Rifā'a, too, incarnates the good in his request to the people to trust him, and heed his preaching. Rifā'a, as we have seen, pays the ultimate penalty and is cudgelled to death by Khunfis. Qāsim brings a message of equality and the end of tyranny, and is eventually able to inaugurate a new age of peace and love. But that age becomes enshrouded in myth and 'Arafa, more magus than prophet, arrives. Killed in his turn, his life and activities incarnate a warning about the dangers of science which, nonetheless, will continue down the ages to fascinate the ordinary people and, perhaps, lead them astray as they search desperately for salvation.

In all this, then, the themes of reward and punishment are played out on earth. The 'prophet-figures' of Maḥfūẓ's allegory are not only incarnated warnings but, in some cases, they receive the reward of their labours, or are punished by death, unjustly, because of them. The message they bring, as is so often the case in the Qur'ān – the stories of the Arabian prophets Ṣāliḥ and Shu'ayb are notable examples – frequently precipitates anger, and rejection of the messenger.[47]

The 'God-figure' is another vital aspect of the intertext we are seeking to establish, from the point of view of the semiotics and symbols of the three novels under discussion. In *Awlād Ḥāratinā*, al-Jabalāwī is a brooding, frequently invisible figure, often unknown like the classical deity of Neoplatonism. Yet he casts the shadow of his powerful presence over all the events of the novel. If the 'prophet-figures' of Maḥfūẓ's text are the main 'sacred links' between the natural and the supernatural, al-Jabalāwī is the sign *par excellence* of the latter. He *is* the divine, just as the Trustee is the (typical?) human. The death of al-Jabalāwī signals also, in a very real way, the death of the 'sacred link'; with whom will the prophet-figures of the future now communicate? Man is thrown back on his own devices, his own science, and on those, like the magus 'Arafa, who both incarnate and use that science. He is disconnected from the Creator of his universe and his age-old belief in that creator. Maḥfūẓ, through his novel, signals a vivid and deep-seated pessimism about the future.

The third major feature of our semiotic and symbols based intertext is the role of the miracle. As a literary feature, or motor, it is rather less prominent in Maḥfūẓ's text than in those of Rushdie and Kazantzakis. What we do have in Maḥfūẓ's work is a scattering of miraculous, and what might be labelled 'quasi-miraculous', events: thus Adham, at the end of his life, is visited and forgiven by al-Jabalāwī; Rifā'a claims to have heard al-Jabalāwī's voice in the desert; Rifā'a casts out evil spirits, and gives physical and spiritual healing; later his body disappears from its grave. Qāsim encounters al-Jabalāwī's servant at Hind's Rock; and while 'Arafa's magic should not be confused, perhaps, with the miraculous, it forms part of an undercurrent in the book where reality and the surreal or supernatural or inexplicable are never far apart and sometimes merge. This narrowness of distance between corporeal and divine, secular and sacred, mundane and magical – incarnated or articulated best in the 'sacred link' of the 'prophet-figures' of Maḥfūẓ's novel – is a fourth intertextual feature which we will have cause to note in Rushdie's and Kazantzakis' texts too. It signals a fluid world of body and spirit which is, perhaps, more monolithic or one-dimensional than the usual Cartesian paradigm with its rigid divisions.

Fifthly, and finally, we may note the messianic impulse, the desire for salvation via a saviour figure, which permeates Maḥfūẓ's novel. This is seen, most clearly and dramatically, right at the end of the work where the people yearn again for the end of tyranny and the saviour figure of Ḥanash.[48] But it is a motif which occurs elsewhere as well: the oppressed people look towards the future, hoping for deliverance by al-Jabalāwī,[49] confident that the morrow will bring a better day.[50] The next saviour is just round the corner.

He is the classical *sign* of salvation, and the prophet-figures of the novel are not only heralds of salvation like John the Baptist, but, each time, saviour figures in their own right, unlike John. They forecast and *bring* salvation. The 'sign of impending salvation' may thus be said to be a key motif in Maḥfūẓ's allegory.

If we turn now to Rushdie's *Satanic Verses*, we find that the 'sacred link' between celestial and terrestrial, divine and human, is the angel rather than the prophet or the messenger. In the Qur'ān, the role of the key angel – Archangel as he would be termed in the Western tradition – Jibrīl (Gabriel) is to be the vehicle of the revelation, the medium through which the Qur'ān is revealed to Muḥammad. Jibrīl is the sacred link *par excellence* between God and man in Islam, for not only does he bring the Qur'ān but he is the key agent, for example, in the Islamic annunciation to Maryam. Jibrīl's Qur'ān-bearing role is illustrated in the following verses:

Say: Whoever is an enemy
To Gabriel – for he brings down
The (revelation) to thy heart
By God's will, a confirmation
Of what went before
And guidance and glad tidings
For those who believe, –
Whoever is an enemy to God
And his angel and apostles,

To Gabriel and Michael –
Lo! God is an enemy to those
Who reject faith.[51]

Jibrīl's role at the Islamic annunciation to Maryam, mother of the prophet 'Īsā (Jesus), is also highlighted in the following Qur'ānic verses:

Then We sent to her
Our angel [litt.: Our spirit, Arabic: *rūḥanā*], and he appeared
Before her as a man
In all respects.[52]

Jibrīl, of course, is by no means the only Islamic angel though, because of his association with the Qur'ān, he is considered to be the most important. There are many others who are allocated a variety of functions: for example, Isrāfīl[53] stands ready to blow the final trumpet to signal the Judgement; Munkar and Nakīr[54] interrogate the dead in their tombs; 'Izrā'īl[55] is the principal angel of death; and every person has his or her personal or guardian angels.[56] Whatever the role allocated to them, however, all the angels are celestial servants of God and obedient to Him.[57]

Rushdie's Gibreel in *The Satanic Verses* is a highly ambiguous figure. Very much a 'sacred link', he is also portrayed as a *flawed* link, sometimes seeming to merge with, or at least be reflected by, his very human namesake Gibreel Farishta who is, in any case, 'a symbolic angel.'[58] Rushdie's angel, controversially, accepts that *he* is responsible both for the initial acceptance of the three deities at the heart of the Satanic Verses issue and their later repudiation. The angel portrayed here arrogates to himself a power which is quasi-divine. Later Gibreel flies with the Imām to the City of the Empress, and Ayesha in Chapter Four claims that the Archangel has told her that Mishal has breast cancer. In the latter, then, Gibreel is not only a messenger but a messenger of bad news.

At the end of Rushdie's novel, there is a change of sacred link, a subtle but distinct shift in emphasis from the angel Gibreel whose presence has overshadowed the entire novel up to this point, towards the angel 'Izrā'īl whose name Rushdie anglicises as Azraeel. The change is specifically signalled by the title of Chapter Seven: *The Angel Azraeel*. As we have seen, it is in this Chapter that Saladin suffers his heart attack. From now on, death is in the air. In Chapter Eight, Khadija, wife of the Sarpanch, sees Azraeel in a dream and, soon afterwards, lies down and dies. A baby is stoned to death and many appear to be drowned in the

Arabian Sea. The Zamindar Mirza Saeed Akhtar starves himself to death. Saladin attends his father's death in Chapter Nine and the body of the film mogul S.S. Sisodia is found, murdered. Alleluia Cone falls to her death from a skyscraper and Gibreel Farishta commits suicide. It is, perhaps, fitting that this long catalogue of death which brings the novel to its conclusion, should be presided over (at least in a chapter heading!) by the Islamic angel of death himself, 'Izrā'īl, who links not only the human and the divine, but who is given responsibility by God for *severing* the link with life in every human being.

Turning to the second major feature of the possible intertext which we are exploring, the presence of a 'God-figure', we find that this is absent from Rushdie's novel if we seek a parallel to Maḥfūẓ's Jabalāwī or Kazantzakis' Christ. There is neither a brooding figure behind the scenes nor an overt and questioning Messiah. What Rushdie does, however, is to incarnate the supreme forces of good and evil in two humans, Gibreel Farishta and Saladin Chamcha, and allow them to play out a long cosmic drama in the manner of an Ahura Mazda and Ahriman.[59] The real 'God-figure' in *The Satanic Verses* must surely be Gibreel himself whose role here exceeds anything portrayed either in the Qur'ān or the Bible.

Within the dimensional fluidity of Rushdie's text, miracles and extraordinary occurrences are almost commonplace, whether they be in life, dream or film sequence. The whole text begins with an amazing miracle, the salvation of Gibreel Farishta and Saladin Chamcha after falling thousands of feet from a blown-up aircraft. Later, Saladin grows hooves, horns and a monstrous penis; Gibreel Farishta is endowed with a halo. The ghost of Rekha Merchant flies around on a carpet. The angel Gibreel moves easily between the earth and the supernatural sphere. The Imām flies with Gibreel to the City of the Empress. In Chapter Eight, *The Parting of the Arabian Sea*, four survivors claim a miracle does occur and the sea *does* actually part. It is clear from all this that the narrowness of the gap between corporeal and spiritual, secular and sacred, positively resonates throughout the text, and sometimes seems to dissolve totally in a new plane where such Cartesian distinctions are inapplicable and where all forms of reality merge.

Finally, we might ask whether a messianic impulse, with its concomitant associations of deliverance and redemption, is identifiable in Rushdie's text. The answer must be that such an impulse is present only occasionally. There is certainly neither the messianism articulated in the people's yearning in Maḥfūẓ's novel, nor the increasingly overt messianism of Kazantzakis' work. Each of the principal protagonists,

Saladin and Gibreel, it is true, seeks a salvation and redemption but only through and for himself. Gibreel, mega-stalwart of the Indian film industry, seeks and achieves temporary immortality on the faithless advertising hoardings of Bombay. He is his own egocentric Messiah but his own demon as well, as his awful end indicates. The anglophile actor Saladin finds satisfaction and redemption in a sense of place, first of all England; by the end, Saladin, initial incarnation of evil, has been redeemed and given a second chance. The air disaster which both men survive gives each a new lease of life, literally; it also gives each a fresh set of problems epitomised graphically in hooves and halo. They each course through Rushdie's text, not as great Messiah figures intent on saving the world, but as minor bumbling seekers and travellers, concerned only with their own fate and hoping for a deliverance from the strange aftermath of the air disaster. The essence of their missions is egocentricity. Similarly, the figure of Gibreel is too ambiguous to endow with any kind of Messianic connotations. Only the shadowy figure of the exiled Imām in Chapter Four comes really close to representing a saviour figure in whom the hopes of many others are inexorably invested, and who embodies the classic soteriological aura of exile and return. However, on a more minor level, the figure of Ayesha in Chapter Eight (*The Parting of the Arabian Sea*) may also be said to be endowed with a certain messianic charisma. Certainly, she seems to be a Messiah to the cancer-striken Mishal.

Kazantzakis' novel *The Last Temptation* possesses the five suggested facets of our projected intertext in abundance, if we examine it from the point of view of semiotics and symbols. The Greek author's 'sacred link', as in *The Satanic Verses*, is the angel. For example, in major episodes, Matthew records his Gospel at the dictation of an angel. An angel appears to Jesus with a silver chalice as the latter begins His Passion in the Garden of Gethsemane. Most significantly, however, it is an angel, claiming to be Jesus' guardian angel, who comes to Him at the beginning of the last temptation of the title, and who leads Him to a wedding with Mary Magdalene and finally abandons Him. As we have seen, the dazzling archangel of the three temptations in the book is portrayed by Scorsese as a column of fire and it is into that column of fire that Jesus' 'guardian angel' turns in the film. For Scorsese at least, and, indeed, Levitt,[60] the angelic figure has a sublime ambiguity and is here revealed as Lucifer himself. (We may compare this ambiguity with that inherent in the figure of Rushdie's Gibreel in *The Satanic Verses*). The figure of the angel in Kazantzakis' novel, however, frequently signals the presence of the divine, whose messenger he is, and the meeting, or interface of two dimensions, earthly and supernatural. In this the angelic role is very much akin to that portrayed in the Bible where the angels again mediate two distinct worlds, carry God's messages (for example, at the Annunciation) and similarly signify the infusion of a seemingly entirely corporeal world by an eternal divine milieu.

The presence of a 'God-figure' in Kazantzakis' novel requires no intensive quest here: the figure of Christ is the *sine qua non* of the novel and an ubiquitous presence. We may move, therefore, immediately but briefly to the role of miracles in the text. While, as we have seen, there is an Arian tendency on the part of the author to 'play down' the role of miracles,[61] such occurrences are by no means totally eschewed. For example, Jesus cures a Roman centurion's paralysed daughter. This is perhaps just one example of a general atmosphere which pervades the entire novel of Kazantzakis, an atmosphere where the distance between the physical and spiritual worlds is very narrow, and the Greek author's text shares this feature closely with those of Rushdie and Maḥfūẓ. Kazantzakis' text 'hums' with signs and signals of other worlds, of the divine.

Finally, we note the fundamental nature of the 'messianic impulse' in Kazantzakis' Christ. It is an impulse which is confusing to the Christ figure Himself at first but which becomes clearer and stronger as the novel progresses.

To summarise, if we examine our three novels from the perspective of semiotics and symbols, it is easy to discern an intertext whose fabric is woven from such aspects as: (1) a 'sacred link', (2) a 'God figure', (3) miracles, (4) the narrowness of the divide between the corporeal and the spiritual, and (5) the messianic impulse. Together they sometimes seem to signify a unity of being, a monism, in which the old dualism of body and soul disappears and the supernatural walks hand in hand with earthly reality. If we take the above block of five points as a 'sign system' of such a unified universe, then there is no doubt that in Kristevan terms we have established the existence of an intertext for our three novels: that fivefold sign system may be transposed from the one to the other with little difficulty. We remain aware that none of our texts is an island, unique unto itself, but that each has a relation to other texts. And with Barthes we note, as we analyse the works of Maḥfūẓ, Rushdie and Kazantzakis, the 'music' of the text, articulated as it is through our list of five key signs. Our comparative knowledge of the *three* texts, in terms of their semiotics and symbols, as opposed to just *one*, adds immeasurably to our appreciation and understanding of each individually.

Myth

The three texts which we are examining each create their own myth and their own mythical worlds. If we take myth here 'in a strictly technical sense to designate a narrative vehicle for a primal event, or series of events, which may function as essential dogma, paradigm or key referent in the future development of any culture, religion or philosophy',[62] then it will be our task here to identify briefly the nature of the myth in each of our three novels, and the message conveyed through its medium. It is recognised, of course, that there may be many different interpretations of the latter.

For Maḥfūẓ the myth is a world of prophetic leaders who play out their allotted roles against the backdrop of a largely hidden Overlord who may or may not be immortal. The novel shows us at the end that he is not. One of the messages among many conveyed by Maḥfūẓ here, is that weak, squabbling man rises and falls down the generations, hoping in a figure larger than himself, al-Jabalāwī, who eventually proves to be mortal (the invention of man's mind?) and subject to death itself. Yet the death of *the figure of Hope* does not destroy *all* hope as the last pages of what is, admittedly, a fairly pessimistic novel show. Maḥfūẓ's myth, in a very real sense, is a profound vehicle for the portrayal of a struggle between despair and hope. It articulates a desperate theology which proves to be an illusion but permits a twilight of hope.

Rushdie, by contrast, presents a mythic world of dream and reality where things, and beings, are not what they seem. This world is a vehicle for the articulation of, among other things, the theme – indeed, *theology* – of alienation, itself only too real, and a kaleidoscope where the natural and supernatural, good and evil and their incarnations, coalesce, merge and, sometimes, change roles. It features an almost Manichaean or Zoroastrian struggle and we recall the mythic vehicles employed in the theologies of those two dualist systems of belief.

Finally, Kazantzakis too, uses his myth, as he himself tells us, as a narrative vehicle to present 'a supreme model to the man who struggles.'[63] His myth also, then, gives us a mighty struggle between the forces of good and the forces of evil, played out on a cosmic scale in the mind of his Man-God. Kazantzakis himself was well aware of the role of myth. Levitt quotes him as follows: 'I wanted to renew and supplement the sacred Myth that underlies the great Christian civilization of the West.'[64] And Levitt believes that *The Last Temptation* treats 'the Old and New Testaments as a storehouse of mythic possibilities.'[65] He adds: 'Virtually every incident originates in the New Testament, but all are filtered through the screen of comparative myth . . .'[66]

This brief examination of the role of myth in the three novels under discussion suffices to reveal that myth is the bonding cement in the intertext which we have sought to establish. The primary messages – on whose interpretation scholars will argue anyway – may differ, but the role of myth as a fundamental vehicle for those messages in each of our texts is beyond dispute.

The Heart of the Intertext

Having established the existence of our intertext, there remains one final feature of it which we must examine. It lies at the heart of the intertext and, like much of the above, is common to all three texts. This is *the allegation of blasphemy*. All three texts, as we have seen, have precipitated cries of blasphemy, and shouts of anger, by a faithful in Islam and Christianity outraged at what is perceived as a gratuitous attack on religion. Each author has suffered too in one way or another, to a greater or lesser degree. This arena of suffering – authorial and 'readerly' – should be borne in mind, for the circumstances – political, physical and other-caused by the text will inevitably have an impact on future readings of that text. A further element, then, in the intertext thus identified, must be that of *controversy*. The consequences for future readings are obvious: the controversy thus engendered will 'insinuate' itself into the very fabric of the text and become a feature which cannot be ignored. No one, for example, except the most uninformed, will ever again come to Salman Rushdie's *Satanic Verses* without reading it through the spectacles of the Ayatollah Khomeini's *fatwā*.

NOTES

1 See Julia Kristeva, *Revolution in Poetic Language*, (New York: Columbia University Press, 1984), pp. 59–60; see also idem., 'Revolution in Poetic Language' in Toril Moi (ed.), *The Kristeva Reader*, (Oxford: Basil Blackwell, 1986), p. 111; Michael Payne, *Reading Theory: An Introduction to Lacan, Derrida and Kristeva*, (Oxford: Basil Blackwell, 1993), p. 240.
2 See John Lechte, *Julia Kristeva*, Critics of the Twentieth Century, (London & New York: Routledge, 1990), pp. 14, 66, 79 ff, 91.
3 Payne, *Reading Theory*, p. 163.
4 Julia Kristeva, *Sēmeiōtikē: Recherches pour une Sémanalyse*, (Paris: Éditions du Seuil, 1969), p. 146; see Payne, *Reading Theory*, p. 240.
5 Payne, *Reading Theory*, p. 240; Kristeva, *Revolution in Poetic Language*, p. 60.
6 Kristeva, *Revolution in Poetic Language*, pp. 59–60.
7 Ibid., p. 60.

8 Kelly Oliver, *Reading Kristeva: Unraveling the Double-bind*, (Bloomington & Indianapolis: Indiana University Press, 1993), p. 93.
9 Kristeva, *Revolution in Poetic Language*, pp. 59–60.
10 Ibid., p. 146, see Payne, *Reading Theory*, p. 240.
11 See Payne, *Reading Theory*, p. 178; Judith Still & Michael Worton, 'Introduction' to Worton & Still (eds.), *Intertextuality: Theories and Practices*, (Manchester & New York: Manchester University Press, 1990), p. 1.
12 Still & Worton, 'Introduction' to Worton & Still (Eds.), *Intertextuality*, p. 1.
13 Cited in ibid., p. 18.
14 Michael Riffaterre, 'Compulsory reader response: the intertextual drive' in Worton & Still (eds.), *Intertextuality*, p. 56 (my italics).
15 El-Enany, *Naguib Mahfouz: The Pursuit of Meaning*, pp. 129, 141.
16 Ibid., p. 129.
17 See 'Yūsuf (2)' in Netton, *Popular Dictionary of Islam*, pp. 261–262.
18 Kazantzakis, *LT*, p. 454.
19 David Thompson, [Review of] 'The Last Temptation of Christ', p. 37.
20 Bien, *Nikos Kazantzakis, Novelist*, p. 73, see also p. 67.
21 Ibid., p. 7.
22 See also Levitt, *The Cretan Glance*, p. 79.
23 Bien, *Nikos Kazantzakis*, p. 41.
24 Levitt, *The Cretan Glance*, p. 60.
25 Ibid., p. 79.
26 See Leonard Maltin (ed.), *Movie and Video Guide, 1993 Edn.*, p. 478 s.v. 'Gospel According to St. Matthew'; Michael Singer, 'Cinema Savior', *Film Comment*, vol. 24, no. 5 (September–October 1988), p. 46.
27 Milne (ed.), *Time Out Film Guide*, 2nd edn., p. 264 s.v. 'Gospel According to St. Matthew'.
28 Bien, *Nikos Kazantzakis, Novelist*, p. 67.
29 See Ott, *Fundamentals of Catholic Dogma*, pp. 130 ff.
30 See also Levitt, *The Cretan Glance*, p. 80.
31 See ibid., pp. 70, 82.
32 Henry Wansbrough (ed.), *The New Jerusalem Bible*, p. 1606.
33 Ibid., pp. 1605–1606; see also Benedict T. Viviano, 'The Gospel According to Matthew' in Brown, Fitzmyer & Murphy (eds.), *The New Jerome Biblical Commentary*, p. 631.
34 See *The New Jerusalem Bible*, p. 1606.
35 See Francis Watson, *A Guide to the New Testament*, (London: Batsford, 1987), pp. 148–149 s.v. 'Son of Man'.
36 See *The New Jerusalem Bible*, p. 1606.
37 See David Michael Stanley, *The Gospel of St. Matthew*, 2nd rev. edn., New Testament Reading Guide, no. 4, (Collegeville, Minnesota: The Liturgical Press, 1963), p. 16; see also Viviano, 'The Gospel According to Matthew', p. 631.
38 *The New Jerusalem Bible*, p. 1606.
39 See Stanley, *The Gospel of St. Matthew*, p. 16; see Watson, *Guide to the New Testament*, pp. 147–148 s.v. 'Son of God.'.
40 *The New Jerusalem Bible*, p. 1606.
41 Bien, *Nikos Kazantzakis, Novelist*, p. 67.
42 Ibid.

43 Viviano, 'The Gospel According to Matthew', p. 631.
44 Ibid., see also p. 674.
45 See W. Montgomery Watt (ed.), *Bell's Introduction to the Qur'an*, (Edinburgh: Edinburgh University Press, 1970), pp. 28–29.
46 El-Enany, *Naguib Mahfouz: The Pursuit of Meaning*, p. 142.
47 See the seventh *Sūra* of the Qur'ān, *Sūrat al-A'rāf*, for the histories of the two prophets Ṣāliḥ and Shu'ayb.
48 See El-Enany, *Naguib Mahfouz: The Pursuit of Meaning*, pp. 143–144.
49 See *AH*, p. 117; *CG*, p. 75.
50 See *AH*, pp. 305, 449; *CG*, pp. 198, 288.
51 Q.2:97–98, trans. by Yusuf Ali, *Qur'an*, pp. 43–44. See J. Pedersen, art. '*D*jabrā'īl', *EI*², vol. 2, pp. 362–364; 'Jibrīl' in Netton, *Popular Dictionary of Islam*, p. 136.
52 Q.19:17, trans. by Yusuf Ali, *Qur'an*, p. 771.
53 See 'Isrāfīl' in Netton, *Popular Dictionary of Islam*, p. 129.
54 See 'Munkar and Nakīr' in ibid., p. 180.
55 See ''Izrā'īl' in ibid., pp. 131–132.
56 See 'Kirām al-Kātibīn' in ibid., p. 149.
57 See, for example, Q.66:6, Q.19:64.
58 Akhtar, 'Art or Literary Terrorism?', p. 2.
59 The two principal protagonists in the Zoroastrian religion. 'The world, Zoroastrians believe, is the arena for the battle between Ohrmazd [Ahura Mazda] and Ahriman . . . It is only when good ultimately triumphs that Ohrmazd will become omnipotent.' (John R. Hinnells (ed.), *The Penguin Dictionary of Religions*, (London: Penguin Books, 1984), p. 28 s.v. 'Ahura Mazda'). See also R.C. Zaehner, *The Dawn and Twilight of Zoroastrianism*, History of Religion Series, (London: Weidenfeld & Nicolson, 1961).
60 Levitt, *The Cretan Glance*, p. 73.
61 Ibid., p. 66.
62 Netton, *Allāh Transcendent*, pp. 234, 254 n.267.
63 Kazantzakis, 'Prologue', *LT*, p. 9.
64 Levitt, *The Cretan Glance*, p. 62.
65 Ibid., p. 61.
66 Ibid., p. 66.

5

ANTITEXT

All excavation is destruction.

Kenyon, *Beginning in Archaeology*, p. 68.

In this book we have surveyed and analysed three texts, products of *the stratum of the present*, which stand accused, in one way or another, of having undermined a sacred or other archetypal text produced in *the stratum of the past*. Although not always articulated as such in each case, these texts have, to all intents and purposes, been interpreted as rivals or *antitexts*, and therein lies their primary offence for those who have been hurt by their appearance.

The Ur-Antitext *par excellence* must surely be that of the blind Syrian poet to whom we have referred earlier, Abū 'l-'Alā' al-Ma'arrī: he called his work *al-Fuṣūl wa 'l-Ghāyāt* (*The Chapters and the Endings*). Of al-Ma'arrī and this work, Nicholson observed: 'He thought so well of the style [of the Qur'ān] that he accepted the challenge flung down by Muḥammad and produced a rival work (*al-Fuṣúl wā-'l-Gḥáyáṭ*), which appears to have been a somewhat frivolous parody of the sacred volume, though in the author's judgement its inferiority was simply due to the fact that it was not yet polished by the tongues of four centuries of readers.'[1] Although at least one author maintains that al-Ma'arrī did not intend 'his work as a whole to be an imitation of the Qur'ān, let alone to surpass it'[2] it is clear from the careful attempts to imitate the Qur'ānic style[3] that this is precisely what the poet *did* intend.[4] A.M. Zubaidi characterises *al-Fuṣūl wa 'l-Ghāyāt* neatly as 'an ascetic work devoted to the praise of God and the expression of the poet's fear of Him and hope in His forgiveness and mercy.'[5] This, then, is the *real* beginning, regardless of what Musaylima and Ibn al-Muqaffa' might have attempted before, of a perceived heretical tradition of trying to emulate or rival the Qur'ān.[6]

The famous Italian semiotician, Umberto Eco, once wrote: 'The author should die once he has finished writing. So as not to trouble the path of the text.'[7] With this statement Eco stresses the primacy of the text and the primacy of the reader who is free to interpret that text more or less as he or she wishes.

Robert Scholes, stressing that reading is 'an intertextual activity'[8], maintains that 'we are never outside the whole web of textuality in which we hold our cultural being and in which every text awakens echoes and harmonies.'[9] For Scholes 'reading is always, at once, the effort to comprehend and the effort to incorporate. I must invent the author, *invent his or her intentions*, using the evidence I can find to stimulate my creative process . . .'[10] The reader, then is a 'co-producer.'[11] The obvious consequence, of course, of such a method of reading is that the reader's interpretation may vary from that of the author. A reader may, for example, perceive blasphemy where none is intended.

There is a very real sense in which each of the three main literary texts which constitute the subject matter of this book has been read, or at least perceived, as an antitext, regardless of authorial intention. Thus, opponents have seen *The Last Temptation* as a rival *New Testament*, *Awlād Ḥāratinā* as a new or rival Qur'ān, and *The Satanic Verses* as an obscene species of *Sīra* or *Life* of the Prophet Muḥammad like that produced by Ibn Isḥāq (*circa* 704-*circa* 767).[12]

The identification of our three texts as 'antitexts', or rather, the realisation that others have regarded them as such, highlights *three major gulfs:* the first is *the gulf between author and individual reader.* We noted in an earlier chapter the context of these texts and the conditioning of the stratum of the past. It is clear that every text may be read differently according to the different conditioning and cultures of author and reader, not to mention differences in education, prejudice and a vast variety of other areas. In other words, there is, or can be, a clash between authorial intention and reader's perception and reception. There can be two dissonant registers of perceived intention and meaning.

On the one hand, the author, or film producer for that matter, may proclaim a deeply felt intention regarding the work: Of *Awlād Ḥāratinā* Maḥfūẓ observed: 'The stories of the prophets provided an artistic framework, *but my intention was to criticize the revolution and the existing social system.*'[13] Kazantzakis, too, made his intentions plain: '[*The Last Temptation*] isn't a simple 'Life of Christ'. It's a laborious, sacred, creative endeavour to reincarnate the essence of Christ, setting aside the dross – falsehoods and pettinesses which all the churches and all the cassocked representatives of Christianity have heaped upon His figure, thereby distorting it.'[14] And a screen note at the beginning of Scorsese's film of *The Last Temptation of Christ* insists that the film is not based upon the Gospels.

On the other hand, the text or film may be metamorphosed in the mind of the reader into the grossest blasphemy. There is a certain danger in Eco's dictum cited above, since, in the absence of any authorial 'control' or 'sustained ownership' (from the point of view of literary intent), *any* intention can be read into any text or film. Authors too, may play into their opponents' hands all too easily: we note, once again, Maḥfūẓ's division of his novel into 114 chapters, for example.

The second gulf which might usefully be elaborated here is that which may arise *between the author and the establishment*. It is a truism that every country has its élite establishment, or establishments, political, religious, academic and other, official and unofficial, often possessed of considerable power. Such power may be based on quite undemocratic principles and traditions, as R.H.S. Crossman suggested some time ago.[15] On the other hand, it can be democratised if, with Tom Bottomore, we define democracy 'as a type of society in which the élites – economic and cultural, as well as political – are "open" in principle, and are in fact recruited from different social strata on the basis of individual merit.'[16] Whatever our definition, however, and however much it may lend itself to crude Marxist analysis,[17] the existence of élite establishments cannot be doubted. They may include politicians, intellectuals, industrialists and senior civil servants.[18] Martin Jacques claims that 'every society has and *requires* elites',[19] even though his central argument deals with the erosion of the establishment in Britain.[20]

An élite establishment is the custodian of a range of weapons: these may include physical power, the power of patronage, arcane or esoteric knowledge, even the control of *all* knowledge, or the formulation and implementation of law. Such facets of power are self-evident. Above all, however, an establishment often has the power, in one form or another, *to proscribe*. Set against all this may be the alienated 'Outsider' (to borrow a term from Albert Camus[21]), often political or authorial, or even administrative,[22] who sees it as his or her *duty to protest*. Concrete success on the one side *may* lie in the imposition of penalties, and, on the other, in their avoidance. The real gulf between the two sides is one of perception and may be expressed in terms of right and responsibility: an establishment of whatever kind and shade may believe that it has the (collective?) right to rule and thus to impose its own idea of responsible citizenship. The 'Outsider' may believe that he or she has the (individual?)

right to object, regardless of consequences, or imposed and seemingly alien responsibilities. The whole debate may be articulated in a variety of other apparent antitheses such as assimilation versus integration, and artistic licence versus artistic responsibility.

In the light of all this, it is salutary to remember that religions, too, all have their various élites, often filling the upper echelons of a very hierarchical establishment. These may range from the Archbishops and Bishops and Synod of the Church of England, to the Grand Ayatollahs and the '*ulamā*' (so often mistakenly termed 'clergy' by the Western media) of Iran, to the Brahmins of India.[23] Often, too, such élite establishments regard themselves as the jealous custodians of a true 'orthodoxy' enshrined in theologies articulated by themselves, based on sacred texts to which they alone hold the master exegetical keys. Religious knowledge, the guardianship and articulation of it, thus becomes intertwined ineluctably with religious power. It is small wonder, then, that the producers of texts regarded by the establishment as antitexts become primary victims of those establishments' wrath and that a massive gulf may open up between author and establishment.

The third gulf which may be referred to briefly here is that which opens *between one religion and another*. This is an indirect, unintended, but perhaps inevitable, consequence of the debates over the blasphemous, or otherwise, nature of the three texts which we have been examining. For these works have forced religious leaders everywhere, and a number of authors as well,[24] to focus on the whole definition of blasphemy. What becomes rapidly obvious, from the theological perspective, is the impossibility of a mutually acceptable definition across inter-faith lines. Thus, for the Muslim, the idea of the incarnation of God is pure blasphemy, and it is described as such at the beginning of the Eighteenth Chapter of the Qur'ān.[25] Yet, for most Christians, to describe Jesus Christ as anything else *but* the Son of God is equally blasphemous. Lawton notes: 'If religions find each other's beliefs blasphemous and blaspheme each other, how can a statute of blasphemy be framed that will protect all religions equally? This is a logical objection that seems to me insuperable, and I have not seen it answered.'[26]

In this book we have examined a text (*The Satanic Verses*) considered by some to be an extended exploration of the theme of cultural alienation, and by others to be an atheistic and blasphemous attack on a major world religion, Islam, and its holy Founder, the Prophet Muḥammad. We have surveyed a text (*The Last Temptation*) regarded by its author as an attempt 'to offer a supreme model to the man who struggles'[27] but by others as an Arian attack on the Gospel, its message and its central Figure. We have analysed a text (*Awlād Ḥāratinā*) held by some to be a mythic, allegorical work, and by others to be an attempt at producing a blasphemous 'new Qur'ān.'

We have not attempted to find a final definition of blasphemy but only to present the evidence on which such allegations have been based. Our methodology in this book has been founded upon five Braudelian-style layers: *Pre-Text*, *Text*, *Context*, *Intertext*, and *Antitext*. The problem of how to produce a definition of blasphemy that will please everyone remains, and it has not been perceived as the task of this book to try and solve it.

What we can say, by way of conclusion and using David Lawton's elegant phrase, is that 'the discourse of blasphemy is one devised and practised by orthodoxy.'[28] Now it is clear, as we have suggested before, that if the author is on the outside of that orthodoxy or the establishment in which it is embedded, then neither he nor she will feel bound by establishment discourse and categories. For such an author the word 'blasphemy' is emptied of meaning.

NOTES

1 Nicholson, *Literary History of the Arabs*, p. 318.

2 R. Paret, 'The Qur'ān-I' in Beeston *et al.* (eds.), *Arabic Literature to the End of the Umayyad Period*, p. 213.

3 See ibid., and A.M. Zubaidi, 'The Impact of the Qur'ān and *Ḥadīth* on Medieval Arabic Literature' in Beeston *et al.*, *Arabic Literature to the End of the Umayyad Period*, pp. 337–338.

4 For the Arabic text, only part of which has survived (see Paret, 'The Qur'ān-I', p. 213), see *al-Fuṣūl wa'l-Ghāyāt*, ed. Maḥmūd Ḥasan Zanātī, Kitāb al-Turāth, no. 1, (Cairo: al-Hay'a al-Miṣriyya al-'Āmma li'l-Kitāb, 1977).

5 Zubaidi, 'The Impact of the Qur'ān and *Ḥadīth*', p. 337.

6 See Paret, 'The Qur'ān-I', pp. 212–213.

7 Umbert Eco, *Postscript to 'The Name of the Rose'*, trans. by William Weaver, (San Diego & New York: Harcourt Brace Jovanovich, 1984), p. 7. For objections to 'Death of the Author' theory, see Seán Burke, *The Death and Return of the Author: Criticism and Subjectivity in Barthes, Foucault and Derrida*, (Edinburgh: Edinburgh University Press, 1992).

8 See Robert Scholes, *Protocols of Reading*, (New Haven & London: Yale University Press, 1989), esp. pp. 1–49.

9 Ibid., p. 6.

10 Ibid., p. 9 (my italics).

11 Still & Worton, 'Introduction' in Worton & Still, *Intertexuality*, p. 2. See also Lechte, *Julia Kristeva*, pp. 107–108.

12 See 'Ibn Isḥāq' in Netton, *Popular Dictionary of Islam*, p. 112. See also Ibn Isḥāq, *al-Sīra al-Nabawiyya*, ed. M. Saqqā *et al.*, (2 vols., Cairo: al-Ḥalabī,

1955); idem., *The Life of Muhammad: A Translation of Isḥāq's Sīrat Rasūl Allāh*, with introd. and notes by A. Guillaume, (Karachi: OUP, 1955, 1980); Martin Lings, *Muhammad: His Life Based on the Earliest Sources*, (London: Allen & Unwin/Islamic Texts Society, 1983).

13 Cited in El-Enany, *Naguib Mahfouz: The Pursuit of Meaning*, p. 100 (my italics).

14 Cited in Levitt, *The Cretan Glance*, p. 62.

15 See R.H.S. Crossman, *Plato Today*, 2nd rev. edn., (London: Unwin Books, Allen & Unwin, 1963), esp. pp. 91–92. See also Anthony Simpson, *The Anatomy of Britain 1992*, esp. p. 15 in *The Independent on Sunday*, 29th March 1992.

16 Tom Bottomore, *Élites and Society*, 2nd edn., (London & New York: Routledge, 1993), p. 9.

17 See ibid., p. 15.

18 See ibid., pp. 15–34, 52–71.

19 Martin Jacques, 'The erosion of the Establishment', *The Sunday Times: Section 9: The Culture*, 16th January 1994, p. 6 (my italics).

20 Ibid.: Jacques' point is that 'Britain now needs a different kind of elite.' He lists 'the values that inform Establishment culture.' They are: 'a belief in continuity, tradition, permanence, experience, careers for life, and age; amateurishness, obtuseness, Britishness, a literary education, old-style generalism and a traditional and narrow range of intelligences; hierarchy and paternalism; background, the club mentality, the closed world and male values; effortlessness, safety, uniformity, conservatism and pragmatism.'

21 See Albert Camus, *L'Étranger*, ed. by Ray Davison, Twentieth Century Texts, (London: Routledge, 1988); idem., *The Outsider*, trans. by Joseph Laredo, Penguin Modern Classics, (Harmondsworth: Penguin, 1983).

22 See Clive Ponting, *Secrecy in Britain*, Historical Association Studies, (Oxford: Basil Blackwell, 1990).

23 See Bottomore, *Élites and Society*, pp. 53–54.

24 See, for example, Richard Webster, *A Brief History of Blasphemy*, (Southwold: The Orwell Press, 1990); David Lawton, *Blasphemy*, (London & New York; Harvester Wheatsheaf, 1993); Commission for Racial Equality & Inter Faith Network of the United Kingdom, *Law, Blasphemy and the Multi-Faith Society*, (London: Commission for Racial Equality/The Inter Faith Network for the United Kingdom, 1990).

25 See Q.18:5.

26 Lawton, *Blasphemy*, p. 9; see also CRE/IFN, *Law, Blasphemy and the Multi-Faith Society*, p. 37.

27 Kazantzakis, 'Prologue', *LT*, p. 9.

28 Lawton, *Blasphemy*, p. 202.

BIBLIOGRAPHY

Arabic Sources

(In this section 'al-' and 'el-' have been omitted from proper names at the beginning of an entry. Translations of texts are also included here.)

Ahrām: 28th March 1990.

Ākhir Sā'a (Egyptian Weekly Magazine): 10th May 1989.

Ali, Abdullah Yusuf *see* Qur'ān.

Arberry, A.J., *see* Qur'ān; *see also* under Other Written Sources.

'Aẓm, Ṣādiq Jalāl, '"Ayāt Shayṭāniyya" Karnifāl Sākhir', *al-Nāqid*, no. 54 (December 1992).

—— *Dhihniyyat al-Taḥrīm*, (London & Cyprus: Riad El-Rayyes Books, 1992).

—— *Naqd al-Fikr al-Dīnī*, 6th impression, (Beirut: Dār al-Ṭalī'a, 1988).

Enany, Rasheed, 'al-Shayṭān al-Sākit: al-Kashf 'an al-Mafqūd bayn al-Nāqid wa 'l-Manqūd', *al-Nāqid*, vol. 6, no. 63 (September 1993).

—— *See also* under Other Written Sources.

Guillaume, A., *see* Ibn Isḥāq.

Ḥallāj, *Kitāb Akhbār al-Ḥallāj*, ed. Louis Massignon & Paul Kraus, (Paris: Éditions Larose, Imprimerie 'au Calame', 1936).

—— *See also* Massignon (trans.).

Ḥāmid, 'Alā', *Masāfa fī 'Aql Rajul*, (Cairo: n.p., 1988).

Hava, J.G., *al-Farā'id Arabic-English Dictionary*, (Beirut: Dār al-Mashriq, 1970).

Ḥayāt: 2nd July 1990.

Ḥusayn, Ṭāhā, *Fī 'l-Shi'r al-Jāhilī*, (Cairo: Maṭba'a Dār al-Kutub al-Miṣriyya, 1926).

Ibn Isḥāq, *The Life of Muhammad: A Translation of Isḥāq's Sīrat Rasūl Allāh*, with introd. & notes by A. Guillaume, (Karachi: OUP, 1955, 1980).

—— *al-Sīra al-Nabawiyya*, ed. M. Saqqā *et al.*, (2 vols., Cairo: al-Ḥalabī, 1955).

Kraus, Paul, *see also* al-Ḥallāj.

Lane, Edward William, *An Arabic-English Lexicon, Part 2 Jīm-Khā'*, (Beirut: Librairie du Liban, 1968).

Ma'arrī, *al-Fuṣūl wa 'l-Ghāyāt*, ed. Maḥmūd Ḥasan Zanātī, Ḳitāb al-Turāth, no. 1 (Cairo: al-Hay'a al-Miṣriyya al-'Āmma li 'l-Kitāb, 1977).

—— *Risālat al-Ghufrān*, Dhakhā'ir al-'Arab, no. 4, 3rd edn., ed. 'Ā'isha 'Abd al-Raḥmān Bint al-Shāṭi', (Cairo: Dār al-Ma'ārif, 1963).

Mahfouz, Naguib, *see* Maḥfūẓ.

Maḥfūẓ, Najīb, *Awlād Ḥāratinā* [*AH*], (Beirut: Dār al-Ādāb, 1967; 5th imp., 1986).

—— *Children of Gebelawi* [*CG*], trans. by Philip Stewart, Arab Authors 15, (London: Heinemann, 1981).

Massignon (trans.), Louis, *The Passion of al-Ḥallāj*, trans. with a biographical foreword by Herbert Mason, Bollingen Series, no. 98, (4 vols., Princeton: Princeton University Press, 1982).

—— *See also* al-Ḥallāj.

McDonald, M.V., *see* Watt & McDonald (trans.).

Munīf, 'Abd al-Raḥmān, *Cities of Salt*, trans. by Peter Theroux, (London: Cape, 1988).

—— *Mudun al-Milḥ*, (Beirut: Arab Institute for Research and Publishing, 1984).

—— *See also* under Other Written Sources.

Quds al-'Arabī: 14th–15th April 1990; 30th December 1991; 6th January 1992; 8th January 1992; 20th January 1992; 25–26th January 1992; 28th January 1992; 2nd April 1993.

Qur'ān: *The Holy Qur'an: Text, Translation and Commentary* [Q.] by Abdullah Yusuf Ali, (Kuwait: Dhāt al-Salāsil, 1984) [Arabic and English Text].

—— *The Koran Interpreted*, by A.J. Arberry, (2 vols., London: Allen & Unwin/ New York: Macmillan, 1971) [English translation].

Stewart, Philip, *see* Maḥfūẓ.

Ṭabarī, *Jāmi' al-Bayān fī Tafsīr al-Qur'ān*, (Beirut: Dār al-Ma'rifa, 1972 [repr. of AH 1328 edn. of Būlāq: al-Maṭba'a al-Kubrā al-Amīriyya]), vol. 17.

—— *Ta'rīkh al-Rusul wa 'l-Mulūk*, ed. Muḥammad Abū 'l-Faḍl Ibrāhīm, Dhakhā'ir al-'Arab, no. 30 (Cairo: Dār al-Ma'ārif, 1961), vol. 2.

—— *See also* Watt & McDonald (trans.).

Ṭabarsī, *Majma' al-Bayān fī Tafsīr al-Qur'ān*, (Beirut: Dār Iḥyā' al-Turāth al-'Arabī, AH 1379), vol. 7.

Watt, W. Montgomery & McDonald, M.V. (trans.), *The History of al-Ṭabarī (Ta'rīkh al-rusul wa 'l-mulūk): Volume VI: Muḥammad at Mecca*, SUNY Series in Near Eastern Studies (Bibliotheca Persica), (Albany, N.Y.: State University of New York Press, 1988).

Watt, W. Montgomery, *see also* under Other Written Sources.

Wehr, Hans, *A Dictionary of Modern Written Arabic*, ed. J. Milton Cowan, 2nd Printing, (Wiesbaden: Otto Harrassowitz/London: Allen & Unwin, 1966).

Yaḥyā, Muḥammad & Shukrī, Mu'tazz, *Al-Ṭarīq ilā Nūbil 1988: 'Abra Ḥāra Najīb Maḥfūẓ*, (Cairo: Umma Press li 'l-Ṭibā'a wa 'l-Nashr, 1989).

Other Written Sources

Abbott, Nabia, *Aishah, the Beloved of Mohammed*, The Middle East Collection, (New York: Arno Press, 1973 [repr. of University of Chicago Press, 1942 edn.]).

'Abd al-Raḥmān ("Bint al-Shāṭi'"), 'Ā'isha, 'Abū 'l-'Alā' al-Ma'arrī: *see* Ashtiany *et al.* (eds.), *'Abbasid Belles Lettres*.

Bibliography

Ahsan, M.M., 'The Muslim Argument: The 'Satanic' Verses and the Orientalists': *see* Ahsan & Kidwai (eds.), *Sacrilege Versus Civility.*

Ahsan, M.M. & Kidwai, A.R. (eds.), *Sacrilege Versus Civility: Muslim Perspectives on The Satanic Verses Affair*, (Leicester: The Islamic Foundation, 1991).

Akhtar, Shabbir, 'Art or Literary Terrorism?': *see* Cohn-Sherbok (ed.), *The Salman Rushdie Controversy in Interreligious Perspective.*

Allegro, John, *The Dead Sea Scrolls: A Reappraisal*, (Harmondsworth: Penguin, 1956; 2nd edn., repr. 1972).

—— *The Sacred Mushroom and the Cross: A Study of the Nature and Origins of Christianity within the Fertility Cults of the Ancient Near East*, (London: Hodder & Stoughton, 1970).

Ally, Muhammad Mashuq ibn, 'Stranger Exiled from Home': *see* Cohn-Sherbok (ed.), *The Salman Rushdie Controversy in Interreligious Perspective.*

Alrawi, Karim, 'Farag Fouda Murdered', *Index on Censorship*, no. 7 (1992).

—— *See also The Guardian*: 3rd March 1989.

Altizer, Thomas J.J., *The Gospel of Christian Atheism*, (Philadelphia: Westminster Press, 1966).

—— (ed.), *Towards a New Christianity: Readings in the Death of God Theology*, (New York: Harcourt, Brace & World Inc., 1967).

—— *et al.*, *Deconstruction and Theology*, (New York: Crossroad, 1982).

Ammerman, Nancy T., 'North American Protestant Fundamentalism': *see* Marty & Appleby (eds.), *Fundamentalisms Observed.*

Amuzegar, Jahangir, *The Dynamics of the Iranian Revolution: The Pahlavis' Triumph and Tragedy*, (Albany, N.Y.: State University of New York Press, 1991).

Andrew, Geoff, *The Film Handbook*, (Harlow: Longman, 1989).

Al-Ani, S.M., *The Early Representations of the Prophet Muhammad with Special Reference to the Mi'rāj Scenes*, 2 vols., PhD Thesis, University of Edinburgh, 1979.

Anthonakes, Michael A., *Christ, Freedom and Kazantzakis*, PhD Thesis, University of New York, 1965.

Appignanesi, Lisa & Maitland, Sara (eds.), *The Rushdie File*, (London: Fourth Estate, 1989).

Aran, Gideon, 'Jewish Zionist Fundamentalism: The Bloc of the Faithful in Israel (Gush Emunim)': *see* Marty & Appleby (eds.), *Fundamentalisms Observed.*

Arberry (ed.), A.J., *Religion in the Middle East: Three Religions in Concord and Conflict*, (Cambridge: Cambridge University Press, 1969), vol. 1.

—— *See also* Qur'ān (Arabic Sources).

Armstrong, Karen, *A History of God*, (London: Mandarin, Reed Consumer Books, 1994).

Arnold, Sir Thomas, *Painting in Islam*, (New York: Dover, 1965 [repr. of OUP edn. of 1928]).

Ashtiany *et al.* (eds.), Julia, *'Abbasid Belles Lettres*, Volume 2: The Cambridge History of Arabic Literature, (Cambridge: Cambridge University Press, 1990).

Badawi, M.M., 'Microcosms of Old Cairo': *see* El-Batrik (ed.), *The World of Naguib Mahfouz.*

—— *Modern Arabic Literature and the West*, (London: Ithaca Press, 1985).

Barker, Elspeth, 'True Stories of Good and Evil', *The Independent on Sunday: The Sunday Review*, 20th September 1992.

Barr, James, *Escaping from Fundamentalism*, (London: SCM Press, 1984).

—— *Fundamentalism*, 2nd edn., (London: SCM Press, 1981).

Barrowclough, Susan, 'Godard's Marie: The Virgin Birth and a Flurry of Protest . . .', *Sight and Sound*, vol. 54, no. 2 (Spring 1985).

El-Batrik (ed.), Younes A., *The World of Naguib Mahfouz*, (London: Egyptian Education Bureau, 1989).

Bauke, Hermann, 'The History of Christological Doctrine': *see* Pelikan (ed.), *Twentieth Century Theology in the Making: Vol. 2*.

Bauvy, Jacques, 'Dans l'Affaire "Je Vous Salue Marie"', *FILMéchange*, no. 32 (1985).

Bayat, Mangol, 'Ayatollah Sayyid Ruhullah Musawi Khumayni and *Wilayat-i Faqih*': *see* Nasr, Dabashi & Nasr (eds.), *Expectation of the Millenium*.

Bea, Augustin, '"Divino Afflante Spiritu": De Recentissimis Pii PP.XII Litteris Encyclicis', *Biblica*, vol. 24 (1943).

—— 'Foreword to *The Jerome Biblical Commentary* (1968)': *see* Brown, Fitzmyer & Murphy (eds.), *The New Jerome Biblical Commentary* (1989).

Beatrice, Pier Franco, *Introduction to the Fathers of the Church*, (Vicenza: Edizioni Istituto San Gaetano, 1987).

Beeston *et al.* (eds.), A.F.L., *Arabic Literature to the End of the Umayyad Period*, Volume 1: The Cambridge History of Arabic Literature, (Cambridge: Cambridge University Press, 1983).

Bhatia, Shyam, 'Broad Path, Courageous Heart', *The Observer*, 8th March 1992.

—— 'Unadulterated Islam says couple must face divorce', *The Observer*, 12th December 1993.

Bible, The Holy: *see* Wansbrough (ed.), *The New Jerusalem Bible*.

Bien, Peter [P.A.], *Kazantzakis and the Linguistic Revolution in Greek Literature*, Princeton Essays in European and Comparative Literature, no. 6, (Princeton: Princeton University Press, 1972).

—— *Nikos Kazantzakis*, Columbia Essays on Modern Writers 62, (New York & London: Columbia University Press, 1972).

—— *Nikos Kazantzakis, Novelist*, Studies in Modern Greek, (Bristol: British Classical Press/New Rochelle: Aristide D. Caratzas, 1989).

—— 'Translator's Note on the Author and His Language': *see* Kazantzakis, *The Last Temptation*.

Bottomore, Tom, *Élites and Society*, 2nd edn., (London & New York: Routledge, 1993).

Bourdeaux, Michael, *Gorbachev, Glasnost and the Gospel*, (London: Hodder & Stoughton, 1990).

Bowden, John, *Edward Schillebeeckx: Portrait of a Theologian*, (London: SCM Press, 1983).

Bowen (ed.), David G., *The Satanic Verses: Bradford Responds*, (Bradford: Bradford & Ilkley Community College, 1992).

Bowker, J.W., [Review of] Martin E. Marty & R. Scott Appleby (eds.), *Fundamentalisms Observed* in *BSOAS*, vol. LVI: 3 (1993).

Braudel, Fernand, *Civilization Matérielle, Économie et Capitalisme (XVe*–XVIIIe Siècle), (3 vols., Paris: Librairie Armand Colin, 1979).

—— *La Méditerranée et le Monde Méditerranéen à l'Époque de Philippe II*, (Paris: Librairie Armand Colin, 1949; 2nd rev. edn., 1966).

Brennan, Timothy, *Salman Rushdie and the Third World: Myths of the Nation*, (London: Macmillan, 1989).

Brown, Raymond E., Fitzmyer, Joseph A., & Murphy, Roland E. (eds.), *The New Jerome Biblical Commentary*, (London: Geoffrey Chapman, 1989).

Brown, Robert, [Review of] 'Je Vous Salue, Marie (Hail Mary)', *Monthly Film Bulletin*, vol. 52, no. 620 (September 1985).

Bullock, Alan, Stallybrass, Oliver & Trombley, Stephen (eds.), *The Fontana Dictionary of Modern Thought*, 2nd rev. edn., (London: Fontana Press, Harper Collins, 1988).

Burke, Seán, *The Death and Return of the Author: Criticism and Subjectivity in Barthes, Foucault and Derrida*, (Edinburgh: Edinburgh University Press, 1992).

Burrell (ed.), R.M., *Islamic Fundamentalism*, Royal Asiatic Society Seminar Papers, no. 1, (London: Royal Asiastic Society, 1989).

Burton, J., 'Those are the High-Flying Cranes', *Journal of Semitic Studies*, vol. 15, no. 2 (1970).

Buss, Robin, *The French Through Their Films*, (London: Batsford, 1988).

Cachia, Pierre, *Ṭāhā Ḥusayn: His Place in the Egyptian Literary Renaissance*, (London: Luzac, 1956).

Campbell, J.K., 'Traditional Values and Continuities in Greek Society': *see* Clogg (ed.), *Greece in the 1980s*.

Camus, Albert, *L'Étranger*, ed. Ray Davison, Twentieth Century Texts, (London: Routledge, 1988).

—— *The Outsider*, trans. by Joseph Laredo, Penguin Modern Classics, (Harmondsworth: Penguin, 1983).

Caplan (ed.), Lionel, *Studies in Religious Fundamentalism*, (London & Houndmills: Macmillan, 1987).

Carpenter, Humphrey, 'Unwrapping the Presence', *The Sunday Times Books*, 20th September 1992.

Catechism: *Catéchisme de l'Église Catholique*, introd. Jean-Paul II, (Paris: Mame, Plon, 1992).

—— *Catechism of the Catholic Church*, (London: Geoffrey Chapman, 1994).

The Catholic World Report: March 1992; February 1994 ('Start the Presses!').

Cawardine, Richard, 'Christianity in North America from the Sixteenth Century': *see* Sutherland *et al.* (eds.), *The World's Religions*.

Chadwick, Henry: *see The Tablet*, 26th September 1992.

Choueiri, Youssef M., *Islamic Fundamentalism*, Twayne's Themes in Right-Wing Politics and Ideology Series, (Boston: Twayne Publishers, 1990).

Clogg (ed.), Richard, *Greece in the 1980s*, (London: Macmillan in association with the Centre of Contemporary Greek Studies, King's College, University of London, 1983).

Cohn-Sherbok (ed.), Dan, *The Salman Rushdie Controversy in Interreligious Perspective*, Symposium Series, vol. 27, (Lewiston/Queenston/Lampeter: The Edwin Mellen Press, 1990).

Commission for Racial Equality and Inter Faith Network of the United Kingdom, *Law, Blasphemy and the Multi-Faith Society*, (London: CRE/IFN, 1990).

Cook, Pam, [Review of] 'The Last Temptation of Christ', *Monthly Film Bulletin*, vol. 55, no. 657 (October 1988).

Corliss, Richard, 'Body . . .': *see Film Comment.*

Cross (ed.), F.L., *The Oxford Dictionary of the Christian Church*, (London: Oxford University Press, 1957).

Cross, Lawrence, *Eastern Christianity: The Byzantine Tradition*, (Philadelphia/ Newtown, NSW: E.J. Dwyer, 1988).

Crossman, R.H.S., *Plato Today*, 2nd rev. edn., (London: Unwin books, Allen & Unwin, 1963).

Cupitt, Don, *The Long-Legged Fly: A Theology of Language and Desire*, (London: SCM Press, 1987).

—— *See also The Independent.*

Dabashi, Hamid, *Theology of Discontent: The Ideological Foundations of the Islamic Revolution in Iran*, (New York & London: New York University Press, 1993).

Darwish, Adel, 'Egypt Islamists try to force foe to divorce', *The Independent*, 10th July 1993.

—— 'The Hydra grows another head', *Index on Censorship*, vol. 21, no. 6 (June 1992).

Davies, Michael, *Partisans of Error: St. Pius X Against the Modernists*, (Long Prairie: The Neumann Press, 1983).

Davison, John, 'The family man who told Hollywood "your soul is sick"', *The Sunday Times*, 7th February 1993.

De Lubac, Henri, *The Splendor of the Church*, trans. by Michael Mason, (San Francisco: Ignatius Press, 1986).

Dieckmann, Katherine, 'Godard in His "Fifth Period": An Interview', *Film Quarterly*, vol. 39, no. 2 (Winter 1985–86).

Dietrich, Angela, 'The *Khalsa* Resurrected: Sikh Fundamentalism in the Punjab: *see* Caplan (ed.), *Studies in Religious Fundamentalism.*

Dinges, William D., '(1) Roman Catholic Traditionalism': *see* Dinges & Hitchcock, 'Roman Catholic Traditionalism and Activist Conservatism in the United States' in Marty & Appleby (eds.), *Fundamentalisms Observed.*

Dinges, William D. & Hitchcock, James, 'Roman Catholic Traditionalism and Activist Conservatism in the United States': *see* Marty & Appleby (eds.), *Fundamentalisms Observed.*

Douin, Jean-Luc, 'Jésus Superstar, Certains préfèrent l'invisible', *Cinémation*, 49 (October 1988).

Eco, Umberto, *Postscript to 'The Name of the Rose'*, trans. by William Weaver, (San Diego & New York: Harcourt Brace Jovanovich, 1984).

Elley, Derek, [Review of] 'Hail Mary', *Films and Filming*, no. 372 (September 1985).

Ellis, Jane, *The Russian Orthodox Church: A Contemporary History*, (London & New York: Routledge, 1988).

El-Enany, Rasheed, 'An Introduction [to Munif]', *Review Guardian*, 14th May 1992.

—— 'Naguib Mahfouz' in El-Batrik (ed.), *The World of Naguib Mahfouz.*

—— *Naguib Mahfouz: The Pursuit of Meaning*, Arabic Thought and Culture Series, (London & New York: Routledge, 1993).

—— 'Religion in the Novels of Naguib Mahfouz', *British Society for Middle Eastern Studies Bulletin*, vol. 15, nos. 1–2 (1988).

—— *See also* under Arabic Sources.

Enayat, Hamid, 'Ayatullah Sayyid Ruhullah Musawi Khumayni and *Wilayat-i Faqih*': *see* Nasr, Dabashi & Nasr (eds.), *Expectation of the Millenium*.

Encyclopaedia of Islam, New Edition [*EI*^{2}], ed. H.A.R. Gibb *et al.*, 7 vols., cont., (Leiden: E.J. Brill/London: Luzac, 1960–).

The European: 21st–24th May, 1992.

Fessio, Joseph: *see* De Lubac, *The Splendor of the Church*.

Film Comment, vol. 24, no. 5 (September–October 1988) ('For Christ's Sake').

Flannery (ed.), Austin, *Vatican Council II: The Conciliar and Post-Conciliar Documents*, rev. edn., Vatican Collection, (Dublin: Dominican Publications/ Leominster: Fowler Wright Books/New Town, NSW: Dwyer, 1988), vol. 1.

—— *Vatican Council II: More Postconciliar Documents*, Vatican Collection vol. 2, (Northport, New York: Costello Publishing Company, 1982).

Ford (ed.), David, F., *The Modern Theologians: An Introduction to Christian Theology in the Twentieth Century*, (2 vols., Oxford: Basil Blackwell, 1989).

Fox, Matthew, *Original Blessing: A Primer in Creation Spirituality*, (Santa Fe: Bear & Company, 1983, 1990).

Freeman, Anthony, *God in Us: A Case for Christian Humanism*, (London: SCM Press, 1993).

Gardet, L., art. 'Allāh', *EI*^{2}, vol. 1.

—— art. 'Al-Asmā' al-Ḥusnā', *EI*^{2}, vol. 1.

—— *See also* Massignon & Gardet.

Gavin, Frank, *Some Aspects of Contemporary Greek Orthodox Thought*, (London: AMS Press, 1970 [repr. from 1923 Milwaukee edn.]).

Gibb, H.A.R., *Mohammedanism: An Historical Survey*, 2nd edn., Home University Library of Modern Knowledge, no. 197, (London: Oxford University Press, 1964).

—— (ed.), *See also Encyclopaedia of Islam, New Edition*.

Gibb, H.A.R. & Kramers, J.H. (eds.): *see Shorter Encyclopaedia of Islam*.

Gifford, Paul, [Review of] Martin E. Marty & R. Scott Appleby (eds.), *Fundamentalisms Observed* in *British Association for the Study of Religions Bulletin*, no. 70 (November 1993).

Gilley, Sheridan, 'Christianity in Europe: Reformation to Today': *see* Sutherland *et al.* (eds.) *The World's Religions*.

Gledhill, Ruth, 'Bishop [Jenkins] feels the heat over views on hell', *The Times*, 15th December 1993.

Glicksberg, Charles I., *Modern Literature and the Death of God*, (The Hague: Martinus Nijhoff, 1966).

Gold, Daniel, 'Organized Hinduisms: From Vedic Truth to Hindu Nation': *see* Marty & Appleby (eds.), *Fundamentalisms Observed*.

Graham, Billy: *see The Guardian*, 2nd June 1989.

Graham, Robert, *Iran: The Illusion of Power*, rev. edn., (London: Croom Helm, 1979).

Griffin, Jennifer, 'Boy faces death for "blasphemy"', *The Observer*, 28th November 1993.

The Guardian: 23rd September 1988; 3rd March 1989; 2nd June 1989; 12th March 1992; 8th December 1993.

—— *See also* El-Enany, Montefiore, Munīf, Odone, Schwarz.
Haddad, S.A., 'The Assassination of Fuda', *The Arab Studies Journal*, vol. 1, no. 1 (Spring 1993).
Haley, Alex, *The Autobiography of Malcolm X*, (New York: Ballantine Books, 1964).
Hallett, Paul. H.: *see* Davies, *Partisans of Error*.
Halliday, Fred, 'The Genesis of the Iranian Revolution', *Third World Quarterly*, vol. 1:4 (October 1979).
Hardy, Daniel W., 'Theology Through Philosophy': *see* Ford (ed.), *The Modern Theologians*, vol. 2.
Heikal, Mohamed, *The Return of the Ayatollah: The Iranian Revolution from Mossadeq to Khomeini*, (London: André Deutsch, 1981).
Henderson, Elaina, 'Sympathy for the Virgin: Hail Mary', *Stills*, no. 21 (October 1985).
Hick, John Harwood, *The Metaphor of God Incarnate*, (London: SCM Press, 1993).
—— *The Myth of God Incarnate*, (London: SCM Press, 1977; 2nd edn. with new preface 1993).
Hinnells (ed.), John R., *The Penguin Dictionary of Religions*, (London: Penguin Books, 1984).
Hiro, Dilip, *Iran Under the Ayatollahs*, (London: Routledge & Kegan Paul, 1985).
—— *Islamic Fundamentalism*, Paladin Movements and Ideas, (London: Collins, Paladin Grafton Books, 1989).
Hitchcock, James, '(2) Catholic Activist Conservatism in the United States': *see* Dinges & Hitchcock, 'Roman Catholic Traditionalism and Activist Conservatism in the United States', in Marty & Appleby (eds.), *Fundamentalisms Observed*.
Impact International: 28th October–10th November 1988.
The Independent: 15th October 1988; 19th January 1989; 21st February 1989; 16th January 1992; 9th March 1992; 8th July 1992; 11th February 1993 ('The Hunter Davies Interview'); 12th May 1993; 7th July 1993 (Letter from Salman Rushdie); 8th July 1993 (Letter from Kalim Siddiqui); 22nd September 1993 (Letter from Don Cupitt).
—— *See also* Darwish; Maccoby; Morris; Said.
The Independent Magazine: 10th June 1989.
The Independent on Sunday: 4th July 1993.
—— *See also* Barker; McGirk; Simpson.
Index on Censorship: no. 7 (1992).
Indian Post (Bombay): 2nd October 1988.
Inter Faith Network for the United Kingdom: *see* Commission for Racial Equality.
Interpreters' Dictionary of the Bible: An Illustrated Encyclopedia, vol. 1 A–D, (New York & Nashville: Abingdon Press, 1962).
Ithaca Times: 2nd–8th March 1989.
Ivens, Martin, 'A brief history of hell', *The Times*, 15th December 1993.
Izutsu, Toshihiko, *Ethico-Religious Concepts in the Qur'ān*, McGill Islamic Studies 1, (Montreal: McGill University Press, 1966).
—— *God and Man in the Koran: Semantics of the Koranic Weltanschauung*,

Studies in the Humanities and Social Relations, vol. 5 (Tokyo: Keio Institute of Cultural and Linguistic Studies, 1964).

Jacques, Martin, 'The erosion of the Establishment', *The Sunday Times: Section 9: The Culture*, 16th January 1994.

Jeanrond, Werner G., 'Hans Küng': *see* Ford (ed.), *The Modern Theologians*, vol. 1.

Jenkins, Steve, 'From the Pit of Hell', *Monthly Film Bulletin*, vol. 55, n.659 (December 1988).

John Paul II, Pope, *Veritatis Splendor: Encyclical Letter . . . Regarding Certain Fundamental Questions of the Church's Moral Teaching*, (London: Catholic Truth Society/Dublin: Veritas, 1993).

Josephus, Flavius, *The Destruction of the Jews*, trans. by G.A. Williamson, (London: Folio Society, 1971 [repr. from Penguin edn. of 1959]).

Kabbani, Rana, *Letter to Christendom*, (London: Virago Press, 1989).

Kauffmann, Stanley, 'Stanley Kauffmann on Films: A Mission' [A Review of *The Last Temptation of Christ*], *The New Republic*, 12th–19th September 1988.

Kazantzakis, Nikos, *Christ Recrucified* [in Greek], 2nd edn., (Athens: Dífros, 1955).

—— *The Last Temptation* [in Greek], (Athens: Dífros, 1955).

—— *The Last Temptation* [*LT*], trans. into English by P.A. Bien, (London: Faber & Faber, 1991).

Keating, Maurice with Keating, H.R.F., *Understanding Pierre Teilhard de Chardin: A Guide to The Phenomenon of Man*, (London: Lutterworth Press, 1969).

Keddie (ed.), Nikki R., *Religion and Politics in Iran: Shi'ism from Quietism to Revolution*, (New Haven & London: Yale University Press, 1983).

Kelly, J.N.D., *Early Christian Doctrines*, 5th rev. edn., (London: Adam & Charles Black, 1977).

Kelly, Mary Pat, *Martin Scorsese: A Journey*, (London: Secker & Warburg, 1991–92).

Kenyon, Kathleen M., *Beginning in Archaeology*, rev. edn., (London: Phoenix House/New York: Frederick A. Praeger, 1961).

Kramer (ed.), Martin, *Shi'ism, Resistance and Revolution*, Collected Papers Series of the Dayan Centre for Middle Eastern and African Studies, The Shiloah Institute, (Boulder, Colorado: Westview Press/London: Mansell, 1987).

Kramers, J.H.: *see Shorter Encyclopaedia of Islam.*

Kristeva, Julia, *Revolution in Poetic Language*, (New York: Columbia University Press, 1984).

—— 'Revolution in Poetic Language': *see* Moi (ed.), *The Kristeva Reader.*

—— *Sēmeiōtikē: Recherches pour une Sémanalyse*, (Paris: Éditions du Seuil, 1969).

Küng, Hans, *Infallible? An Enquiry*, (London: Collins, 1971).

Lawton, David, *Blasphemy*, (London & New York: Harvester Wheatsheaf, 1993).

Lechte, John, *Julia Kristeva*, Critics of the Twentieth Century, (London & New York: Routledge, 1990).

Le Gassick (ed.), Trevor, *Critical Perspectives on Naguib Mahfouz*, (Washington: Three Continents Press, 1991).

Le Morvan, Michael, *Pierre Teilhard de Chardin: Priest and Evolutionist*, (London: Catholic Truth Society, 1969).
Le Roux, Hervé, 'Le Trou de la Vierge ou Marie telle que Jeannot la Peint', *Cahiers du Cinema*, no. 367 (Janvier 1985).
Levitt, Martin P., *The Cretan Glance*, (Columbus: Ohio State University Press, 1980).
Lings, Martin, *Muhammad: His Life Based on the Earliest Sources*, (London: Allen & Unwin/Islamic Texts Society, 1983).
Llewelyn, John, 'Value, Authenticity and the Death of God': *see* Parkinson (ed.), *An Encyclopaedia of Philosophy*.
Lochman, Jan Milic, art. 'Atheism': *see* Lossky *et al.* (eds.), *Dictionary of the Ecumenical Movement.*
Lonergan, B.J.F., *Method in Theology*, (New York: Herder & Herder, 1971/2nd edn.: London: Darton, Longman & Todd, 1973).
Longford, Frank, 'Was Jesus just a Good Jew?', *The Times*, 19th September 1992.
Lossky *et al.* (eds.), Nicholas, *Dictionary of the Ecumenical Movement*, (Geneva: WCC Publications/London: Council of Churches for Britain and Ireland, 1991).
Lossky, Nicholas, art. 'Orthodoxy': *see* Lossky *et al.* (eds.), *Dictionary of the Ecumenical Movement.*
Lustick, Ian, *For the Land and the Lord: Jewish Fundamentalism in Israel*, (New York, N.Y.: Council on Foreign Relations, 1988).
Maccoby, Hyam, 'Obituary: Dr. John Allegro', *The Independent*, 24th February 1988.
Madan, T.N., 'The Double-Edged Sword: Fundamentalism and the Sikh Religious Tradition': *see* Marty & Appleby (eds.), *Fundamentalisms Observed.*
Malik, C.H., 'The Orthodox Church': *see* Arberry (ed.), *Religion in the Middle East*, vol. 1.
Maloney, George A., *A History of Orthodox Theology since 1453*, (Belmont, Mass.: Nordland Pub. Co., 1976).
Maltin (ed.), Leonard, *Movie and Video Guide, 1993 Edition*, (London/Harmondsworth/New York: Signet, Penguin, 1992).
Marsden, Eric, 'Jews Stand up for Jesus', *Sunday Times*, 20th December 1970.
Martin, Malachi, *The Jesuits*, (New York: Simon & Schuster, 1988).
Marty, Martin E. & Appleby, R. Scott (eds.), *Fundamentalisms Observed*, The Fundamentalist Project, vol. 1, (Chicago & London: University of Chicago Press, 1991).
Massignon, L. & Gardet, L., art. 'Al-Ḥallādj', *EI*², vol. 3.
—— *See also* under Arabic Sources: al-Ḥallāj; Massignon (trans.).
Mazrui, Ali, 'Novelist's Freedom vs Worshipper's Dignity': *see* Ahsan & Kidwai (eds.), *Sacrilege Versus Civility.*
—— *See also Ithaca Times.*
McAndrew, Francis, 'Christ's Self-Knowledge', *Christian Order*, vol. 34, no. 6/7 (June/July 1993).
McGirk, Tim, 'Fatwa is a feminist issue in Dhaka', *Independent on Sunday*, 5th December 1993.
Medved, Michael, *Hollywood Vs. America: Popular Culture and the War on Traditional Values*, (New York: Harper Collins, 1992).

Menas Associates' Egypt Focus, vol. 2, no. 3 (March 1992).
Meynell, Hugo, 'Bernard Lonergan': *see* Ford (ed.), *The Modern Theologians*, vol. 1.
Miles, Helen, 'Zealots set time bomb under Egypt's law', *The Sunday Times*, 27th June 1993.
Milne (ed.), Tom, *The Time Out Film Guide*, 2nd edn., (London/ Harmondsworth: Penguin Books, 1991).
Moaddel, Mansoor, *Class, Politics and Ideology in the Iranian Revolution*, (New York: Columbia University Press, 1993).
Moi (ed.), Toril, *The Kristeva Reader*, (Oxford: Basil Blackwell, 1986).
Montefiore, Hugh, 'Obituary: John Allegro', *The Guardian*, 20th February 1988.
Morgan, Robert, 'Rudolf Bultmann': *see* Ford (ed.), *The Modern Theologians*, vol. 1.
Morris, Jan, 'Believe It or Nor', *The Independent*, 19th September 1992.
Munīf, 'Abd al-Raḥmān, 'Moving beyond Lines in Sand', *Review Guardian*, 14th May 1992.
—— *See also* under Arabic Sources.
Nasr, Seyyed Hossein, Dabashi, Hamid & Nasr, Seyyed Vali Reza (eds.), *Expectation of the Millenium: Shi'ism in History*, (Albany, N.Y.: State University of New York Press, 1989).
Netton, Ian Richard, *Allāh Transcendent: Studies in the Structure and Semiotics of Islamic Philosophy, Theology and Cosmology*, (London & New York: Routledge, 1989).
—— (ed.), *Arabia and the Gulf: From Traditional Society to Modern States*, (London & Sydney: Croom Helm, 1986).
—— 'Arabia and the Pilgrim Paradigm of Ibn Baṭṭūṭa: A Braudelian Approach': *see* Netton (ed.), *Arabia and the Gulf.*
—— *A Popular Dictionary of Islam*, (London: Curzon Press/Atlantic Highlands: Humanities Press, 1992).
New Jerusalem Bible: *see* Wansbrough (ed.).
Nicholson, R.A., *A Literary History of the Arabs*, (Richmond: Curzon Press, 1993 [repr. of 1930 CUP edn.]).
—— *Studies in Islamic Poetry*, (Cambridge: Cambridge University Press, 1921, repr. 1969).
Nielson, Jørgen S. (ed.), *The "Rushdie Affair" – A Documentation*, Muslims in Europe Research Papers Series, No. 42 (June 1989), (Birmingham: Selly Oak Colleges, CSIC, 1989).
Nietzsche, Friedrich, 'Passages on the Death of God, from *The Gay Science* and *Thus Spoke Zarathustra*': *see* Altizer (ed.), *Towards a New Christianity.*
—— *Thus Spoke Zarathustra*, Penguin Classics, (Harmondsworth: Penguin Books, 1969).
The Observer: *see* Bhatia; Griffin; Rushdie.
O'Collins, Gerald, 'Selling Jesus', *The Tablet*, 26th September 1992.
Odone, Cristina, 'The Impertinent Conception', *The Guardian*, 19th September 1992.
Oliver, Kelly, *Reading Kristeva: Unraveling the Double-bind*, (Bloomington & Indianapolis: Indiana University Press, 1993).
Ostle, Robin, 'Urban Form, Literary Form: Conflict and Polarity in the Work of Naguib Mahfouz': *see* El-Batrik (ed.), *The World of Naguib Mahfouz.*

Ott, Ludwig, *Fundamentals of Catholic Dogma*, (Rockford, Illinois: Tan Books, 1974 [repr. of Cork: Mercier Press, 1960 4th English edn.]).

Paret, R., 'The Qur'ān-1': *see* Beeston *et al.* (eds.), *Arabic Literature to the End of the Umayyad Period.*

Parkinson (ed.), G.H.R., *An Encyclopaedia of Philosophy*, (London: Routledge, 1988).

Parsa, Misagh, *Social Origins of the Iranian Revolution*, (New Brunswick & London: Rutgers University Press, 1989).

Paul VI, Pope, *Humanae Vitae: see* Flannery (ed.), *Vatican Council II: More Postconciliar Documents.*

Pawlikowski, Paul, 'The Greatest Story Never Made?', *Stills*, no. 18 (April 1985).

Payne, Michael, *Reading Theory: An Introduction to Lacan, Derrida, and Kristeva*, (Oxford: Basil Blackwell, 1993).

Paz, Francis Xavier, *The Novels of Najīb Maḥfūẓ*, PhD Thesis, University of Columbia, 1972.

Pedersen, J., art. 'Djabrā'īl', *EI*^{2}, vol. 2.

Peled, Mattityahu, *Religion My Own: A Study of the Literary Works of Najîb Maḥfûẓ*, PhD Thesis, University of California, Los Angeles, 1971.

Pelikan (ed.), Jaroslav, *Twentieth Century Theology in the Making: Vol 2: The Theological Dialogue: Issues and Resources*, The Fontana Library: Theology and Philosophy, (London: Collins/New York: Harper & Row, 1970).

Pius X, Pope, *Encyclical Letter "Pascendi Gregis" . . . On the Doctrines of the Modernists*, (London: Burns & Oates, 1907 [repr. Long Prairie: The Neumann Press, 1983]).

—— *Lamentabili Sane: see* [Appendix 2 of] Davies, *Partisans of Error.*

Pius XII, Pope, *Divino Afflante Spiritu* in *Acta Apostolicae Sedis* (Rome), vol. 35 (1943).

—— *Encyclical Letter of . . . Pope Pius XII . . . on the Most Opportune Way to Promote Biblical Studies*, (Vatican: Tipografia Poliglotta Vaticana, 1943).

—— *Mediator Dei* in *Acta Apostolicae Sedis* (Rome), vol. 39 (1947).

—— *Mystici Corporis* in *Acta Apostolicae Sedis* (Rome), vol. 35 (1943).

—— *Mystici Corporis Christi: Encyclical Letter on the Mystical Body of Christ*, with discussion club outline by Gerald C. Treacy, (New York: Paulist Press, 1943).

—— *On the Sacred Liturgy: Encyclical Letter "Mediator Dei" of Pope Pius XII*, with Introd. and Notes by Gerald Ellard, (New York: America Press, 1948).

Ponting, Clive, *Secrecy in Britain*, Historical Association Studies, (Oxford: Basil Blackwell, 1990).

Positif: 'L"Affaire" Scorsese', no. 333 (November 1988).

Ramsey, Paul: *see* Vahanian, *The Death of God.*

Raschke, Carl A., 'The Deconstruction of God': *see* Altizer *et al.*, *Deconstruction and Theology.*

Riffaterre, Michael, 'Compulsory reader response: the intertextual drive': *see* Worton & Still (eds.), *Intertextuality.*

Rinvolucri, Mario, *Anatomy of a Church: Greek Orthodoxy Today*, (London: Burns & Oates, 1966).

Robinson, B.W., art. '(5) The *Mi'rādj* in Islamic Art' in art. 'Mi'rādj', *EI*^{2}, vol. 7.

Robinson, Neal, 'Reflections on the Rushdie Affair – 18th April 1989': *see* Bowen (ed.), *The Satanic Verses: Bradford Responds.*

Rose, Gregory, '*Velayat-e Faqih* and the Recovery of Islamic Identity in the Thought of Ayatollah Khomeini': *see* Keddie (ed.), *Religion and Politics in Iran.*

Rushdie, Salman, *Midnight's Children*, (London: Jonathan Cape, 1981).

—— 'Out of the Shadows', *The Sunday Times Magazine*, 7th February 1993.

—— 'Pawn in a Wider Game', *The Observer*, 4th July 1993.

—— *The Satanic Verses* [*SV*], (London & New York: Viking Penguin, 1988).

—— *The Satanic Verses*, 1st US paperback edn., (Dover, De.: The Consortium, Inc., 1992).

—— *Shame*, (New York: Vintage/Aventura, 1984).

—— *See also The Independent.*

Ruthven, Malise, *A Satanic Affair: Salman Rushdie and the Rage of Islam*, (London: Chatto & Windus, 1990).

Saffari, Said, 'The Legitimation of the Clergy's Right to Rule in the Iranian Constitution of 1979', *British Journal of Middle Eastern Studies*, vol. 20:1 (1993).

Said, Edward, 'Intellectual exile: expatriates and marginals', [Edited text of one of his 1993 Reith Lectures], *The Independent*, 8th July 1993.

Sanders, E.P., *The Historical Figure of Jesus*, (London: Allen Lane, The Penguin Press, 1993).

Sardar, Ziauddin & Davies, Merryl Wyn, *Distorted Imagination: Lessons from the Rushdie Affair*, (London: Grey Seal, 1990).

Schillebeeckx, Edward, *Jesus: An Experiment in Christology*, trans. by Hubert Hoskins, (London: Collins, 1979) [first published in Dutch in 1974].

Scholes, Robert, *Protocols of Reading*, (New Haven & London: Yale University Press, 1989).

Schwarz, Walter, 'Wide eyed and Godless', *The Guardian: Outlook*, 4th–5th September 1993.

Scruton, Roger, *A Short History of Modern Philosophy from Descartes to Wittgenstein*, (London: Ark Paperbacks, Routledge & Kegan Paul, 1984).

Second Vatican Council: *see* Flannery (ed.); Vatican II.

Séguy, Marie-Rose (ed.), *The Miraculous Journey of Mahomet: Mirâj Nâmeh*, Bibliothèque Nationale, Paris, (Manuscrit Supplément Turc 190), (London: The Scolar Press, 1977).

Seligsohn, M., "Ā'isha Bint Abī Bakr': *see Shorter Encyclopaedia of Islam.*

Shorter Encyclopaedia of Islam [*EIS*], ed. H.A.R. Gibb & J.H. Kramers, (Leiden: E.J. Brill/London: Luzac, 1961).

Siddiqui, Kalim: *see The Independent.*

Sigal, Clancy, 'Hail Storm', *The Listener*, 17th October 1985.

Simpson, Anthony, *The Anatomy of Britain 1992* in *The Independent on Sunday*, 29th March 1992.

Simpson, J.A. & Weiner, E.S.C., *The Oxford English Dictionary*, 2nd edn., (Oxford: Clarendon Press, 1989), vol. 2.

Singer, Michael, 'Cinema Saviour', *Film Comment*, vol. 24, no. 5 (September–October 1988).

Smart, Ninian, *The Phenomenon of Religion*, Philosophy of Religion Series, (London: Macmillan, 1973).

Smith, Wilfred Cantwell, art. 'Aḥmadiyya', *EI*[2], vol. 1.
Somekh, S., 'The Sad Millenarian: An Examination of Awlad Haratina': *see* Le Gassick (ed.), *Critical Perspectives on Naguib Mahfouz.*
Sproxton, Vernon, *Teilhard de Chardin*, (London: SCM Press, 1971).
Stanley, David Michael, *The Gospel of St. Matthew*, 2nd rev. edn., New Testament Reading Guide, no. 4, (Collegeville, Minnesota: Liturgical Press, 1963).
Stern, J.P., *Nietzsche*, Fontana Modern Masters, (London: Fontana Press, Harper Collins, 1985).
Stewart, (trans.), Philip: *see* Maḥfūẓ (Arabic Sources).
Sullivan, Francis, A., *Salvation Outside the Church?*, (London: Cassell, Geoffrey Chapman, 1992).
The Sunday Times: 4th July 1993.
—— *See also* Carpenter; Davison; Jacques; Marsden; Miles; Rushdie.
The Sunday Times Magazine: *see* Rushdie.
Sutherland *et al.* (eds.), Stewart, *The World's Religions*, (London: Routledge, 1988).
The Tablet: 26th September 1992; 28th August 1993.
—— *See also* O'Collins.
Taheri, Amir, *The Spirit of Allah: Khomeini and the Islamic Revolution*, (London: Hutchinson, 1985).
Taylor, Donald, 'Incipient Fundamentalism: Religion and Politics among Sri Lankan Hindus in Britain': *see* Caplan (ed.), *Studies in Religious Fundamentalism.*
Teilhard de Chardin, Pierre, *The Phenomenon of Man*, (London: Fontana Books, Collins, 1969).
Thiering, Barbara, *Jesus the Man: A New Interpretation from the Dead Sea Scrolls*, (London: Doubleday, 1992).
Thompson, David, [Review of] 'The Last Temptation of Christ', *Films and Filming*, no. 409 (October 1988).
Thompson, David & Christie, Ian (eds.), *Scorsese on Scorsese*, (London: Faber & Faber, 1990).
The Times: 22nd February 1988 ('Obituary: Dr. John Allegro'); 26th November 1993; 15th December 1993 (Editorial: 'To Hell from Durham: More Thoughtful Provocation from the Bishop').
—— *See also* Gledhill; Ivens; Longford; Wilson.
Vahanian, Gabriel, *The Death of God: The Culture of Our Post-Christian Era*, (New York: George Braziller, 1961).
Vatican II, *Dei Verbum*: *see* Flannery (ed.), *Vatican Council II*, vol. 1.
—— *Lumen Gentium*: *see* Flannery (ed.), *Vatican Council II*, vol. 1.
—— *Sacrosanctum Concilium*: *see* Flannery (ed.), *Vatican Council II*, vol. 1.
Vermes, Geza, *The Religion of Jesus the Jew*, (London: SCM, 1993).
Viviano, Benedict T., 'The Gospel according to Matthew': *see* Brown, Fitzmyer & Murphy (eds.), *The New Jerome Biblical Commentary.*
Voll, John O., 'Fundamentalism in the Sunni World: Egypt and the Sudan': *see* Marty & Appleby (eds.), *Fundamentalisms Observed.*
Von Balthasar, Hans Urs, *The Theology of Henri de Lubac: An Overview*, (San Francisco: Ignatius Press, Communio Books, 1991).
Von Grunebaum, G.E., art. 'I'djāz', *EI*[2], vol. 3.
Wace, Henry & Schaff, Philip (eds.), *A Select Library of Nicene and Post-Nicene*

Fathers of the Christian Church, Second Series, Volume XI: Sulpitius Severus, Vincent of Lerins, John Cassian, (Oxford: James Parker & Co./New York: The Christian Literature Company, 1894).
Wansbrough (ed.), Henry, *The New Jerusalem Bible* (Standard Edition), (London: Darton, Longman & Todd, 1985).
Ware, Kallistos [Timothy], 'The Church: A Time of Transition': *see* Clogg (ed.), *Greece in the 1980s*.
Ware, Timothy, [Bishop Kallistos of Diokleia], *The Orthodox Church*, (London: Penguin Books, rev. repr. 1993).
Watson, Francis, *A Guide to the New Testament*, (London: Batsford, 1987).
Watt, W. Montgomery, art. ''Ā'isha Bint Abī Bakr', *EI*², vol. 1.
—— (ed.), *Bell's Introduction to the Qur'an*, (Edinburgh: Edinburgh University Press, 1970).
—— *Muhammad at Mecca*, (Oxford: Clarendon Press, 1972).
—— *Muhammad at Medina*, (Oxford: Clarendon Press, repr. 1968).
—— *Muhammad, Prophet and Statesman*, (London: Oxford University Press, 1967).
—— *See also* under Arabic Sources.
Webber, Jonathan, 'Rethinking Fundamentalism: The Readjustment of Jewish Society in the Modern World': *see* Caplan (ed.), *Studies in Religious Fundamentalism*.
Webster, Richard, *A Brief History of Blasphemy*, (Southwold: The Orwell Press, 1990).
Wildiers, N.M., *An Introduction to Teilhard de Chardin*, The Fontana Library of Theology and Philosophy, (London: Fontana Books, 1971).
Williams, Rowan, *Arius: Heresy and Tradition*, (London: Darton, Longman & Todd, 1987).
Wilson, A.N., 'Faith to Face', *The Times Saturday Review*, 19th September 1992.
—— *Jesus*, (London: Sinclair-Stevenson, 1992).
Worton, Michael & Still, Judith (eds.), *Intertextuality: Theories and Practices*, (Manchester & New York: Manchester University Press, 1990).
Wybrew, Hugh, 'Eastern Christianity since 451': *see* Sutherland *et al.* (eds.), *The World's Religions*.
Zaehner, R.C., *The Dawn and Twilight of Zoroastrianism*, History of Religion Series, (London: Weidenfeld & Nicolson, 1961).
Zonis, Martin & Brumberg, Daniel, 'Shi'ism as Interpreted by Khomeini: An Ideology of Revolutionary Violence': *see* Kramer (ed.), *Shi'ism, Resistance and Revolution*.
Zubaida, Sami, 'The Quest for the Islamic State: Islamic Fundamentalism in Egypt and Iran': *see* Caplan (ed.), *Studies in Religious Fundamentalism*.
Zubaidi, A.M., 'The Impact of the Qur'ān and *Ḥadīth* on Medieval Arabic Literature': *see* Beeston *et al.* (eds.), *Arabic Literature to the End of the Umayyad Period*.

Cinematic and TV Sources

Akkad, Moustapha (director), *The Message* (1977).
——*Al-Risāla*: *see* above.
BBC2 (TV), *The Late Show*, Monday 9th March 1992.
Godard, Jean-Luc (director), *Je Vous Salue, Marie* (1984).
Scorsese, Martin (director), *The Last Temptation of Christ* (1988).

INDEX

In this Index the Arabic definite article ('al-'/'el-') has been omitted at the *beginning* of an entry. Characters etc. from the three major novels discussed in this volume are listed here with the name of the novel in brackets i.e. (*AH*), (*SV*) or (*LT*). (*See* ABBREVIATIONS page).

Aristotle 5
Arius 90
Article 19 21
Ashland, Wisconsin 41; Ashland Public Library 41
Ashraf, Syed Ali 40
Athens 41, 42
Averroism 46; *see also* double-truth doctrine
'Awāṭif (*AH*) 16
Awlād Ḥāratinā see Maḥfūẓ
Ayesha (*SV*) 22, 30–3, 36, 37, 123, 125
Ayesha, Empress (*SV*) 31, 32, 123, 124
'Aysha (*AH*) 14
Azhar 71, 80, 82, 83; Islamic Research Council 83
Azraeel (*SV*) 22, 23, 33–6, 37, 123, 124
Azrael *see* Azraeel

Baal the Poet (*SV*) 28, 34, 35
Bachan, Amitabh 23
Badawi, Mustafa 11, 17
Baghdad 79
Bakhtin 115
Bangladesh 20, 104 n.91
Baptists 96, 99
baqā' 73
Bāqī see eternity of God
Barabbas (*LT*) 65 n.228
Barthes, Roland 115, 116, 126
Basra 36
Battuta, Billy (*SV*) 33, 34
Bayūmī (*AH*) 14
BBC 52, 82
Bea, Cardinal Augustin 94
Beirut 10
Bethany (*LT*) 44, 47
Bethlehem 46, 47
Bhatia, Shyam 10
Bhutto, Benazir 19
Bible 2, 46, 96, 98, 124, 126; *see also Acts of the Apostles*; Joseph story in Bible and Qur'ān; *Leviticus*; New Testament; Old Testament
Biblical Archeology Review 55
bid'a 79
Bien, P.A. 41, 42, 50, 51, 117, 118
Bilal (*SV*) 27, 28, 31
Bilāl b. Rabāḥ 28, 40
Bilal X *see* Bilal (*SV*)
birth control *see* Paul VI, Pope
Blackstone 1
blasphemy ix, x, 1–7, 9, 39, 41, 49, 51, 52, 57, 69, 70, 71, 78, 79, 82, 86, 99, 128, 132, 133, 134, 135; punishment for 1–2, 77–8; *see also sabb*; *tajdīf*
Bloom, Verna 51
Bombay 20, 22, 23, 25, 26, 27, 38, 39, 125
Booker Prize 19, 60 n.61
Bostan (aeroplane) (*SV*) 25, 38
Botticelli 54, 81; *The Birth of Venus* 81
Bottomore, Tom 133
Bradford 20
Braudel, Fernand ix, x, 135
Brennan, Timothy 19, 22, 23, 24, 26
British-Iran Parliamentary Group 21
Broadcasting Standards Council 52
Brown, Raymond E. 94
Brueghel 51
Bultmann, Rudolf 91
Bunyan, John 10, 24, 117; *Pilgrim's Progress* 10, 24
Burton, John 86
Bustān 25

Cachia, Pierre 80
Caetani, L. 86
Caiphas (*LT*) 48
Cairo 10, 11, 18, 70, 80, 83
Cairo International Film Festival 81
Cairo University 76, 83
Cambridge, U.K. 77
Camel, Battle of the 30
Campbell, J.K. 97
Camus, Albert 133
Cana (*LT*) 45
Canada 96
Capernaum (*LT*) 47
Carmel, Mount (*LT*) 47
Carpenter, Humphrey 77
Carter, Angela 40
Catechism, Universal *see* John Paul II, Pope